MIXED

BLESSINGS

By

Sonya L. M. Hill

C O N T E N T S

THIS BOOK IS DEDICATED TO

My Mom,
And in loving memory of
Dad, Auntie, Nan & Granddad
Without whom I just wouldn't have
achieved any of the things
I can do today
x

Also special thanks
to my nephew,
Ellis A. Leverton-Hill
for helping with the photography
x

1

First Breaths

Hi folks, I'm Sonya.

I was born on the tenth of May 1967 and preceding the events which I will describe for you in a minute, due to a lack of oxygen and the circumstances surrounding my birth, I am confined to a wheelchair suffering from Cerebral Palsy.

For me, I suppose the first thing that often springs to mind, when reflecting upon the relatively short space of time in which my problems must have arisen, probably a little over an hour, is how fragile the tapestry of life is and how the events which took place had such an enormous and powerful impact in shaping how I was going to live out the remainder of my days.

It is pointless to dwell in self-pity, I have no time for that, but sometimes I can't help but peruse over exactly what kind of person I would have turned out to be had I not been disabled?

What kind of jobs would I have had? Maybe I would have chosen a career in teaching or perhaps I would have elected to study the law? Would I be married now? Have kids? Well, by this time I would probably have had a boisterous brood of naughty teenagers, who emptied my fridge at three or four in the morning, lounged in bed till dinner, and then threw a wobbly because there was nothing to eat.

All speculation and dreams set aside though, when disability does strike, there is little choice available to you other than to do your best in promoting new skills and to return the love you are shown. Of course, I have a broad array of stories to convey which you will hopefully find amusing, intriguing, or of use in some small way, but let's start with a tour around my local district and by unfurling the first few leaves of my family tree.

I spent my childhood living in Dudley, which is considered to be the heart of The Black Country, renowned for being a heavily populated area and named as such for its black, industrious smog of the nineteenth century. Contrary to this, the outskirts of the town were surrounded by farming land and hills and I remember that as a small child, when taking the short car journey necessary to reach my grandparents' house, I always loved to peer out of the window over the fields to see the horses and cattle having their afternoon graze. Sadly, like most places these days, much of this spare land has been built upon, now being home to a small modern housing estate.

Although probably not being so widely heard of as Birmingham, Dudley has always been richly characterized and best known for its unique, regional language, humour, history, and tradition. For me, I think I always felt a certain amount of pride in Dudley and during my early years, although I would quite often be taken on shopping trips around other small nearby areas such as Blackheath, Cradley Heath or Kingswinford, unless we just fancied going somewhere a little more adventurous, then we could always track down what we were looking for in Dudley's town centre.

There are a few special landmarks too, which I always associate as being unique to this area and in the centre of the town, sitting next to the end of its outdoor market, one such iconic feature which you can't miss is the 140-year-old Triumphal Arch Fountain, which was ornately sculpted by the Scottish-born sculptor James Forsyth and brought to the area during the nineteenth century for William Ward, the first Earl of Dudley. Towering to a height of 27 feet, the fountain also depicts another character from Greek legend, majestically riding upon his winged horse, Pegasus.

By trade, my father worked as a haulage contractor and, for many years, he spent long hours on the road, transporting hardcore road

2

materials from one end of the country to the other. He could drive any vehicle with ease and no matter how long and cumbersome the lorries were to manoeuvre, irrespective of the weather and we used to get some really harsh winters, nothing seemed to faze him. Of course, like most lorry drivers, during his long excursions up and down the lonely motorways, he was seldom without a bag of boiled sweets as his solitary companion.

My mom has always been a wonderful mother. As a young girl, she trained in shorthand and typing; this was her first job, and then she worked as a typist and clerical assistant for Dad. She is also very artistic, being interested in anything to do with cake decorating or gardening. She is not just a mom; she is my best friend, and it is only Mom's steadfast determination to which I can truly accredit the things I can do today. When I came along, my parents just had one little girl; my older sister who is my senior by 4½ years.

Moms side of the family all played an enormous role in my life, this consisting of my nan, Granddad, and Mom's younger sister. Auntie, at this point, had one little boy who is just two years older than me, so from an early age, he turned out to be my special playmate.

Somewhere around my sisters' fourth birthday, Mom discovered she was expecting another baby, me, so as the weeks progressed, she excitedly began to plan for my forthcoming arrival.

It was at some stage during Mom's pregnancy with me, whilst attending a routine check-up at the doctor's that the GP observed that I was breached. He very quickly referred her to the hospital, because without wanting to cause unnecessary alarm, he knew of the potential risks this could incur and he felt confident that her needs would be dealt with. Mom diligently kept up with all her appointments. She was assured by the hospital staff that they were used to dealing with this kind of problem, so despite her trepidation, she trusted that everything would be alright.

In the early hours of the day I was born, Mom started to feel uncomfortable and she knew it was time to go to hospital. On the way, my parents dropped my sister off at my grandparents' house to be looked after and to excitedly wait for news of my arrival. With Mom safely in the hospital, Dad carried on to work. In those days, fathers were not encouraged to be present at a child's birth, so he set off in his car again.

At first, several medical staff were milling around, but shortly afterwards, Mom could not hear a sound and then she became aware that she was completely deserted. She frantically rang the bell for the next hour, but no-one came. By this time she was very distressed, but finally, a nurse arrived.

A doctor of oriental origin arrived on the scene, and observing Mom's dreadful predicament, he started angrily bawling orders at the nurses.

The medical team attempted to head off pushing my mother's bed down the corridor and into the nearest delivery room realizing the urgency. Shortly afterwards I was delivered. I was totally white and just managing to catch a quick glimpse of me, Mom saw I had a crop of thick, black hair, just like my sister and cousin had when they were born.

I was born at 5:10 pm, I was not breathing, and I made no murmur.

They wrapped my limp body in tissue paper and took me away. Mom just lay in a total daze, awash with sheer exhaustion, confusion and grief. Her baby had been born, but was it a boy or a girl?

Now, for the second time, Mom found herself alone. So many unbearable thoughts must have been drumming through her head. Had she had a boy, or maybe it was another daughter? Where had everyone gone again? Oh well, there was only one thing to deduce at this point - I was stillborn, or why else could she not hear my first cry?

Gradually she became aware that she could hear a very faint, muffled sound, which was coming from the room next door. She realised afterwards that this was their ardent attempts to resuscitate me.

Seconds ticked on into minutes, the minutes relentlessly droned on into what must have felt like an eternity, and still Mom hadn't even been given basic treatment following her labour.

Eventually, however, the doctor returned.

"You have a daughter", he said, "but she is gravely ill and it is not expected that she will survive the night".

Mom said nothing, she turned her face towards the opposite wall and just lay there, in dazed silence.

Later that night Dad arrived, and obviously, his reaction was one of shock and disbelief.

"Well, what's happened?", Dad demanded, "what now?"

No-one seemed to offer a reply, so he just sat by Mom's bedside for a while, neither knowing what to say or how to react. He finally concluded that nothing could be done that night, so he returned home in the hopes that perhaps Mom could get some sleep.

The next day, Dad visited again, also accompanied by Nan and upon walking into Mom's room they saw that she had got dressed and was sitting on her bed. Mom asked if Nan could go down to the nursery to see me. The nurse said that normally only parents were allowed into the nursery, but on this occasion, she would make an exception.

Peering through the window, Nan observed my tiny white form lying in the incubator. Just like my parents, feeling totally helpless and robbed of the privilege of those first special moments of holding the new baby in her arms, smelling all those beautiful newborn aromas and feeling my warm body against her skin, Nan knew all she needed to do was to say prayers to the Lord, so when they got home this was to be their first task.

"Just get me out of here", Mom said, angrily brushing her hair, "my little girl is waiting for me."

By this, she was referring to my older sister, now making a hopeless attempt to completely disassociate herself from those heavy, oppressive walls of the maternity ward. Their mottled greyness seemed to be closing in on her and in stark contrast, she was also surrounded by happy mothers nuzzling their new babies in their arms and pottering in and out of the nursery and she hadn't even been allowed to touch me yet.

The most recent twist to the situation, which added to its bitter poignancy even further, was that the nurse had just told her that during the night, they had baptized me Mary, as they hadn't expected me to see daybreak.

Mom's only comment following the news of my christening was, "I don't care if they call her Ria as long as she survives". She hated this name. Before this problem had arisen with my birth, my parents had already agreed that if they had another daughter, then I should be called Sonya Louise. Dad was particularly pleased with the suggestion of Louise, as this was the name of his mother.

Finally, they decided that the only answer to this quandary would be to tag Mary on the end, as it was, after all, the first name I had been given.

On reflection, Mom must have felt in total despair. All the natural instincts and joys that a new mother ought to be experiencing had been taken away and they had even given me my first name. At least now, by returning to the privacy of her own home, she could snatch a few hours break, to grieve, to wash her face away from prying eyes, but more important than ever now, she needed to feel like a parent again to my waiting sister.

Now all she yearned was to return to some semblance of normality, simply to pour a cup of tea and to resume looking after my big sister. I think the word "normality" is probably a strange choice of wording here because she just felt incomplete.

The next morning at 8:00am Mom rang the ward, and she was relieved to hear that I had survived the night. Upon this news, their hearts were lifted. During the day, the telephone rang several times from a combination of anxious relatives and Dad's business associates, but my family had to request that the line must be kept open for the hospital and my mother was too upset to go to the phone in case it was the news she feared.

In those days, it was customary for women to pay a visit to their local vicar after the birth of a baby to participate in a short ceremony known as being "churched". This was merely a time of prayer to thank the Lord for a safe delivery and had to be performed before a new mom could go out into the community and carry out her normal, day-to-day life. Nan suggested this should now be done as Mom would be going to and from the hospital to visit me. Mom and Dad went to the local vicarage and the vicar answered the door.

Upon hearing what had happened, the vicar took my parents into the church where he prayed for them both and for my recovery.

The next few days were critical. There seemed no improvement in my condition so the only existing thread that now remained for my family to cling on to was the fact that currently, I was still alive.

Our family home was situated right at the top of a steep hill. The view from our lounge window was something spectacular. You could observe many buildings, trees, and the tiny multi-coloured dots on the horizon of vehicles heading for their chosen destination. Being so high up, it was a very healthy spot or, at least, it should have been, but looking back, there were quite a few families who seemed to experience hardships of one type or another. Although housing a closely-knit community, I would never describe the neighbours being of the nosey, curtain-twitching variety, but if something went wrong, then the tale quickly circulated from one household to the next and as you can imagine, word soon got around that Mom had returned home without me.

Most of the neighbours were similar in the age range to my parents; there were several couples with one or two small children, and it was an extremely pleasant area in which to grow up. Many of them had a polite and sensitive disposition but it was now apparent to them all that something was amiss. They did not venture around for a few days however, allowing the family some much-needed space.

Gradually, of course, as there was still no sign of my arrival, they started to make their enquiries. Upon news of my illness, many warm wishes and kind gestures began to trickle in; some would bring a cake or a plant, but they were all very keen to offer support.

Despite Mom's ongoing turmoil, she continued to journey into the hospital each day to visit me. To minimize the risk of infection, she was always requested to wear a mask and gown before entering the nursery. She would bring the masks home to my sister, who promptly utilized them as hammocks for her dolls.

Things still looked bleak though, and during the next few days, I had a number of seizures and so I had to be heavily sedated until this was under control. This was particularly upsetting, as the staff then shaved off my hair, enabling them to draw fluid from my head to relieve the pressure from my brain and to stop my convulsions.

Epilepsy is a common occurrence following a head injury and I suspect that I would be exhausted now after the trauma of my birth.

Mom then noticed that when I opened my eyes, instead of looking clear blue, they appeared cloudy so she feared I may be blind but she dare not bring this up with the staff dreading possible confirmation.

One day when Mom was there for my next feed, the nurse casually commented, "Don't worry about her eyes as most of the babies have contracted an eye infection which is being treated with drops and should clear up in a few days".

"Thank God that's one problem we don't have to deal with", Mom later said when reporting what had happened to Nan. Tears of sheer relief followed: this happened on most days as life was like a constant roller coaster of highs and lows.

A week after my birth my parents requested an appointment with the paediatrician, as they needed to inquire what the prognosis was. He explained that they had had to resuscitate me and the treatment I had been given since. Mom then asked him the most difficult question of all, "Will she live?", to which he replied, "Oh, she'll live", but went on to say that any development would be very slow and very poor, so the best thing Mom could do was to go away and have another baby. That was all Mom wanted to hear and immediately dismissed his heartless suggestion thinking where there is life there is hope.

For the first three weeks of my life, the family has conveyed to me that there seemed no proper definition of time. Day and night seemed to simply blur into one monotonous continuation, consisting only of Mom commuting between the hospital and home, just praying that brighter prospects would soon dawn.

I was unable to suck from a bottle so Mom had to learn the painstaking art of spoon-feeding me my milk. When the doctor was finally satisfied that my fits had stabilized and Mom was competent in managing my feeds, I was finally discharged to head home.

Dad came to collect me in his car and for my big sister and the rest of my relatives, through the power of prayer and by the amazing goodness of God, the long wait to meet me finally drew to a close.

2

Home Improvements

Mom's daily journeys to and from the hospital had finally come to an end, or at least for a short while but, at this stage, I don't think either she or the rest of my family, had fully comprehended that the real journey, which now lay before them, was only just about to begin.

As Dad rolled his car into the steep drive, the front door opened and Nan appeared on the doorstep, closely trailed by a little girl, her hair tied in ponytails with pink and white ribbon. It was, of course, my big sister.

"Oh look Nan", she chirped in delight, "they're back" and with this, she promptly began to yank at the car door, as she could hardly wait to see me.

"Hello Sonya", she whispered, "I'm your sister".

Mom slowly carried me indoors and through to the lounge, where she sank into the nearest armchair and exhaled, letting out a huge sigh of relief.

My granddad started to busy himself and immediately went through to the kitchen to put the kettle on. I think it was apparent that cups of tea would be of great use all round.

It was such a relief that I was home and at last, the family was all together. Mom knew that initially, there would be some difficult days ahead, but for the meantime, at least for the foreseeable future, the one prominent obstacle which rapidly seemed to preside over all else was the continual and tedious task of feeding me.

I still couldn't suck from my bottle so to keep my milk warm, Mom would stand it in a jug of boiling water and then she would slowly pour small amounts into an eggcup to spoon into me.

Days went into weeks and the weeks seemed to endlessly drone on, but my monotonous routine perpetuated and Mom did little else during the day except for two basic and relentless chores: feeding me and mopping up my vomit.

This sounds as if she was dealing with a child suffering from an eating disorder like Bulimia, but the only difference is that, in my case, I was trying desperately to retain my food.

I would cry with the sheer frustration of not being able to swallow properly and so at the point at which I breathed in, Mom would throw the next spoonful down my throat, but because I was gulping so much air down at the same time, the whole lot was soon projected again into my bib.

In those days we had quite a few family members living close by, so apart from my grandparents and my auntie, whose ongoing support never wavered, Nan's sisters were never too far away either. Following my birth, news of my problems had travelled down the great family grapevine and so, shortly after I came home, my great aunties, one by one, began to ascend our steep hill.

"Oh, somebody's wearing a very pretty dress today", my auntie said as she peered at me, cradled calmly in Mom's arms. Most of my body remained limp, but my right arm always visibly jutted out to my side.

As I was to discover in later years, my nan's branch of the family consisted of the kindest, funniest, and the most influential characters you are ever likely to meet. They each came to see me, but upon observing the persistent battle to get me fed, none of them could stand to stay with us for too long and they would soon start to get their coats on, probably making some polite excuse such as, "I'm sorry but I'd best get going now, as I need to pop into town for a loaf of bread". Mom knew, however, that this wasn't the real reason for their hurried departure at all. They just didn't like to admit that they simply couldn't stand to watch me being fed, as it was too difficult for them to comprehend that there was just no other way to feed me. In their eyes, it just seemed like I was being tortured, but however gruesome its appearance, this continual ritual was playing the vital role of keeping me alive.

There was no sign of improvement from here on in. Although I must have been retaining adequate nutrients, it was now becoming increasingly obvious to my parents that I just wasn't reaching all the normal milestones.

By eighteen months of age I still wasn't showing any indication of being able to sit up and while I was enjoying a wide and varied diet of liquidized food, neither could I swallow anything that was at all lumpy.

One day Mom decided it was time to discuss these concerns with the family and it was unanimously concluded that the only way forward from here, was to request an urgent appointment with a paediatrician at The Children's Hospital in Birmingham, so Mom promptly went to ask the GP for a referral.

Anyway, a few more weeks went by and the usual routine continued and then one morning, a brown envelope was deposited through the letterbox. At last, the date of my long-awaited consultation was confirmed and I was to be at the hospital on 8 December 1968, at 10:40 am. Mom recorded this information at once on the kitchen calendar and, pulling out a leaf of the heavy oak dining table, she resolutely began to compile her very lengthy and comprehensive list of questions.

It was a ten-mile drive to the hospital, but to this day, the knowledge still sickens me that I was now one and a half years old and the first question, right at the top of the page was, "What is the name of Sonya's condition?"

I mean, almost immediately and most certainly during the process of trying to resuscitate me after birth, it must have been clear to the hospital staff that as a result of being starved of oxygen, both before and during my delivery, which had then been proceeded by the problems I'd presented, that I suffered from Cerebral Palsy.

Nonetheless, before the impending appointment with the paediatrician, Mom had never even heard of this term. She knew little of disability and the only brief encounters which she had experienced were with people who had Downs Syndrome and there was also a spastic boy who went to the same school as she did. Physically, he had a milder form of Cerebral Palsy than me, but in earlier years, little was understood about different disabilities and the facilities for handicapped children were incredibly sparse. The teachers, being in an ordinary school, had no knowledge of what the young boy required, so he spent most of his schooldays simply wandering around the corridors, leaving any educational potential which he could have shown if given the appropriate encouragement, to go unnoticed.

Just a few generations before mine, it was a common notion that if anyone was unable to walk, people automatically concluded that they must have had Polio. By the time I came along, however, I was extremely lucky that a clearer understanding of the requirements of children with special needs was in its infancy, but as I will explain in more detail later, there was still huge scope for further improvement.

Anyway, finally the time came for our all-important meeting with the specialist, so Mom fastened me securely in my car seat and headed for the throng of busy carriageways, leading into the city of Birmingham.

I continued for quite some time going to see the doctor here, so it is these visits that form one of my earliest memories.

The hospital was huge, very old, and from the outside had the appearance of a large, decaying mansion; its pitted brickwork also resembled that of a sea wall sculpted by the crash of many incoming tides. Mom pushed me through the rusty wrought iron entrance gates, up the sloping driveway and soon we entered the first long corridor that led to the reception desk.

I always enjoyed going for a ride up this walkway as the walls were brightly painted with all my favourite Walt Disney characters. There was Bambi, Dumbo and then the Seven Dwarves went trailing through the woods in their search for Snow White. If the traffic hadn't been too bad when motoring into Birmingham and Mom felt we had a few minutes extra to spare before our appointment, it was great fun to see how many of the dwarves I could name. There was Dopey, Bashful, Sleepy, Happy, but our time had soon elapsed and Mom told me that we must hurry along now, or we would be late to see the doctor and trying to neatly intercept my mounting protest, she earnestly assured me that if I was a good girl, then I'd be able to see them all again on our way back to the car.

However, the merry welcome of the fresco soon faded, because the last set of double doors we had to negotiate, were the most creepy doors I'd ever seen, for they were not made of wood, but bendy, transparent plastic. With this, together with the overwhelming stench of disinfectant which was now not only piercing through my nasal passages but also producing a nasty, metallic taste in my mouth, I just knew in my little heart that there must be something ghastly lurking within to get me.

Finally, we reached our appropriate waiting area and I began to scan around the room for toys. Soon I'd made my decision and I began to earnestly draw Mom's attention to the big, pink and white rabbit which was propped up in the corner, by pointing and exhibiting my cheeky, appealing grin again.

This slight lull in my growing anxiety was only short-lived though as unbeknown to me, there were even worse horrors waiting for me behind the next door, despite its aesthetic camouflage of being the regular wooden type to which everyone with common sense was routinely accustomed.

Upon entering the examination room, the doctor seemed friendly enough: he confirmed what my name was and shook my hand, but after this, his mood just seemed to change. He reached into the drawer of his desk and I thought, in my childish innocence, that just like my own GP, he was about to courteously offer me a sweet to thank me for my visit, but I should have known better, for instead he went on to retrieve a big silver and black reflex hammer with which he then proceeded to bash my thin little kneecaps which caused me to jump.

This was followed up by a thorough medical examination and then he made immediate arrangements for me to attend our local clinic, as he concluded that physiotherapy must be employed at once to strengthen my floppy limbs and also, to develop my communication skills, he booked me in with the speech therapist.

He then explained at great length exactly what Cerebral Palsy was and, armed with this new information, Mom felt far better equipped to plan for the horizon ahead.

We started on our homebound trip and feeling uplifted by the successful outcome, we decided to call into Nan's house to pay her a surprise visit.

My grandparents lived just a few streets away from our house and, around this time, it was extremely limited as to where Mom could feasibly take me because apart from trips to see either my grandparents or my auntie, we were unable to go to many other places because my mealtime routine was now consuming such a large proportion of our day.

Mom carried me through Nan's kitchen, dragging my huge bag stuffed with all my favourite toys and at once I detected that lovely warm aroma of a jam sandwich cake rising in the oven. Like most grandmothers, my nan was always renowned for being an excellent cook and her freshly baked cakes and scones provided a beautiful banquet fit for royalty.

Nan greeted me, as usual, with a big kiss and a pleasantry which often went something like, "Come on and bring the little rascal in."

Even at this early stage, it was apparent that despite my difficulties, I was beginning to develop a very active mind and I forever needed to be occupied in some way. Nan's cheery greeting would promptly be knocked back, however, as the only thing I said in response was, "I'm bored" and my sad little mouth would turn down and down and down.

"Wait a minute you monkey", Nan laughed, "you haven't even got over the threshold yet."

It was often Granddad who, with his usual big smile on his face, would quickly come to the rescue.

"I know what Sonya", he said, now following us into the house armed with the last few carrier bags, "Let's have a look what's on the TV" and he reached over to retrieve a crumpled old magazine from beneath the smoked-glassed, nest of tables. "Er, what time is it?", he paused, glancing over to the clock above the fireplace.

The clock was a minute or two slow but Granddad told me that Mary, Mungo and Midge had just started; it was a favourite of mine, but failure to catch the opening caption didn't really matter anymore, as I knew by now that every episode always began with the same boring explanation of who they were and where they lived. The main storyline was based around a girl, a dog and a mouse who all resided right at the top of a tall block of flat, their abode being noted by the pretty flowerbox in the window, so they obviously shared similar interests to Mom.

My T.V. programme kept me out of mischief for the next twenty minutes, but as soon as the credits began to roll, I looked up and inquired chirpily, "What can we do next then Granddad?"

"Well the sun is shining", he said, "so I wonder if Kimmy is ready for a treat?"

Kimmy was my grandparents' old collie. She had curly white fur, the only exception being a small, brown patch which covered her ear, also being charmingly swirled around one eye. When it was a nice sunny day, like today, Granddad would sit by my side, supporting me on the garden bench and I would be contented for hours then, just stroking Kimmy and sharing the contents of Nan's biscuit barrel with her.

A few more weeks rolled by and eventually, as a result of going to see the specialist at the hospital, I was sent for assessment at the local clinic, where now, our new weekly schedule began, consisting of trips to the Physiotherapy Department on two days and also the speech therapist.

This old clinic is still in operation today and in appearance it has changed very little, sitting right at the top of the hill, just before you reach the infants' school, surrounded by its sweeping grass verge.

In the beginning, the most pressing difficulty for my new physiotherapist to tackle, without delay, was my inability to accomplish a sitting position. She placed me on a foam mat and with a little assistance from Mom, she would encourage me to reach in front of me, to try to select a toy of my choice.

My problem in this respect was that although I was showing a healthy interest in wanting to be able to grasp out at the toys, instead of possessing the ability to reach in front of me, my left hand, which vaguely seemed to be emerging as the one I was attempting to use, was still involuntarily being thrust out to my side and so obtaining the desired object proved impossible.

Progress was extremely slow and I found it incredibly frustrating. Now that this new method was realised, my family rigorously practiced with me at home, by encircling me with cushions. On some days, I simply couldn't be bothered with any more physio, I would start to cry and deliberately throw myself backwards in temper, so Mom would have to try and ignore me then, till my rage had subsided. She did, of course, try to coax me out of it, by singing to me or showing me new toys, but by now my stubbornness had fully manifested itself so her efforts were all in vain.

By whatever means were available to me, I was successfully starting to convey my feelings and needs to Mom. She lovingly devoted all her waking hours to my care and all the other things which she used to be able to associate as being the normal, everyday life of a housewife and mother, were being carried out obliviously around her by Auntie, Nan and Granddad. Dad still went to and from work each day, driving his big oily trucks. My sister was dropped off at the local primary school, meeting up in the playground with my cousin. Auntie worked part-time in a hairdressers' salon and Granddad was still working for a large and well-known car manufacturer.

After just a few sessions of physiotherapy, Mom began to gather many new ideas about the importance of carefully selecting suitable toys to encourage me to use my hands as much as possible to develop my fine motor skills and so next she launched into her mammoth toy search.

I think my dad probably found her efforts quite extraordinary, as within days, she had exhausted the telephone directory, actively scouring around not only all the toyshops in Dudley, but continuing her mission throughout the whole of The Midlands. She sent for as many toy mail-order catalogues as she could get her hands on. In those days, family homes were not so often submitted to the vast quantity of postal advertisements which are in circulation today but, when Mom had finished, our house soon became the singular exception.

By this time, reports of my condition, now being passed around by my aunties, had also filtered overseas to our Canadian relatives and Mom had recently discovered that there was one particular toy, which was a marble sorting game, assembled within a plastic windowed tower, but it was currently unavailable in this country. She wrote to her cousin to report on my progress and she enclosed my first photographs and just a few weeks later, a cylindrical-shaped parcel arrived via airmail which had been posted in Vancouver.

The physiotherapist now advised Mom that she should contact Scope, formerly known as The Spastics Society, for further information, so next, one of their representatives called in to meet me and to establish how she could help.

Specializing in Cerebral Palsy, her immediate reaction after watching me rolling around on the hearth chewing on Prince, my fur dog, was that they must provide a special chair for me and she would arrange for this as a matter of urgency. She told Mom that she had seen children with similar problems to mine many times and if I had a chair to hold me in a firm sitting position, then I would only need to concentrate my efforts around manipulating toys and I could also try to feed myself.

Only about three weeks later, as promised, the doorbell rang and a blonde, ruddy-faced man stood at the bottom of the driveway, with an enormous wooden chair in his arms.

"Sonya Hill?" he inquired.

"Oh yes", Mom replied, "just drop it down anywhere in the hall, it will be fine".

"I've just got to pop back to the van", the driver told her, "as there's a tray to go with it".

Mom then placed her signature on his greasy clipboard and he went on his way.

"Right Sonya, let's see how we get on with this posh new chair", Mom said, now trying to fit my skinny little legs in my new seat, one either side of the central padded stump to prevent me from slipping down under the table.

She had just managed to get me settled when we heard the back door being opened again. This time, it was Auntie. My cousin had got tired with playing in the garden, so she had decided to catch the bus which stopped just at the bottom of our hill and she had bought him to play. He stood at the side of her, excitedly jumping from one foot to the other, noisily blowing on his plastic trumpet.

I looked up and started to laugh. I knew instantly, simply by the din, who had just bounced through the door.

"I can see someone's got a lovely new chair", Auntie said to me and then regarding my mom, she added, "It is just the thing to hold her in a good position as well. I will be able to come and easily cut her hair now."

My cousin ran behind the settee and pointed down into the back garden. "Rhubarb!", he cried with excitement.

"I wonder if Sonya could eat rhubarb?", Mom pondered. "It looks just about ripe enough now, so I think I'll go down and cut a few stalks off and see if I can do a bit of feeding practice with her."

Auntie agreed that this was an excellent idea, so she said, "Go on, I'll watch her for a minute while you go and get some."

My sister had heard all the commotion now: she had been playing with her dolls' house in her bedroom with her friend, the one with the strange croaky voice, but now she appeared in the kitchen doorway, having just realised that my cousin had arrived.

She pulled on her black school trainers, which lay under the telephone table in the hall and then bounded down the steep flight of steps, to join the others in the back garden.

The process of teaching me to feed myself was going to be another messy, long, and difficult one.

Mom rolled up the sleeves of my dress, fastened one of those revolting, plastic Pelican bibs around my neck and then brought out a new pack of kitchen roll in readiness to clean up my horrendous mess.

She placed a saucer of sugar on my tray and next proceeded to wrap a short length of rhubarb in a sheet of the kitchen towel, now pressing it into the palm of my left hand. I didn't really have the ability to chew it, but once I had established a firm grip, I learnt to dip it into my sugar and elevate it to my mouth.

It soon became clear to everyone that my new chair would prove to be invaluable, as holding me in a secure sitting position, I could at last concentrate all my efforts on playing with toys, rather than trying to prevent myself from accidentally toppling over every few minutes.

Of course, just like the rest of my family, my nan was always on the lookout for new toys too. As you can see, they were all very kind and each time we went on a family shopping trip, a regular three-way dispute would often flare up between my mom, Nan and Auntie as to which one was to pay for our treat that day.

Anyway, a day or two later, I was seated in my new chair again and I could hear Mom rustling about in the hall. I didn't know what she was doing, but soon she came in, carrying a big, paper packet.

"Here", she said, "see what Nanny's sent for you".

I gave it a quick prod with my thumb, but nothing happened, so it kept me quiet for the next five minutes trying to force a multi-coloured, metal tin to fall out of the packet. I still hadn't the foggiest idea what it was supposed to be, but there was an ominous-looking button on the side, labelled "Press Here", so I looked at Mom again, just to make sure that it was safe to follow the instructions. She just nodded and smiled at me, so I reached forward and bashed the red button with my clenched fist.

I heard a funny squeak, and I threw my head back and chuckled, as now, a red and white clown donned in a yellow trilby, concertinaed out of its secret hiding place. It was, of course, a Jack-In-The-Box.

I have always been encouraged to use both hands, but the fact was now slowly emerging, that my left hand was going to become the dominant one although, following the enormous difficulties which Mom had seen me through up to this point, to learn that I was now developing into a left-handed child was an absolute thrill.

3

What Can I Do Next Mom?

Time was moving on fast and Dave Edmunds topped the British Single Charts with "I Hear You Knocking", marking the close of 1970. The radio was on in the dining recess and I was just watching Mom through the kitchen doorway, as she busied herself going about her regular daily chores.

"I'm going to do some baking a little later", Mom said, "so if you're good while I finish the last bit of tidying up, you can help me if you want."

"O.K. Mom", I agreed. I thought this sounded like a reasonable bargain and I always loved the chance to make a mess.

In the meantime, however, I continued to amuse myself, and today I'd chosen to play with my big red shape-sorter letterbox. It contained about half a dozen different coloured shapes, but it had no other particularly interesting quality, except boasting the educational capacity of teaching me about shape matching and for me, of course, it was useful to practice the fine, skilful hand movements necessary to post each shape through its corresponding hole. The only slight downside to the post-box, however, was that, with me being me, every five seconds I would inadvertently get my fingers stuck in the posting holes and then I would accidentally pull the lid off trying to shake myself free again, scattering its contents all over the floor.

"I won't be long now", Mom called a few moments later. "I've just got to put the next load of washing in."

Back then Mom still used one of those old-fashioned, twin-tub washing machines, one side was the actual washer and then adjacent to this, sat the spinner. In those days, doing the weekly wash was a case of using a large set of wooden pincers to transfer the soaking wet laundry from the washer and jostle it into the spinner. It was somewhat of a performance and then at the end, she would need to rest the pipe at the back of the machine in the kitchen sink to drain the water out.

I wonder how the young women of today would manage in carrying out this time-consuming procedure? but at least times had moved on from the metal tub and wooden maid.

Depending upon my mood, or whether I felt reasonably well that day, it was a bit hit and miss as to whether in fact, Mom could settle me for long enough to be able to do the washing.

On some occasions, she would simply bundle our clothing into a bag and take me down to the launderette and then sit there, desperately trying to keep me interested in watching the soap suds splash around in the window of the washing machine and when that idea began to wear thin, she could always resort to the tedium of counting how many cars of a particular colour drove passed the shop.

I'd been very good this morning, however, so after taking a little time longer to have our mid-morning drink and a few chocolate biscuits, Mom set to work, this time making some pastry in her big, orange mixing bowl.

I loved to watch Mom cook, but my favourite thing of all, was when she decided to bake homemade jam tarts with some leftover scraps of pastry, as this was one of the first culinary tasks I could join in with. She put on my apron, sprinkle my tray with flour and after a little practice, I learnt to roll out my dough. Next, it was time to cut out the pastry rounds with the little pastry cutter so Mom would position it in the correct place for me and then the only thing I had to do was to whack the target with my fist and then the deed was done, all ready for Mom to carefully tease out, next transferring my pastry cutter into a new position. My hand would excitedly take to the air again, as I tried to prepare myself to punch out the pastry case.

The second task Mom found for me to do was to grease the tin. It was difficult to decide what got the most generous coating of fat, the baking tray, my table, or me, but it was all good fun, and I was taking an interest in trying to help around the home.

Despite the convenience of my new chair, it soon became apparent that another dilemma which needed to be addressed was that objects tended to slide around on my table, making it more difficult for me to do things.

At first, Mom used to hold items still for me and then she sometimes employed the technique of spreading out a damp cloth on my table, which gave a non-slip effect. It was quite a considerable time afterwards, in fact, not until I started school, that we were introduced to non-slip mats, but in the early days, the notion of using the cloth or sometimes, even a warm tea towel did the trick.

As soon as our jam tarts were in the oven and my brain had registered that for the whole of the last five seconds my table had been empty, except for the last few tiny remnants of pastry, which you almost needed a magnifying glass to spot, I looked up and inquired, "Are we going out anywhere today Mom?"

I realise now that I must have been so tiring at times, but my mom and the rest of the family saw my eagerness to learn how to do different things as a positive attribute because it was the possession of this strong desire to become as independent as I could, that was going to see me through.

"We've got to go out in three parts of an hour", she answered, "to pick your sister up from school, so we haven't got a lot of time left now. Tell you what though, I think there's just enough time for you to play with your train while I finish off getting ready. Would you like that?"

"Yes, that sounds cool", I nodded.

At the time I had a lovely train set, which was based upon The Magic Roundabout. This had a small plastic base and included miniatures of all the characters including Ermintrude, Dylan, Florence and not forgetting, of course, Dougal the friendly sausage dog, who just seemed to glide around the set aimlessly, as if he were being blown along by some invisible, underground gust of wind. The main feature, of course, was the little locomotive itself and I would spend many happy hours just winding the handle to propel it around the track. I could never turn the cog very quickly, but I would repeatedly hit it with my thumb and eventually, the train would complete its steady revolution.

Well, just like my little train, the time was fast chugging on too and although it was clear to see that I was progressing all the time, Mom felt that I now really needed to mix with other children who perhaps had a similar range of needs to my own.

During one of my visits to see the paediatrician at the hospital, Mom had told him of her concerns about my educational future and she enquired how much progress he felt could be realistically expected of me. He advised her that given the correct encouragement, in his experience, he had seen many youngsters go on to achieve great things although my physical development would probably be slow. His opinion had yielded in Mom a refreshing new optimism. He also provided her with some highly informative literature on dealing with the needs of children with Cerebral Palsy so she now felt that, in one way or another, my immediate needs were being met.

However, there was still one crucial question weighing very heavily on Mom's mind and that was, "How was she going to set about finding a suitable school for me?

As time passed, this problem was becoming ever more urgent and she knew she would have to come up with a solution as quickly as possible. She still hadn't any spare time in the day though as when I hadn't got appointments, each day was evenly divided between three main activities and they were: to increase my mobility, to encourage me to manipulate things with my hands, and to improve my communication skills.

I would awake early in the morning and soon Mom decided to move me into my own bedroom, as she felt I would sleep better. I think one of my first memories is of being in my cot, as I can still clearly recall that it was painted white, decorated at each end with images of a lamb and a rabbit.

Despite my problems, I was still finding new ways all the time, to be a little imp. I knew perfectly well what people expected of me, but it was hard work, so I attempted to show Mom, to little avail however, I was going to do everything in my way and in my own time. Poor Mom used to spend all day trying to coax me into a sitting position, with my levels of willingness to do so constantly fluctuating, but as soon as it was time for bed, the rules changed.

After kissing me good night, Mom tucked me up, switched on my bedside lamp which shone through the lacy skirt of a fairy and then, as soon as I heard my door shut, I decided it was time to conform to Moms request which she had made earlier in the day and sit up.

I would wait a few minutes, however, cunningly giving her just enough time to reach the bottom of the stairs and then I would kick off all the bedclothes. I continued to strenuously pull myself up, clinging on to the bars of my cot sides and then, complacently wanting to show off my new skill, I would hoot for Mom to come and tuck me in again, "Mmmoooommm!"

"Oh look, Sonya, what have you done this for again?" Mom inquired, as she observed that my covers were now in total disarray. Remaining oblivious to the true impact of my childish prank, however, behind my cheeky smile, this was simply my smug little way of saying, "Ha! well if you want me to sit up, I'll sit up, but only when it's time to lie down, OK?".

During the day, my time was still separated between sitting in my wooden chair so that I could play with toys on my tray and crawling around the lounge. I don't think at this stage it really mattered to Mom what I was doing, just as long as I was learning to use my hands and so as a result, at times, I used to be engaged in some quite bizarre pastimes.

It is probably a common trend for mothers to give their small children a wide range of kitchen utensils or indestructible ornaments to coax them into eating a meal or to distract their attention from spiralling into a brewing tantrum. However, when it came to encouraging my hand control, Mom's imagination seemed boundless.

I was quite young and I remember that on one occasion I was sitting on the floor next to Mom's chair and she was arduously shelling peas into a basin ready for that night's tea. She could probably tell by my face that I was about to start grumbling that I had nothing to do again when she came up with yet another idea. "Would you like to hang the washing out? I'll show you what I mean", she asked and then smiling, she began to rummage through the sideboard drawers.

Back then, our rotary washing line stood in the back garden. I could always observe it through the lounge window, but I seldom went down there, as it could only be accessed by a very steep flight of steps.

"I don't know what Mom's thinking about now", I thought, "because how can she carry me down to the line when she's got a big basket of wet laundry in her arms? What's going on?"

Finally, she bought out the spotted tin, which had probably once held a paper tray of assorted biscuits and been given as a Christmas present but was now home to a jumble of coloured cotton reels. She tore off a length of thread and then proceeded to arrange two dining chairs so that they faced each other, one on either side of the hearth rug.

Next, she tied a long piece of cotton around one chair leg and then trailing it across the room, she tore off an appropriate length, knotting it tightly around the second chair.

"Here we are, Sonya", she said, "why don't you try to hang the peapods across the cotton and then it will look like a line of washing, just like mine."

This was, without a doubt, one of my most bizarre pastimes and I also recall that I soon developed a strange fondness of the smell of raw peas, but I suppose it was healthier than sniffing glue and at least it kept me quiet for a while longer, or until all the peapods had ripped in two, no longer being able to be hung up to dry.

I don't know how I'm going to get by after all these ludicrous declarations, so anyway, I think we'd better move on again...

The following day was Wednesday, and time for my next session of speech therapy.

Communication was still proving quite a significant difficulty and although I had been able to easily communicate with Mom for some time, my voice was very indistinct. The other members of my family were still finding it extremely difficult to understand me. It was simply impossible for me to converse with strangers and there were times when I just appeared to be withdrawn, engrossed in my own little world.

At around the age of three, Mom could see that my inability to quickly articulate how I felt or what I needed, was a major cause of me starting to throw temper tantrums. I think the problem was that I had such an active mind that despite having the mental capacity to know exactly what I wanted to do, I lacked the physical ability to act upon it. I was still unable to fully make sense of what was wrong with me but I was becoming increasingly aware that my sister and cousin were taking part in activities that I couldn't.

Of course, as soon as I started to talk at all Mom could understand me, and she started to try to convey to me how my problems had arisen. I think this early ability to communicate with Mom was attributed to several factors: a mother's natural instinct, and part of the bonding process; the fact which I have already explained, in that she committed all her time to looking after me and also, although I think it sounds very similar to the first, she was emotionally and almost physically willing me to start speaking, so I think I agreed that this was kind of important too.

For quite a long time, my dad hadn't got a clue what I was saying, and he also tried to deny that Mom could, but of course, Dad spent many hours at work, so hadn't as much time as my mom to sit listening to me.

Mom expressed her concerns about my great struggle to communicate to the speech therapist, as her main worry was that I would soon be starting school and she feared that from the time I left home in the morning until I arrived back at teatime, no-one was going to be able to understand me. How was I ever going to cope?

The speech therapist reinforced the great importance of simply talking to me and she assured Mom that in time, by keeping up with loads of practice, she felt that I would improve. She said that Mom must now break my habit of thinking it was acceptable to simply point at what I wanted and even though Mom understood these gestures, she must insist that I said all my words properly before giving a response.

Oh dear, it looked like someone else was cottoning on to my laziness, so there was only one thing for it now, which was to plan my next line of revenge and clever trickery. I think I always have wanted to improve, but my sense of humour was now starting to come to the fore, so I decided to just tease Mom a little by cooperating with my speech practice only in short bursts.

I then started to deliberately miss out all the consonants in my words and for some bizarre reason, which I am now presuming I must have formulated, boredom probably being the greatest contender, this idiosyncrasy usually occurred during a recital of my unique and very strange version of "Baa, Baa Black Sheep". An even stranger revelation was the fact that I always tried my best to say the first two lines of the nursery rhyme as clearly as possible, but as soon as I reached the line, "Yes sir, yes sir, three bags full", I totally lost the plot and from here on in, I would just pronounce the vowel sounds exclusively, but nothing more. This comical rendition would then end up sounding something like, "Baa Baa Black Sheep, Have you any wool? E IR, E IR, EE A OO", as this was far easier to say than "Yes sir, yes sir three bags full" and what was the point, as Mom knew all the words anyway?

Regretfully though, I soon learnt that my cunning little ploy had failed as Mom then took enormous delight in insisting that I chant the whole thing again, this time, however, with the addition of each and every sound.

She then decided to persist in practicing my speech therapy for a while longer and she suggested that maybe I would like to read a few stories.

Some of my earliest books were the ones made of fabric and I also had a collection of cardboard pop-up books.

I remember one of my favourite stories that Mom would read to me over and over, began, "Ten little rabbits, hopping in a line. One hopped into a bush. Then there were nine".

There was hardly any improvement in the storyline from here on in and it monotonously continued, with a similar corny little riddle on every page, the rabbits slowly diminishing, as they each fell victim to some unexpected, ill-fated peril. At this point, I was beginning to convey my great love for animals so by the time we got to the final page where the last bunny was about to be lured into its final dark burrow, I was always eager to turn straight back to the beginning again just to reassure myself that all ten rabbits were really still in that line. Maybe this book is the origin for my more recent intrigue for horror stories.

My fascination with the real animal world was now showing in other ways too. I started to exhibit intense anger towards the subject of animal cruelty and from an early age, if I managed to catch any bulletin on the news that any creature had been mistreated at all, I would be reduced to tears, too furious to talk for the next hour and this characteristic remains with me today.

Mom had a plastic blancmange mould in the shape of a rabbit. I used to love to watch the pink rabbit wobbling on the plate, but I only had to see the big spoon going towards his back and the corners of my mouth would begin to droop again and I would look just like a sad clown and inevitably start to cry so it wasn't worth the hassle. Eventually, I advanced to the stage where I could steal myself just enough to cope with the atrocity that its body had to be eaten, but then Mom would have to carry the plate with the rabbit's head fully intact back into the kitchen and I think I used to cajole myself into believing that by saying some magic words, which were a big secret that only Mom knew, she was going to restore him to perfect health. To my dismay, however, I have since discovered that my sister had eaten the remains, even down to the poor thing's brain.

Anyway, the clock was still ticking. Soon I had reached the age of three and the problem remained that Mom, quite urgently now, needed to find a suitable school for me. This was again unknown territory for Mom, as it was plain to see that I would be unable to just be slotted into the ordinary infants' school with my sister, as they weren't equipped to cater for my needs. She began to voice these concerns to Nan and then one day, quite unexpectedly, she received another letter from the clinic, requesting me to attend an educational assessment. It was held in the same building as my other weekly treatments, so would pose no problem to get there.

Within just a few moments of arrival, a tall, lanky woman of about fifty years of age called us into the treatment room. I started to cough a little, in my typical attempt to convey to Mom that I couldn't cope with the nauseating stink of disinfectant. I hated it but being in the company of the assessor and wanting to give a good impression, Mom simply mopped my chin with a handkerchief and pretended not to realise what I meant.

There were a few toys scattered around, a large mound of foam mattresses down the furthest end and also the room was home to various pieces of apparatus and exercise equipment.

The lady doctor tested my hands, she placed a range of toys in front of me to reach for, she held up various pictures for me to identify and test my speech and then she just shook her head in denunciation that I could understand anything at all. Mom could hardly believe what she was hearing, and she was utterly furious. Being completely accustomed to my pattern of speech she knew perfectly well what I was saying and that all the answers I gave were correct. The assessor, however, blatantly denied this and she concluded that Mom simply needed to believe that she could communicate with me, as it was all part of grieving for my condition. Mom then hurried out of the room again, livid and blinded by tears.

A little while afterwards, this resulted in me being granted a place at a local centre for mentally handicapped people where I would have been amused all day with singing and various types of playful activities. What a thrill that would have been!

Still undeterred, Mom's next line of attack was to write to Lord Cadbury, the chocolatier guy, whose child also suffered from Cerebral Palsy, as she had now learnt that he sat on The Board of Governors of the school run by Scope. He promptly replied saying he had no input as far as student selection was concerned, but he sent Mom a very helpful book explaining various things about my condition and soon I was sent to undergo yet more tests.

The Scope school, specializing in my disability, exhibited a totally different approach towards my problems from the onset and they wholeheartedly supported Mom's view that there was no doubt about my educational potential. Unfortunately, at the same time, there was a little boy who had also applied for a place and when compared, his overall score in the test results was identical to mine. There was only one place available but, still only being in the early 1970s, attitudes towards the sexes were a little behind the times, so the young boy was given the priority over me.

Mom had been convincing herself that this school was, without doubt, the place for me, and so upon hearing that my application had been turned down, she felt completely devastated and my future, was dashed once more into uncertainty.

"Come on", she sighed, desperately trying to focus on something more positive, "It's a nice warm day today, so I think I'll take you outside to do a bit of walking practice, we've got to get those little legs of yours working." Mom was advised by the paediatrician to get me a pair of boots which were tightly laced ending just below the knee as this would be ideal to support my thin, floppy legs, as this would help provide me with a little walking practice. Very often, she would support me under my arms and march me along the wall at the top of the garden.

As I clomped back and forth, she would sing...

"Oh, the grand old Duke of York,
He had ten thousand men,
He marched them up to the top of the hill,
And he marched them down again..."

Well, I don't know about me, but poor Mom must have had muscles like Popeye. Also, sometimes if I held my head up, I would spot the lady who lived opposite watching all that was going on and smiling at me through her kitchen window.

My hospital consultant had also provided some very useful information, but Mom still felt that the reason for me not being able to walk was simply due to my weak muscles. If the physiotherapist was capable of strengthening me enough to accomplish a sitting position, then she felt that my inability to walk could be tackled similarly to that of how a bodybuilder strengthens their muscles. She thought it was merely a case of constant stimulation and, sooner or later, I would get the hang of it.

It is believed that by repetitively putting someone who has suffered brain injury into a position which they find difficult, this will often be to accomplish either a sitting or a standing position, depending upon the needs and abilities of each patient, then it may be possible to forge new neurological pathways, hence awakening underlying faculties which could be lying dormant.

My nan's father, although he had passed away long before I was born, had been a keen herbalist. So the story goes, during his lifetime if anyone had any ailments, he would go for a walk along the country lanes gathering all kinds of wild flowers and leaves, then he would amble up the garden path, all set to devise the perfect remedy and I have little doubt that he would have tried to concoct something to benefit me. Mom would also dose me with a herbal medicine, which she had read in a magazine was supposed to improve the learning capacity of brain-damaged children. Well, I don't know about that, but I was certainly very healthy, and Mom did little else each day except trying to stimulate me.

Soon it was time to pick my sister up from school again, so Mom started to put my anorak on, that awful brown one, which had a long piece of elastic threaded down both sleeves with a woollen mitten sewn on each end, so that I could feel it being pulled across my back and while we were getting ready, she tried to keep me amused with a game of "I Spy".

"I spy with my little eye, something the colour of red", Mom began.

"Er...is it tomato sauce?", I asked, now seeing that Mom was now rushing to lay the table at the last minute.

"No Sonya. That was a really good guess though but look a bit harder and try again", she replied.

"Maybe it's the red candles in the candelabra?" was my next guess.

"No, it's not that either", Mom said, "and anyway, they're orange".

After about three more attempts of scanning around the living room for every speck of red I could muster, I finally saw that my red plastic sunglasses were poking out of the top of my big pile of toys.

At last, Mom agreed that she had been thinking of the spectacles all along and with this rewarding conclusion, we set off for my sister's school.

We reached the school gates just about five minutes before the bell went and, living in such a hilly area, within the first week or two of September, there was already a noticeable chill in the air.

"Stop trying to pull the hood of your anorak off, you naughty girl", Mom scolded me, "it's too cold and if you don't stop this instant, then you won't have any sweets".

At this, I would often cease what I was doing and scowl out of the car window to see whether there was any sign of my sister coming dawdling through the gate yet, usually trailing behind that girl who had a voice like a bleating lamb.

When at last she showed up, Mom said that we would soon be home again now, but we would have to call into the bread shop first.

Here we go again, I thought, There's always some kind of detour before going home and I never have been able to fathom out why everyone called it the bread shop, as it was just a small general store, selling everything from tins of baked beans to a sink scourer.

Outside the bread shop stood one of those metal notice boards bobbing to and fro in the breeze, displaying the day's most important headline.

"Fears grow for missing local boy".

Ten minutes later, Mom finally emerged again, with half a dozen stuffed carrier bags in her arms, one with a newspaper in the top, which was almost taking to the sky in the breeze.

"Look", she said to us, "there's another little boy who's disappeared now. You will have to be so careful", she told my sister. "This is why I'm so reluctant to let you take your bike to the park with your friends, as it would be just my luck for you to be the one who was taken."

My sister sighed, but rapidly forgot her disappointment when I remembered to ask, "Did you get us any sweets today Mom?"

"Yes", she said, "but you will have to eat your tea first, or you'll spoil your appetite again like you did the other day".

It was early September and Mom started to prepare for Christmas. She began looking around the shops early, as in those days it was such a problem to find suitable toys for me which I would be able to do. Putting this problem aside though, just like everything else, it never fazed Mom for long, especially when Nan and Auntie decided to hit the town with her too.

Anyway, one Saturday morning, Mom was preparing the lunch and she was just about to lift a joint of pork out of the oven when the phone rang.

"Quick, answer the phone", she called to my sister.

I heard her asking to speak to my cousin, so from that, it became immediately apparent that Auntie was on the line, so Mom went into the hall to see what was going on.

Auntie said, "Turn to page 26 of the newspaper, there's an advert for a nursery that's just opened for disabled and able-bodied children and I thought it might be suitable for Sonya."

Mom agreed that this sounded like a good plan, so she scribbled down the phone number and first thing the following day, she rang it. The lady who answered said that they did accept children with special needs, but there were only a few places left for this term. Mom made immediate arrangements to take me in on the following Monday to have a look round and to assess its suitability. She knew that Auntie would be looking after my cousin and she was still working part-time in the hairdressing salon, so she rang and asked Nan to accompany her, as two heads were better than one and she knew it never took Nan long to reach a wise decision.

They weren't overly impressed by the organizer. Nan said she looked a bit grouchy, but there was a broad array of toys and activities available and they felt that I was now getting to the stage where I needed to be integrated with other children who had similar problems to my own.

I can vaguely remember going to the nursery and one of the first activities that I loved to do, was the large, wooden jigsaws. By this time, the dexterity in my left hand was getting better and better, so it was the ideal challenge for me to try and slide the pieces of puzzle back into their correct destination. It took me quite a while to master this skill, but I was now beginning to enjoy the fact that with a little patience, I could accomplish things and so when another chunk of my jigsaw slid into place, I would throw my head back and start to chuckle, probably thinking something like, "Yes, I've done it!"

In fact, for many years afterwards, doing different puzzles became one of my main hobbies, so this idea was pencilled into my Christmas list without hesitation.

Mom skimmed down the telephone directory and she learnt that there was a major toy outlet in the city and in no time at all, I had built up a collection of about a dozen to fifteen different jigsaws.

However, at home, it wasn't long before I concluded that doing my puzzles one at a time was starting to get a bit dull, so I felt it was time to spice things up a little.

I crawled over to the kitchen doorway, just to see what Mom was doing and to report that I'd just finished the puzzle of the mother pig with her huge litter of hungry piglets when something else caught my eye and my next comical pastime evolved.

"Mom", I chuckled, "have you finished with that empty bread packet on the top of the fridge?"

"Yes", she replied, "but what on earth do you want that for? Here we go, what are you about to concoct now?" Mom smiled... "Oh and keep it away from your face, or you'll suffocate next", she warned.

I dashed back round to the fireplace and shrieking with laughter, I started to tip out all of the pieces from first one jigsaw and then quickly moving from one puzzle to the next, I continued to make my way around the circle, until all the pieces from my jigsaws were mixed up, lying in a huge mound. Next, I took time to ensure that each piece was lying face down, so that I couldn't see its picture, this would take me quite a while, especially as, whilst turning one piece face down, I would often inadvertently flip another one up the wrong way again. Oh dear, I did get myself into some sorry states, but once I'd decided what I wanted to do, I was determined to accomplish it and so eventually my game was all set to play. I then began to gather up the pieces, randomly selecting them a few at a time and then, placing them into the bread packet, I began the huge task of rebuilding my jigsaws. I would draw one piece of the puzzle from the bag and then crawl over to the correct jigsaw to slot it into position. Again, I don't know where this peculiar notion sprang from, but it was certainly another good way of keeping me mobile.

As you can see, I was becoming quite an amusing little character and despite my obvious physical restrictions, I was devising new forms of play all the time and I was slowly developing more patience too, as it gave me an enormous sense of achievement when I accomplished another new skill.

Soon it was time to start my new nursery. I was still very attached to Mom though and up until this point, she had never been anywhere without me. She stayed with me for my first few mornings and then one day, I decided to go over and play in the sandpit. I'd filled the green bucket with sand, but it was too heavy for me to lift to tip my sandcastle out, so I turned around expecting to be able to call Mom over to assist me.

My eyes were met by a sea of faces. With the terror intensifying like a huge, oncoming tidal wave which was about to crash into my consciousness, I gradually realised that I recognized no-one, and one person was missing from the crowd - Mom.

Unbeknown to me, Mom had slipped out for half an hour to go for a cup of tea at the café three streets away. I didn't know quite what to make of Mom's disappearance at first, but as time went on, it was clear that whatever had occurred, her abrupt departure had all been concocted by the teacher, as there was just no way that Mom would have left me with strange people, well, not unless of course, she had been forced. I was sure that there was something sinister about this nursery from the very beginning and Mom has since told me that she couldn't even walk in a straight line without the aid of my pushchair to lean on. She has recalled for me that she hated every minute of this trip and she just felt that she must hurry back to make sure I was alright.

Upon her return, as she peered through the door of the nursery, Mom instantly observed that I was anything but alright, as a little boy was gleefully clobbering me over the head with a plastic hammer. One of the songs they used to sing to us was, "Peter hammers with one hammer", so I think that little rascal decided to mimic Peter's role and put me under the hammer. Needless to say though, this was both the first and last time that Mom ever left me alone at nursery so, in fact, it turned out that the naughty hyperactive boy had done me a good deed, after all, so even at the tender age of three, I made sure that my "girl power" won through.

It was at the nursery, however, that Mom became friends with another lady whose daughter also suffered from Cerebral Palsy and it soon became clear that, at last, I had found my first special playmate. The little girl was physically a bit more able than me and she was just starting to learn to walk by clinging onto the furniture. She soon latched onto Mom too and she used to address her by calling out, "Sonya's Mom!"

For Mom, this was the first time she had met another mother who was toiling with a child similar to me, so I think it was a great experience for both of them to be able to share their problems and feelings from a mother's viewpoint.

A few more weeks went by, somewhat uneventfully, except for keeping up with my regular, everyday activities. When the weekend came around again, of course, I always looked forward to my Saturday afternoon visits to see my grandparents. It was great fun to see everyone and even better on those days when I managed to beat my cousin's score, ricocheting the tiny, metallic balls around the Bagatelle board.

At first, the game comprised of ten balls in total, which were held in an elongated compartment at the bottom of the board but, of course, after many pleasurable hours of use, their numbers slowly diminished and some may even remain to this day, obscured from human sight, having rolled into a dark undiscovered corner or maybe even mashed up at some distant landfill sight, after being sucked into the belly of the vacuum cleaner.

Anyway, Granddad was always in charge of keeping track of our scores and when it was my turn again, he would often position the next ball in front of the trigger.

"YES!", I yelled, as my first ball bounced its journey around several nails, until at last coming to rest in its final destination, allotting me with a final total of 125 points, this being the third highest scoring hole on the board.

Now suitably chuffed, I shot my cousin a very satisfied grin.

"Come on then", I sniggered mischievously, "let's see if you can beat that one."

Mom had made her exit into the kitchen with Nan as usual, where they started preparations for tea, but the door was ajar, so we could hear their pleasant chatter as they began to butter some bread.

"When I was driving down here", Mom said, "I had to pop into the paper shop for a TV paper and I saw that there is a notice up outside the church to say that their Sunday School Anniversary is coming up. I wonder if it would be any good for Sonya?"

"I would most definitely enquire", Nan agreed, "I think that would be a lovely idea. I would take them both", she said, meaning my sister, as she would have to go along to look after me.

Sure enough, Mom went along on the following day to meet the vicar and of course, he extended a very warm welcome and so my sister and I were taken along to the next meeting.

It was late autumn at this point and coincidently, we soon learnt that there were only a few more weeks to go before the anniversary and the children had already started to learn all the lines of their cheery choruses. It would pose quite a task so I would need to practice at home too, or I'd just be rubbish. "Oh no", I thought, "when Mom realizes what is going on, she will use this as another boring speech therapy ploy."

I wasn't the only one whose talents were going to be put to the test though as, around this time, my nan worked as a professional seamstress, so as you can imagine there seemed no finer excuse than the Sunday School Anniversary for Nan to rise to her next creative challenge and within just a few weeks, two matching outfits were sewn up and all ready, give or take the final fittings and adjustments.

In the end, we looked like a couple of decorated Easter eggs, as we were adorned from top to toe in stiff velvet bows and reams of lace. Meanwhile, Mom took us into Dudley again, to seek out the all-important, matching accessories so we would have new slides for our hair, perhaps a little silver bracelet and of course, we were never considered respectable without a pair of shiny, black patent shoes.

Finally, the big day was upon us and we had to have our lunch extra early, just to ensure that Mom had plenty of time to make sure that "we looked respectable", which, of course, I always thought we were anyway, so all that was necessary, was for us to look like us in our extra posh dresses but, every little girl secretly enjoys dressing up, don't they? It's just cool to show a little attitude.

When we arrived, Mom quickly ran the comb through my hair then, pushing me into the small musty church hall, she parked my wheelchair on the end of the first row of children. My memory of this is very hazy, but one detail I can recall is trying to warble along with the others, in the constant knowledge that all the other kids were singing at a rate of about three sentences ahead of me. If I was lucky though, sometimes this would happen to be the point where the lyrics were repeated so everyone else's second performance of a particular line would overlap my first and my slight timing difference would go undetected.

I have always hated the sound of my voice, despite my reputation for being the world's biggest chatterbox and if I ever tried to audition for The X Factor, I wouldn't even make it through to boot camp.

Anyway, the most important thing is in the taking part and Sunday School gave me a great opportunity to join in with my sister and to feel able to make friends with other children in my local community. My mom has always encouraged this and I feel this kind of normal activity has played an important role in encouraging my independence and shaping me into the single-minded character I'm known as today.

We attended this church for some time and on another occasion, it was the Harvest Festival and to raise extra cash, it was only a small place, they auctioned off baskets of fruit and vegetables which had been donated by the congregation. Mom and Nan bought a huge loaf of bread which had been hand-crafted into the shape of a sheaf of corn. Displayed on the stall it had looked very eye-catching but, unfortunately, when Nan came to slice it for tea, the knife wouldn't touch it, as it was as hard as a brick. She did attempt to warm it a little and soften it off in the oven, but I don't know about it being a loaf of bread, it was more like a loofah to scrub your back with. Let's just say that on the following day, the ducks in the park enjoyed a hearty meal, but whether they were still able to fly, is a quandary which I shall never know.

Another weekend had passed and soon it was time to head back to the nursery. I didn't want to go today, as I had more than my fill last week, what with Mom disappearing and then that kid trying to crack my head open with a plastic sledgehammer. Surely I was entitled to some mercy now and Mom would recognize my screamingly obvious need to stay at home? I was really doing well with my physiotherapy and I could even sing almost as well as Pavarotti, so I begged Mom to give me a break and just let me stay at home.

It was no use however and soon I was dressed up like an Egyptian mummy with frostbite again, as she assured me the temperature was below freezing and if I didn't wear several layers, then all my extremities would turn blue and drop off.

"Er, a little too much information, Mom", I thought, now slowly piecing together the horrific graphical consequences of her comment.

I really did think I was having a hard time of it now, but little did I know that my woeful days hadn't even started yet. I'd began with such good intentions too. I mean, I had done everything I could think of to try and be the model daughter. I'd helped Mom with the housework, I'd learnt to do the jigsaw puzzles, not only one at a time like other lazy kids, but I did all mine in one go and I'd even invented a good use for old peapods. Surely that ought to accredit me as a pioneer for future recycling methods and not only that, I'd boldly gone where no other toddler had gone, well not in all my four years of experience anyway, and I'd taken my first battering from the unruly kid at the nursery.

Maybe this was the reasoning behind my friend's pitiful cries of "Sonya's Mom", each afternoon when Mom came to pick me up, as she too was pleading sanctuary from a similar fate.

Well, her mom and mine had obviously been secretly colluding, because one morning, as we arrived at the dreaded nursery gates, her mom came running up to Mom's car window, bearing a big grin on her face. I couldn't quite make out what she was about to say, but whatever it was, it was enough to fill me with dread.

"Good morning Sonya", she said, smiling and then she turned to Mom and began to talk in an excited, but urgent tone.

"I've managed to track down a special school", she said, "It's called The Victoria School and it seems to have excellent facilities, it's just what we need" and then she asked Mom if she would like to accompany her to their forthcoming Open Day.

Of course, Mom didn't hesitate and when the day finally arrived, she practically jumped for joy, as she knew as she drove through the gates, that The Victoria School was, without question, the place for me.

Its facilities were fantastic, incorporating onsite physiotherapists, speech therapists, specialist teachers and an extensive range of aids. Mom's first and lasting impression was, it was simply perfect. It seemed, finally, to be the dream come true she had been longing for.

All the previous disappointment of not being able to get me into the Scope school just flew out of the window. She came home, thoroughly delighted and while my sister was keeping me out of mischief with a few board games, she composed a letter to the local councillors, also sending another copy to my paediatrician at the hospital requesting him to support my application.

God had succeeded once again in magnificently lifting the burden of how I was to be educated. At The Victoria School in Northfield, Birmingham and so what we were going to have to do next, was to prepare for a wonderful Christmas.

4

Toys 'N' A Tangerine

The weekend soon came round again, and Mom stood scraping vegetables at the kitchen sink. She was singing a hymn that she had just been listening to on the Sunday morning service which was being broadcast live from a small chapel in Devon.

Dad came in, he was late getting up and his mop of thick, black hair was still dishevelled, but he had driven several hundred miles in his truck again during the week so, before returning to his regular grindstone again tomorrow, it was time for him to chill out and to enjoy the company of the family.

"You sound chirpy", he commented to Mom, as he grabbed a few digestive biscuits to dunk in his coffee.

"Yes", Mom said, "I just feel like I've had a total weight lifted from my shoulders now I've found Victoria School. I know this is the right choice for Sonya now and it is as though someone has guided me because even I was beginning to wonder where this would all end and I know you thought I was just daydreaming". Dad giggled and replied, "Well at least it has made you happy anyway." He came in the living room and slumped into his armchair to read the paper.

I was on the hearth rug, trying to stick my thumb through the ring, setting off the goofy voice of my big, talking monkey. It held a range of about half a dozen phrases and when Mom and Nan spotted him in the shop window, they agreed it would be another great toy to further stimulate my hands.

I would play quietly for hours now and the only thing that could be heard was my chimp, followed by my cheerful little tone trying to mimic what he had just said.

This would go something like, "Oo oo, I love to eat bananas!", or "Stop that monkey business", or another phrase of an equally stupid nature.

Secretly, I now suspect that my chattering companion may just have been Nan's desperate solution to try to stop me crawling into the hall and trying to telephone the number for the speaking clock or the weather forecast every time Mom's back was turned. I was unable to operate the phone dial, but I was now beginning to cotton on to the fact, that if I couldn't achieve something in one way, then I could generally invent another and I would sneak a pen from Dad's coat pocket, I knew where they kept the blue book with all the silly numbers in, so all that was left to do was to lodge the pen tip in the correct holes on the dial. It would take me a long time but I felt utterly jubilant once I'd successfully inputted the final number and I would elevate the receiver to my ear just to make sure that I could hear that parrot-like recorded message saying, "At the third stroke, it will be 4:15 and 20 seconds, beep, beep, beep. It was great fun until, of course, Mom finally realised why I'd kept so quiet for such a long time. I had been caught out again and so I would slither down the hall in a mood, to see if I could find any ladybirds or woodlice that had managed to creep their way in, under the front door. I would roll the woodlice over on their backs, just to see whether they could manage to correct their position again. This idea may have derived from my physiotherapist who had been playing a similar game with me at the clinic. In order to improve my resistance and to teach me to maintain a strong sitting position, one of the exercises she'd devised was to try to knock me off balance and then see whether I could readjust my posture quick enough to avoid tumbling over. I don't know which of us made a bigger effort, me or the insects.

I wasn't so cruel with the ladybirds however as they were my favourite species of insect, so I just used to encourage them to wriggle in and out of my fingers, making them step up and down onto different surfaces, giving them a varied range of terrains to explore. I thought I was being kind, but the poor things were probably scared witless by me - their gigantic predator: the experience from their perspective was undoubtedly similar to us being pursued through the desert by the pounding footsteps of a Tyrannosaurus Rex.

What are you up to now?", Mom called to me from the kitchen doorway, "as if I didn't know. I wonder where your sister is?"

She was halfway down the hill, as usual, skipping and playing tag with her mates.

Mom walked to the top of the drive. "Oi", she called to my sister. "Come and look after Sonya for half an hour while I just finish the dinner off. I'm very busy here and I've only got one pair of hands. Reluctantly, my sister came plodding up the hill to fetch me. In those days, I don't think I made any secret of the fact that I now felt that I had won. This was what I had wanted all along and despite my problems, I was in no quandary by now of what was meant by the term "sibling rivalry", but she is four years older than I am so, at this point, her grasp of its concept was even greater.

My sister and I would often spar off at each other at mealtimes and if I'm honest here, on these occasions I was often the ringleader, as Mom would tell her to feed me a sandwich while she was busy. She would break off a small lump of bread and I'd watch her hand steadily approaching my mouth and then when my dinner was just about three millimetres away from my hungry, drooling lips, my laid-back temperament would transform into that of a Rottweiler trying to tear a piece out of the postman's leg. Well, I had to get my own back for her constant insolence in some way and this type of banter appeared to work like the bugs in the hall.

All the kids in our road would congregate in the one corner, where the steep hill swerved into its first ninety-degree bend. Some of the houses, particularly those which faced ours, had huge, sheer staircases leading up to the front door, so if we had lived in one of those, it would have been impossible for my parents to keep carrying me up on a daily basis.

My sister took me down to her friends, parked my wheelchair in a safe position and put the brakes on.

"Now, don't touch those brakes or you're dead", she said lovingly. "Look, here's a stone for you, so either draw a picture on the wall or you can just watch us, but be quiet OK? or you will have to go back in again." She nodded right in my face, just to be sure that her instructions had been heeded and she walked away to join her mates.

She then launched into the usual types of play customary during the 1970s, such as skipping, or bouncing her tennis ball against the garden walls, as it was still, of course, long before the age of game consoles, or other modern handheld devices. It is fantastic how things have moved on since then especially as it has opened up so many new and remarkable doorways for disabled people like me who would probably have just vegetated by now, spending each day waiting for the next episode of their favourite soap opera or reading books and crumpled magazines.

Less than three minutes later, however, just allowing my sister long enough to settle contently back into her game, I would drop my stone. On most occasions, I think this was probably a deliberate action, simply to acquire further attention, but I just wanted to be able to join in. Sometimes, one of the little girls would promptly rush over and pick it up for me, although after it had landed on the pavement for about the twentieth time, I think this began to wear thin with the whole gang, but most of all with my sister, who, at this point, would stomp over to me, fuming. She would then place her hands on top of mine and say, "OK, you're freezing now, just as I thought. Come on, no arguing, it's time for you to go in before you've got a bad cold again".

My big sister then embarked upon the strenuous task of pushing me back up the hill, zealously praying all the way, that this time, either the dinner would be ready to be dished up or, at least Mom would have the heart to agree that my hands were too cold and that I now needed to be taken in. I'm mean, come on, let's be honest here, by my sister's judgment, I was suffering from borderline frostbite and she wasn't prepared to carry my blue fingers in a plastic bag to the hospital had they have dropped off.

On this particular occasion, however, much to my sister's relief, Mom did agree to take me back in.

The next day, it was 5th November; Bonfire Night, so on his way back from the office, Dad decided to call for some petrol and he was just about to put the key back in the ignition to drive home when he spotted a great big poster in the window of the paper shop next door. It was advertising an enormous box of fireworks and it was a pretty reasonable price too, as there were loads for just £15, so he decided to bring some home for us.

My dad came bouncing through the door, with a great big grin on his face. I knew instinctively there must be something weird going on, as he started to do his funny little shuffling action again, shifting his weight from one foot to the other, as so often seemed to precede one of Dad's amusing grand announcements. Now I come to think of it though, he also did the same thing when I had a temperature of 104, a thumping headache and I was lying on the settee wrapped in my "sick blanket". He would then burst into song. The doctor really ordered that one.

"Look what I've just bought for you", he said, now pulling the firework selection from the carrier bag.

"I hate fireworks, Dad", I said, crossly.

"What do you mean?" he replied. "I thought you would like to watch all the pretty lights through the window. It was supposed to be a lovely treat for you Sonya, so I'm rather disappointed now."

"No!", I answered angrily. "I hate them. I don't want to watch."

I was losing my temper at this point and one habit which I had now developed, giving uprise to an additional twist to throwing myself backwards in rage and deliberately banging my head on the carpet, is that I would viciously dig my nails into my hands and arms and scratch myself until I had almost drawn blood. Tears were beginning to brim over my eyelids and that notorious mouth expression was emerging again and going down and down and down.

"OK", Mom said, in a desperate attempt to interject before I threw a full-scale tantrum, "I think I've fully ascertained by now that you hate fireworks, so you don't have to watch them if you don't want to. You can help me do some dusting instead, but why don't you like them anyway?"

At this, I just waved my stiff arms towards the television and between my big sobs, she eventually got it out of me that I had been listening to a teatime news bulletin and it had been warning the public to take all their pets indoors and to be sensitive to the fact that they would be frightened of all the bangers and rockets going off.

"What about Winnie and Sandy Mom?" I asked.

"Oh, the guinea pigs will be fine", she replied. "Anyway, they are perfectly safe in the garage and they are both buried beneath so much hay, that I doubt very much if they will hear a thing."

For quite a few years, we kept both a male and a female guinea pig, the lady one was black and white and of the long-haired variety; we named her Winnie and then there was her light brown, short-haired boyfriend, who my sister had decided to call Sandy. Yes, of course, the rule was that it was strictly separate cages. My parents didn't just lay down the house rules, but they stood unanimous that there was not going to be any untoward hanky-panky in our garage either. We would be overrun by cavies.

To this day, I'm still not a great fan of fireworks, but as time went on, I did begin to take pleasure in having my wheelchair parked in the large lounge window as, living on a hill, the view stretched for miles and it was far better than attending any organized firework display would have been and to us, it was totally free.

At 11:00 am on the following day the telephone rang and as usual, I heard that it was Nan, just ringing to check that everything was alright.

Bit by bit, she then relayed to Mom that my granddad had received an unexpected phone call from his brother. He had said that he just happened to be passing by in our area, so he had asked if it was convenient to drop by and see us all. My granddad was delighted by this, as it had been quite some time since the two brothers had seen each other, so they were going to call my auntie and invite them to join in the fun too. I'd figured out in an instant, that much to my delight, this was going to mean seeing my cousin again, for the second time in one weekend. How about that one for a brilliant fluke!

Before we went to Nan's, Mom always gave me a carrier bag, so that I could select a few toys to keep me occupied whilst we were there. I guess most young children do this when they are going to visit their grandparents. Mom flashed me a whimsical smile because instead of asking to take a collection of small toys which I could keep tidy and compact, especially as we were expecting a special visitor, I asked if I could take my easel and pencil case of big, chunky crayons.

Well for a start, although I use the term "pencil case" here, I might as well be honest and admit it was anything but a pencil case, because it was in fact, an enormous bag made from a stiff fabric, fashioned in the shape of a baseball cap, complete with its semi-circular peak. It also had a sizeable zip, because for many years I still lacked the fine motor skills in my hands to be able to grip anything very small, and in this respect, I'm not much better now. However, to address my dilemma with zips, Mom used to thread a loop of string or ribbon through them to make them easier to grasp. The cap's peak was another nifty aid, as while I was tugging at the zip, I used to trap the peak under my knees, hence preventing my pencil case from sliding around.

This clever trick of threading a loop through my zips was not only employed on my pencil cases, but it was further extended to many other things, including my anoraks, my little handbags and at one point, I even had a piece of ribbon tied on the zip of my carpet slippers. Oh no, what am I doing? Fancy owning up to that one, Mom used to dress me up like a toothless granny!

As for my easel, this was also a very useful find for it wasn't the conventional upright type which would have been too high off the floor for me to reach. Instead, it was just a low wooden frame, ideal for me to learn to draw pictures whilst kneeling on the floor and underneath it, lay a rotating, wooden rod which held a roll of wallpaper. I could create my weird and wonderful designs and then when I had filled my paper up with random mess or scribbles, the wallpaper could then be wound on further, so that I could start on my next masterpiece.

Anyway, about four hours later, we were ready to leave the house, so we set off in the car and driving down the hill, we headed for my grandparents' house.

My granddad and his younger brother were both brilliant musicians and between them, they could play a vast range of musical instruments. Collectively, they could turn their hands to virtually anything capable of producing a melodic tune, their varied assortment including accordions, violins, concertinas, mouth organs and to listen to them play their pianos or electronic organs, was a total joy that none of us will ever forget. Who needed Top Of The Pops?

Granddad did have a few books of sheet music which he could read without falter, but to my recollection, he hardly ever touched them, as both he and my uncle used to play everything by ear.

I remember that very often, to keep me quiet for an hour or two, Granddad would pull my high chair up to the piano, open the top, where he kept his great list of songs, many of which dated back to World War II and a few of the numbers were probably even older and he would keep me amused for ages, just letting me select different ones for him to play. There were hundreds to choose from, but I recall that one of my most frequent requests just has to be "Puppet On A String".

By this time, I was too big for a baby's highchair, so Nan managed to get me a tall, wooden chair, suitable for an older child. Unfortunately, however, it came minus a table or any type of harness. This posed no real problem for Nan though, as she was soon at the sewing machine again, stitching me a Velcro strap, so that I could be fastened in securely.

My new seat became of great value at mealtimes too, enabling me to sit up to the dining table, so that I could try to empty my plate before the rest of the gang.

Another similar gift that Nan picked up for me was a low, wooden rocking horse, ideal to keep me quiet and out of mischief and also in a safe sitting position while she was busy in the kitchen.

On this particular occasion, we were the first visitors to arrive, but less than ten minutes later, we heard Kimmy barking and I could now see that she was standing at the gate behind Granddad's car, madly wagging her tail.

"O.K. Kim", my auntie said, "now get back in, it's only us."

Kimmy was a lovely old girl, but everyone knew that they always had to be on their toes when entering the back gate, as she had escaped many times and she could squeeze her way through the merest gap.

Nan said to my granddad, "You'll have to be careful with Kim when your brother comes, as you know what she's like and it'll be no good you worrying when she's bounding up the bank again and she either disappears or is run over on the main road, besides which, it is so embarrassing when people come, especially if she jumps up and she's moulting all over their best clothes."

As it happened, none of this occurred, as my uncle arrived on foot and he approached by walking up the long front path, which was situated on the other side of the house to Kim's kennel, so poor Nan could breathe again.

My memory of my uncle's visit is extremely hazy now, as I was still only a very young child. What I do know, however, is that this incredible musical genius which my granddad and his brother had, has been passed on to many of the younger members of the family.

Also, although I was unaware of it at the time, I must have struck a chord with my uncle too, as just a few weeks later, I think there was another special present added to my Christmas list, but I'll unwrap that one a little later, as let's face it, the best part of Christmas for everyone is that scrumptious tantalization of wondering exactly what you are going to get.

During childhood, I loved Christmastime, but I think most small children do, don't they?

This particular year, however, Mom felt really positive, she'd sorted me out to start The Victoria School in January, so in many ways, the majority of the earliest battles were finally ending.

I don't know if other people share the same opinion, although I think there are probably a number of women who will identify with this, in that very often I think that the build-up to Christmas and all those wonderful dreams of how you expect the festive period to turn out, is often far more enjoyable than the actual event.

As far as we were concerned, living on the brow of what was, indisputably, the steepest hill for miles around, we had little need to receive any Christmas cards depicting a traditional snowy scene, she says, with an embarrassed little cough, not meaning to be discourteous to anyone, because as soon as we had the first blustery day of the winter, we'd got a beautiful and enormous snowscape all of our own.

On the first of December, Mom came into the living room carrying two brown paper packets and she told my sister and me that she had a special present for us both. I was sitting in my new little wheelchair, parked by the fireplace, as I had now grown out of my other chairs. Mom placed the package on my tray and I began to eagerly tear at my bag.

I couldn't wait to see what it was as, at first, it just looked like a stupid bit of cardboard with numbers and pretty patterns on it. Mom then went on to explain that it was an Advent Calendar and that every day from now until Christmas, we would have to open a little door to reveal another secret picture and then if we had been especially good children, upon opening the last magic door, Father Christmas would come to bring lots of new toys.

I thought that sounded like a pretty good deal, but for a couple of years, I couldn't make sense of why we weren't just allowed to rip them all open in one go and then as soon as we'd opened number 24, which Mom was claiming was the special one, then surely Santa would know about it and I would get my toys. Well, it seemed logical to a four year old.

Despite my storyline though, I can't recall believing in the guy in the red suit at all, although Mom says that she has seen the time when I did. I suppose even I haven't always been that shrewd, but what I do remember, is that for several years on the trot, I used to try to cajole my mother into the notion that I did, simply to ensure that admitting my complete mistrust would not in any way decrease my number of presents.

Mom carried me downstairs one morning and sat me in my chair while she boiled the hot milk to pour onto my cereal.

"Look Mom", I said, "it's time to open another door on my calendar again. I wonder what picture we'll get today?"

Number eighteen was a green and red Christmas tree bauble, not very exciting really, but the special day that I was so looking forward to was now fast approaching.

During the last few weeks, of course, I had still been continuing to go to the nursery. I had made a special Christmas card for Mom, Dad and my sister. Another morning had been taken up by sticking shiny paper and glitter onto a calendar for the New Year which Mom could hang in the kitchen, but the most striking change in me, is that I had learnt to sing my first favourite carol. The words went...

> Ding dong merrily on high,
> In heav'n the bells are ringing:
> Ding dong! verily the sky
> Is riv'n with angel singing.
> Gloria, Hosanna in excelsis!

I would now patiently try and croon my way through the whole song, but in complete contrast to my previous habit of shortening all the words in Baa Black Sheep, the word "Glooooooooooooooooooo-ooooooooooooria", would last for an excruciating, blood-curdling eternity.

A few days later, Dad was late coming home from the office, so we began to wonder whether anything had gone wrong.

Presently, however, we heard a strange rustling noise as he came through the hall, the source of which became immediately apparent, as he almost knocked the lounge door off its hinges, coming in heaving an enormous Christmas tree.

"Where do you want it?" he asked Mom. "Say now or I will just have to put it anywhere."

In my opinion, there is nothing quite like a real Christmas tree. I think it's just that beautiful, fresh smell of the pine needles and when the tree is new, it seems to have such a lovely, symmetrical shape. A fine-looking tree just does the festive season for me.

"Just drop it down next to your armchair", Mom replied, "It won't be in anybody's way then if you just leave it in that corner"

"OK", Dad said, "but please move some of these toys out of my way, as this thing is very heavy." I had scattered the entire contents of my toy box all over the floor again.

He then propped the tree up against the wall, just praying that it wouldn't come crashing down on top of the T.V., while he ran to fetch a bucket of sand from the garage in which to sink it.

The next common escapade, which he expected to always occur just to aggravate him, was the fact that he would manhandle it into an upright position in the bucket, only to learn that the Christmas tree was too tall for the lounge and its top would be bending across the ceiling at a ninety-degree angle, so back to the garage he would have to go, this time to fetch his saw to hack five inches off the crown. When this was all sorted, at last, everyone would spend the next quarter of an hour in a lively debate about which side of the tree we considered to be the best and which side should be concealed against the wall.

Amidst all this pandemonium, my sister came running in from upstairs. She was moaning that she couldn't find her curling tongs, but she soon forgot all her irritation and stood by the radiator, surveying the enormity of the tree with delight.

"Our trees get bigger every year", she laughed.

"Now you're here", Mom said, "can you just run up into the storage room and bring down the box of Christmas decorations. It's just behind the door, round to the left, you can't miss it."

Ten minutes later, my sister appeared again carrying an enormous cardboard box, so Mom quickly ran to help her.

I was sitting in my wheelchair at the time, so I asked if I could be pushed closer to the tree so that I could see what was going on.

Everyone began to rummage through the dusty baubles and great lengths of disintegrating tinsel, their shiny, broken strands flying everywhere.

"What can I do Mom?" I asked, "I want to help too".

"Well, you can't very well help to decorate the tree, can you Sonya? There'll be no needles left on it for a start and you'll poke your eyes out, then it'll be another hospital job. Tell you what though", Mom quickly dreamt up by way of recompense, "you can let us know if you spot any bare gaps on the tree, as you will be able to notice them better from where you are sitting. That will be a very helpful little job".

This snappy suggestion saved the day again and my eyes twinkled, as I now felt that I had been appointed a significant duty.

I then began to point out all the flaws and much to my sister's dismay, I soon added another twist too, which was to moan if she placed two baubles of the same colour too close together, as I thought it lacked variety. This was an early sign of the emergence of my Taurean, aesthetic flair.

"Here", Mom said to my sister, "I've bought some bags of chocolate coins and bells to hang on the tree, but be careful you don't snap the plastic loops on the top, or they'll be ruined".

"Is there anything decent to go on the top this year?" was my sister's next question. "Last year, we used this angel, but look at the state it's in. The wings have been all bent up in the box and it just looks horrible now".

We all agreed that the angel had undeniably seen the best of its days, so in the end, we settled for the gold tinsel pompom with its long, shiny streamers, which could be draped across the branches to conceal all the gaps.

Mom trimmed the tree with lights and my sister ran to the switch on the wall to darken the room so that we could survey the full effect in its entire splendour. A rainbow of feathery brightness danced around the room and we knew that the season of Christmas had finally dawned.

It was 9:10 am on the morning of Christmas Eve, 1972 and Mom came into my bedroom, as she could hear that I was in deep conversation with Sindy.

"Hello", Mom said. "How are you today? You know who's coming tonight, don't you Sonya, so are you all ready to hang your stocking up?"

"Yes Mom", I grinned, "I hope I get loads of good stuff".

"Oh, I'm sure you will darling", Mom reassured me, "as you have been a very good girl".

To coax me into accepting the fact that I must be good and try to prevent any more screaming episodes or dashing myself backwards in rage, Nan had richly embellished the tale that, if I wasn't on my best behaviour, then Santa wouldn't bring me toys at all, but just a dirty old pile of ashes and bad nuts. In an attempt to consolidate this point even further, she also backed it up by saying that this had really happened to her naughty brother.

We never did a great deal on Christmas Eve, but would spend most of the day munching varied snacks, freshly baked mince pies and watching a conundrum of films and seasonal shows on the television.

Even as an adult, I still think that there is a special aura about Christmas Eve, maybe it's just that peaceful lull in the proceedings when most of the preparations have been completed and it's just a day of hushed reflection.

As a child, I very often ended up watching Lassie, but I always had to keep a cushion on hand in which to bury my face for all those occasions when I was petrified that she couldn't possibly escape although, inevitably of course, in the magic world of television, she somehow managed to ledge one mighty paw onto the very last precipice of survival.

I would get very excited and knowing that I would have a few very late nights over the holiday, especially as I was usually tucked up in bed by 8 o'clock, on Christmas Eve, Mom always made a special effort to carry me to bed at a reasonable time.

Before I went, however, we would go through the usual ritual of choosing which one of Dad's socks to leave in readiness for the guy in the red suit and I would nominate where I thought was the most convenient place to hang it – not forgetting, as I had found out last year, was definitely the floor space right in front of the settee, neatly enabling me to hog most of the hearth, just leaving a square inch vacant for my sister's gifts. To me, the plan seemed like a good one.

I was almost ready for Dad to carry me upstairs, but the final task of the night was to make sure Mom had left Santa a glass of sherry and a piping hot mince pie on the shelf above the fireplace.

Mom tucked me up in bed and as soon as my door closed, I began to chuckle into Sindy's orange plastic ear that I'd fooled Mom again that I believed in this utter madness. I never did understand why my Sindy doll went bald and turned orange. Oh well, life is full of bizarre, unanswered mysteries, so maybe that will just remain another one.

I would then try to stay awake for hours, lying in complete silence, in a sneaky attempt to build up a mental picture of exactly what I imagined may be taking place downstairs.

"Was that Mom's car door slamming, or perhaps it was the boot? I might be wrong on both accounts though as perhaps Dad was going down the pub? On the other hand, maybe he had gone to my nan's house because it would have been easier to hide stuff in her spare room?"

I can remember that all these mischievous thoughts used to go around in circles through my little head. I would hold a lively and heated debate with Sindy as to what possible clues a lump of discoloured plastic could give me, but upon my eventual acceptance that this tactic was turning out to be just as fruitless and unyielding as my last 5000, my eyelids would eventually start to droop, giving way to sheer exhaustion and my magical Christmas dreams.

I woke up with a start on Christmas morning; as I heard my sister's feet thumping across the landing, heading into my parents' bedroom.

"It's time to get up now", she squealed, "come on, it's Christmas Day!"

I heard a few groans, as it was only 6:00 am and my parents had only had three hours sleep, as there had been so many toys to fit together, so they had been wrapping the last few presents and trying to fathom out how to assemble stuff until early dawn.

"Mommmmmmm", I yelled, and then I heard her starting to scold my sister. "Now look what you've done", she said, "you've wakened Sonya".

Mom dragged herself into my room, barely being able to make out where she was going as she was so tired and the floor appeared to be rising before her bloodshot eyes, as she could hardly keep them open, let alone be consciously able to direct her next footstep. She came in only to find that, I had by this time kicked off my bedclothes and I was lying wide awake, as lively as if it had been in the middle of the afternoon.

"Is it time to get up yet Mom?" I asked, "I think I've just heard a bump, so I bet Santa's been now", I grinned.

After a while and another argument with Sindy, as I now pretended that she had been the real culprit who had awakened me, I catnapped again till 7:30 and on Christmas morning, for a four-year-old, this was really pushing it and was borderline taking the mickey.

"Mommmmm, Merry Christmas". I thought that by now, even if she wasn't quite ready, by adding a cheery greeting on the end, I would suitably bypass any further aggravation.

A few minutes later she came in and much to my relief, this time she was ready to get me up.

"I don't want a bath this morning Mom", I said, "and anyway, I only had one yesterday".

"OK then, you don't have to", Mom replied. "We must get a move on today so that we can go and see what Santa's bought."

I chuckled again and soon I was ready to go downstairs.

As I was carried into the living room, I gave one massive scream of delight. The whole length of the settee and most of the hearth rug were completely obscured in brightly wrapped parcels and bags. Our Christmas stockings overflowed with a varied assortment of small treats and there was hardly a square inch in which to stand. Dad was leaning on the shelf above the fireplace with a coffee mug in his hand because my sister had completely taken over his armchair with all her gifts.

"I want to slither Mom", I squealed, "where's mine?"

"Look, this big gold one is from Nanny and Granddad", Mom said, "try to open this one."

It used to take me forever to rip all the paper off, but at first, I was determined to be independent and I would push Mom's hand away if she tried to assist me to break the sticky tape or coloured ribbon.

I loved it. It was my very own telephone on little blue wheels, so that I could pull it along the carpet and it even chattered to me as it went. Mom said it had come without a telephone directory, so I would just have to improvise my way around that one.

I then began to dial my auntie's number and held a pretend conversation with my cousin, excitedly relaying to him that I had a phone with wobbling eyes.

"You don't have to mess with my phone now", Mom said, "as you've got one all for yourself."

The next big box I pointed to contained a tape recorder, together with a selection of Walt Disney cassettes. "Hooray", I said to my sister, "it's The Aristocats". I also had the story of Black Beauty and fixed to that was a third tape, which contained tracks like "The Ugly Bug Ball" and "You can fly", from the Dumbo film.

"Open this one now", Mom said, "it's a special surprise from Granddad's brother."

I carefully removed the wrapping paper and inside was a beautiful, little, orange piano and on the top, there were several rows of coloured balls with eyes. I began to bang the keys and then I discovered that it was a little choir, as each time I struck a key, another mouth sprang open and began to sing.

The lounge, by this time, had been reduced to a total bomb site with screwed up paper and toys everywhere and I still hadn't started to empty my Christmas stocking, so I reached for this next.

I bashed and battered it on the carpet and one by one, a broad selection of tiny gifts began to drop out. This varied array included a clockwork mouse, a pencil with Scooby-Doo on top, a bag of Maltesers, a little, round handheld puzzle in which the object of the game was to roll the tiny, silver balls into the holes and a red and white candy walking stick. "Er...yuck Mom", I said, "there is something all soggy and horrible stuck in the bottom."

Mom rushed over to see what was going on and she realised that I had pummelled Dad's sock with such vigour on the carpet to try to shake out its contents, that what had started out as a lovely healthy tangerine had now been reduced to just a soggy, mashed-up, inedible pulp. She ran with it into the kitchen, its juice dripping everywhere as she went and then she had to turn the sock inside out to throw the remains of the fruit into the bin and then put my Christmas stocking straight in the washing machine.

She was just checking the turkey in the oven, as it was almost ready to come out now when she heard me screaming and in floods of tears. I was banging my new piano in temper, I was throwing the remains of the crumpled up Christmas paper at my sister and calling her a horrible moron and Dad just stood there with an ashen complexion, not knowing what had happened, let alone how to fix it.

My sister started to cry then and she swore on her life that she hadn't done anything to upset me. Mom tried for the next half an hour to sing to me, show me different toys to gently coax me out of my rage, but in the end, she carried me up to my bedroom to lie me down for a while. This type of reaction reoccurred for a few years and my family deduced that it had proved such an enormous effort to open so many presents all in one go, that it totally blew my little mind and I didn't know what to play with first. In plain English, I think this means I was simply "spoilt", but this became yet another unexpected twist to my early struggle to cope with my disability.

After an hour or two of unwinding and taking a nap on my bed, my awful anger subsided, so Mom fetched me downstairs again and she sat me in my wheelchair.

"I know what", she suggested, "do you fancy opening a tube of Jelly Tots?"

"Yes", I nodded, "I really love those."

Mom then proceeded to roll my sleeves up and put my big apron on, as she could see it was going to be another sticky job, just like the performance of me chomping through my rhubarb. I would tip the sweets into my mouth and as I gradually worked my way down the cardboard tube, Mom would have to keep chopping its top off so I could continue to enjoy my sweets and not just have a mouthful of soggy cardboard.

Later on, we all went to my grandparents' house again, so that I could compare what Santa had left me with my cousin's collection of new toys.

After this, I was a very happy little girl and I loved Christmas, but in the early years, Mom learnt to introduce my new playthings gradually, maybe spanning over a few days, or sometimes even extending into several weeks. In the end, of course, having such a kind and loving family, I still ended up with an equal quantity of surprises as my sister and cousin, but it was simply a case of introducing me to a little and often.

What an explosive Christmas cracker I must have been!

5

A Smile For Victory

It was 7:30 on the morning of the 5 January 1972 and Mom came into my bedroom and briskly threw open the curtains. The window was completely frosted over and all I could make out was the row of dripping icicles which were dangling from the roof. I looked down and as my weary eyes gradually adjusted to the light, I saw that there were about a dozen sparrows clustered on the chimney top of the house below.

"Yes", Mom said, "I know how tired you are but we have to hurry up now as you're not a baby anymore and it is time for big school. You are going to have a lovely day today."

She then dragged me from underneath my Humpty Dumpty duvet and proceeded to get me washed and dressed. Next, she carried me downstairs and sat me in my new, little wheelchair and started to feed me breakfast. I had heard what Mom had said about going to big school, but at first, I don't think I fully understood what she was talking about and thinking we were preparing for another day at the nursery, I silently mused, "Oh well, I don't know what the early start is all about, but everything seems to be pretty normal now, so I think I'd better just pretend I haven't noticed. I must be going to the nursery again."

"Look", Mom told me, "I've bought you a special little satchel to carry all your stuff in. You will know which one is yours, as Mom has written your name on the front." She pointed at the label that was tucked behind a rectangle of transparent plastic and neatly printed in green felt tip I read, "SONYA HILL".

"OK", I thought, "so now she's bought me a new bag. That's pretty cool."

"Come on", Mom said, "don't give me any bother because you'll have to wear your fur hat this morning as it is very cold and we've got to go a long way."

Soon we were ready and while driving to school Mom told me that my friend from the nursery would be waiting to play again, but that I was going to make loads of new friends too.

The journey seemed never-ending, but at last we came to some large double gates and as we entered I saw that there was an island in the centre and the complex was home to three separate schools. There was one for deaf children, the school specializing in partially sighted and blind kids and the final destination as you slowly made your way past all the buses and taxis, was The Victoria School. Many years later, a fourth school was added which was tailored towards the needs of autistic children, so collectively the site housed some wonderful facilities nurturing a very broad spectrum of disabilities.

As Mom started to get me out of the car a group of very friendly staff one jolly character, who I soon learnt was my new headmaster, came breezing out of the front entrance to grant us a very hearty welcome.

"Good morning", the headmaster said, taking hold of my hand, "you must be Sonya and is this Mom?"

"Yes", I grinned from my car seat and then, without further ado, I was assigned a new wheelchair for use in school and smiling a lady pushed me through the main entrance.

Being my first day at school, before I could be settled into my new class, which was of course the school nursery, it was important for me to be assessed by my new physiotherapist and also the school nurse, so they could fully evaluate my requirements.

When talking of my first experiences of becoming a pupil at The Victoria School, Mom often describes how she immediately found a new sense of peace which she had never encountered since I had been born.

Of course now, at four years of age, I had already reached so many encouraging milestones, but as Mom was still to learn in the weeks, months and many happy years which were still to follow, finding this school wasn't just going to be the first victory, but the first of many.

Following all my preliminary medical examinations and checks, I was taken down to meet my new teacher, but to be honest I can't remember much about her other than that she was a very petite lady who was shortly to reach retirement.

My first clear memory of starting school however and one which I feel I just have to mention, is that as soon as I entered the nursery I met a very special little girl who I instantly formed a lovely friendship with and she was always my best pal. Yes, I know I have my difficulties, but when I look back and remember what many of the children had to cope with at The Victoria School and, for me in particular, this one, I can only say that even for me, the experience of being amongst them can only be described as extremely humbling.

Having said this, however, even though my friend was unable to speak to me, it was amazing how she used to convey her cheeky little thoughts. Experiencing communication problems myself, this is one aspect of disability that I've always had tons of patience with so, even at the age of four, I just accepted this and although it was only my first day, I can still vividly remember that she was lying on a foam mat on the floor, so I requested to come out of my wheelchair and I crawled over to speak to her. Within the first few moments of meeting her, it was clear that we both shared the same nutty sense of humour. The warmth in her eyes was incredible - simply transfixing, and from then on we were inseparable and life was just one big laugh.

Sadly she is no longer with us, but I felt it was only right to mention my best friend and I am sure if she is looking down on me from glory, she is probably still laughing at me now, the little monkey!

Anyway, my first morning at school went fine; my friend from nursery had started school too, so after settling in a little, I started to move around on my knees.

I can't be sure whether this was in the nursery or during my first few classes now, but my next vivid memory is of crawling along a row of cupboards which were brightly painted with the numbers 1-10 and having a sly peep into each one to see where the most interesting toys were stashed.

Break-time came and the teachers gathered all the children up and sat us around a little table to have our bottle of milk. They brought around a small box of drinking straws, but as they soon found out, the task of trying to get me to draw liquid up a straw was a non-starter, as I could only blow bubbles as I hadn't the ability to suck. Maybe their efforts would have been more successful if they had flavoured my milk with whisky.

During the years that followed the physiotherapists did explore many different ways of assisting me to drink independently. I've tried cups with spouts; a wide variety of two-handled mugs, drinking straws, being both of the flexible and straight types, but this is one skill that I failed to attain until well into adulthood.

The atmosphere of a special school nursery is a very happy one and each day there was a spell when the teacher arranged everyone in a circle for our singing practice. I remember that one of the old favourites was always "The Wheels On The Bus" and another equally popular choice used to be "If You're Happy And You Know It". The teachers made great use of this type of song, as joining in with all the actions was another great way to increase our physical ability.

Later on, I began to realise that the use of music with disabled children is a very powerful and important medium. Personally, I love music and even as I sit here writing this story, my music centre is my background companion. I don't know if you've ever stopped to contemplate the fact, but music is the only universal form of communication which, as strange as it may be, all human beings seem to emotionally "need".

For instance, a typical example of this can be very clearly illustrated in examining an impoverished nation such as Africa. I feel that people in our Western Society must have hearts of solid stone if, at some point, they haven't been reduced to tears by some of the pitiful images that we have all seen so many times, of all those starving and desperately needy children. From a shockingly young age, children are trained to walk for miles, their hungry bellies distended, the soles of their feet covered in sores, their faces crawling with flies, balancing heavy water urns on their heads, feeding on rice and dry grain alone.

Despite their various hardships, however, whether underprivileged by disability or poverty, these beautiful children are seldom without a big smile on their faces and the one thing they all seem to enjoy and respond to most is the magic of music.

In the early days, it took quite a time for me to adjust to my new routine and to become accustomed to the fact that, whether it pleased me or not, I had no choice now, but to attend school. A considerable number of months went by and I would throw a tantrum each morning as I didn't want to leave Mom. She used to park my wheelchair in the lounge window where I would gaze down towards the bottom of our hill so that I could let her know when my taxi arrived and then the next full-scale protest would begin.

"Please Mom", I would whine, "if you just give me a day off today, I promise I'll be a good girl tomorrow. Pleeeaaassse Mom". At this point I would be forced into the back seat of the taxi and then I would press my red, blotchy face into the window, blubbering and bidding Mom goodbye with a half-hearted wave as we descended the hill.

The school nurse had promptly advised the taxi firm that she felt it was unwise for me and another little boy who had very similar problems, to make our long school trip without an assistant to ensure our safety. After just a few weeks of my broken-hearted sobbing throughout the entire 10-mile trip and constantly griping with Mom that I would do anything at all she wanted if she would just get me out of this unbearable predicament of having to go to school all the time, I began to get the message that she was adamant she was going to keep ignoring me.

Mom found it awfully difficult though, as I used to get so distressed each day. Even on arrival at school, I still couldn't comprehend, why Mom, of all people, seemed to be forcing me to go

68

through so much misery. I simply hated the whole monotonous process. My jigging tantrums didn't seem to be having any noticeable effect so, in my mind, there was only one other avenue available to me now – to feign illness.

Almost on a daily basis and continuing into several months, I would call my teacher over in class, saying, "Miss, I've got a terrible headache and I think I'm gonna be sick in a minute". This would then be accompanied by that sad, down-turned mouth again, so before my brewing naughtiness had the chance to spiral completely out of control, she agreed that I ought to be checked out by the nurse just to acquire her verdict.

At this point, my spirits would slightly lift as I'd be thinking, "Oh well, at least my teacher is taking me seriously so I'm over the first hurdle."

Considering I had been so crafty to swiftly determine that the story about Santa Claus was utter rubbish, you would have expected that after about the five thousandth attempt to pull this same stunt and being catapulted straight back to my classroom with my tail between my legs, I would have got the message that my Please-Release-Me-Let-Me-Go act quite simply wasn't going to work.

Depending upon the nurse's mood that day, however, sometimes she would pretend that she was taking my complaint seriously and she would telephone my mom.

"Hello there", the nurse began when Mom picked the receiver up. "I've got Rubbish here again. What shall I do with her?" she giggled.

Mom soon became as used to this little routine as the nurse did, so she would often speak to me on the phone and between them, they would gradually manage to coax me back to my classroom, as they assured me that it would soon be home-time anyway. Of course, I did realise that this was only a pathetic excuse to send me back to my boring lessons, especially when it was only half past ten in the morning.

In contrast to the grownups, however, at least I was telling the truth, as I was, "really sick", as in, "really sick of school". I did all I could to explain that the symptoms I exhibited were actually terminal, but alas, no-one seemed to be listening to me and eventually I just had to learn to live with it as, pretty much like the common cold, there was no known cure, except for taking an appropriate dose of discipline and encouragement. A spoonful of sugar, sadly, offered no relief either.

Another charismatic stage I went through as part of my initial "settling in period", was the fact that on my arrival home I didn't want any food, that is, unless my favourite delicacy happened to be on the menu. The only winning plate of food just had to comprise of a runny fried egg, chips and beans. Again, this caused added anxiety for Mom, so she contacted the school nurse again to seek further advice.

"My dear", the nurse answered, "do not worry about this at all, as it's only one of Madam's funny little phases again. Just pretend you haven't noticed. Feed her what she requests and sooner or later it will just fizzle out of its own accord. She's just stubborn."

I hated that school nurse as she seemed to have me completely sussed and she talked such nonsense.

Oh, O.K. then, I'm sorry, I might as well come clean here and own up to the fact that at least the nurse's statement is partially true because I am very stubborn and I am definitely not even going to try to deny the fact. However, if you care to take a closer look at the other side of my dogged Taurean coin, you will find my loyalty, a character trait which, until I had been forced to go to school, I had felt that Mom had always returned without falter.

Anyway, this hellish routine of wanting to become a permanent truant continued for what must have felt like an eternity for Mom. She used to tremble each morning as she had to force me into the taxi bawling my brains out, but then, one day, a very kind elderly lady took on the post of taxi assistant. She would sing to me and try to keep me amused with little stories like Goldilocks and the Three Bears or The Three Billy Goats Gruff or just encourage me to watch out for different landmarks which we passed on our way.

There are three distinctive points of my trip to school which I can recall making a specific mental note of every day, as for me, I felt that as soon as we'd driven past these, it signified that the long journey was at last drawing to an end.

"Are you still watching through the window?" the taxi attendant would say. "Can you remember what is coming up next?"

Firstly, just after the garage which faces a large pub on the opposite side of the road, you go down another wide road which is flanked on either side by a line of bungalows. There is one of these dwellings, situated right on the end of the row, and perched on the edge of its roof, was a porcelain cat with its curled tail and one outstretched paw dangling as if he was trying to catch a mouse that had just scampered up the drainpipe. I used to pass that cat twice a day and think, "Oh look, he still hasn't plucked up enough courage to jump down yet."

My next observation which I noted as we passed by, being situated immediately before the stretch of road which passed the reservoir was a huge clock. I can't be sure now whether this building was a church or just some kind of ancient tower, but particularly on my way to school, a destination to which I only ever travelled under complete duress, it reminded me of The Tower of Vlad Dracula. At the end of the long bridge which spans over the reservoir, there is a choice of two roads, both of which lead to The Victoria School. In the years that followed, continuing to travel to school in a taxi, my friends and I would irately bleat at the driver at this point, that we didn't want him to turn left, as we considered this to be the boring route, but as we had all been so good, we needed him to keep going straight ahead and take us down what we called "The Leafy Way". Of course, this wasn't really the name of the road, but for many years all the children in my taxi would use this term to describe a very long, twisting passageway which was densely paralleled on either side by large trees.

The taxi drivers were never awfully thrilled by this request as it was such a narrow lane that should we meet another vehicle which was heading in the opposite direction, it would present them with some extremely tricky driving manoeuvres to safely pass. Our chief motive for wanting to travel down The Leafy Way was that particularly in the autumn, there were very often squirrels scurrying through the trees, so it became a little contest between me and the other children to see who could spot the first one. If we turned left, however, the alternative route was far wider and much easier to negotiate if the traffic was heavy, so we would all flash each other sly little glances around the taxi to indicate whether we thought we had given the driver sufficient earache for him to succumb to the pressure and battle his way across The Leafy Way.

Anyway, my school routine rolled on and it wasn't long before my teachers observed that one thing which was going to cause me a major problem, if not addressed with some urgency, was the fact that due to my poor hand control, I was experiencing difficulties in holding a pencil efficiently enough to complete my schoolwork. Several other children seemed to be struggling with this too, so a letter was composed to the parents requesting their assistance in raising some much-needed funds.

Of course, as soon as Mom received the newsletter, she telephoned Auntie and my grandparents immediately, and together they concluded that the most effective option would be for them to each hold a coffee morning for the neighbours and perhaps they could request them to bring sandwich cakes, the sale of which could also be of great advantage. In the end, all three coffee mornings were a huge success; people were really kind and the money began to roll in.

All in all the level of financial backing was fantastic and it didn't take long for the news of the appeal to reach the organizers of my Sunday School, and after only a few weeks the school was in a position to donate all the proceeds to The Sequal Trust, which is a very helpful and worthwhile charity based in Shropshire whose work is dedicated to providing special equipment designed to enhance the independence of people with physical disabilities and communication problems.

In their early days, The Sequal Trust was formerly known as The Possum User's Association or, more commonly known by its abbreviated form of The PUA and the letters in the word "Possum" originally derived from the term Patient Operated Selector Mechanism.

Today, the communicative and literacy needs of disabled people are amicably addressed with the use of computers and as my skills continued to change and develop throughout my time at school, The Sequal Trust came up with quite an array of useful technology which really were a fantastic help, but keeping things in perspective with my age, my first device was geared towards my biggest problem at the time, which was to provide a method of developing my early skills in English and Numeracy.

My setup comprised of an ordinary electric typewriter, (but if you are too young to know what that is, then just Google it) and it was also accompanied by an additional very large keyboard, known as an "expanded keyboard", for obvious reasons, as its keys were spaced widely apart, each being covered in a large plastic keyguard, enabling me to rest my hand on its firm casing whilst operating the buttons with my thumb, reducing the risk of typing errors.

The other most common form of Possum, which was again, based upon activating a typewriter, came with an electronically activated grid and by pressing a small switch, usually with their foot, or sometimes a knee, some of my friends used to guide a small light around the coordinates of a letter-board, hence producing their essays or mathematics assignments.   It is amazing really how many different variations of these machines are available and although they are all geared to do the same basic job, they can be greatly adapted to best suit the needs of the individual.

The Sequal Trust is still in operation today but, of course, since I was a little girl, the advancements in computer technology have been amazing and it is the kind donations of ordinary people which assist in providing this very important technology, allowing disabled people the freedom to communicate and to reach their educational potential.

During the school holidays, we were avidly encouraged to bring our special equipment home, as it would guard against theft or damage in the event of a school break-in. I used to enjoy this, as Mom would set it up for me on the dining table and I would write short stories, or sometimes, my dad would give me letters to copy. This used to take me a very long time but it was a useful activity to keep me out of mischief.

73

One day, I returned home from school and Mom greeted me with the usual question, which was always, "Well, what have you been doing today, Sonya?"

"I've had a w-hiss" Mom thought I said.

"No", Mom said, "I can't understand that word, you'll have to try again. You've had a what?"

"I went on my Possum and we had a w-hiss Mom"

"I'm sorry Sonya, but I still can't get it", she replied again, "just say it slowly and try once more."

This frustrating conversation dragged on and on, elapsing into a period of several minutes although finally, I managed to convey that I'd attained a completely pathetic score in the General Knowledge quiz, but I couldn't clearly pronounce the word "quiz" so, contrary to me, I think Mom deserved 10 out of 10 for deciphering that correct answer.

At last, I had settled down well at school and I think I must have been around about the age of six, when Mom finally began to feel more relaxed and she suddenly realised she was now looking to the future with refreshing new optimism. Albeit with the aid of my special equipment, I was now making good progress and I was able to interact with family and friends, so the daily routine seemed far less gruelling and time-consuming.

Being so involved with different activities at school had not only helped in providing me with a suitable place of education and the expertise I required, but Mom was able to form relationships with many other families too, who could completely relate to and empathize with her situation.

Despite this though, whilst busying herself with the usual day-to-day routine, Mom still felt isolated. Family gatherings at school were still fairly rare, but whether she was taking me on a shopping trip into town, to the local park to feed the ducks, or just simply standing at the top of the drive talking to one of the neighbours about their children, there was always that same agonizing question that seemed to be continuously hammering on the inside of her head and that was, "Why has this situation had to occur with my child?"

I'm sure this must be a very common feeling shared by most people who have a disabled child. Although I suspect the vast majority of people these days must have connections in one way or another with someone who is disabled, it is never a situation that people expect to happen to them. This then leads on to the embarrassment of their differing circumstances and, in addition to the continual and tiring routine of meeting the needs of a handicapped relative, families like mine don't have the time to explain that, really, as parents, they are still the same people as they always were, just maybe having slightly different jobs to do.

For most parents, I think one aspect to this quandary may lie in the fact that, although your child is happy, probably being fully integrated into a special school, or day centre, their world revolves around their friends and the activities they have participated in that day.

This is good and exactly what they require, of course, but one of the problems from the point of view of the parents and one which is heightened even further if the child experiences speech or communication problems, is they can't actually "say" how they are feeling and how their disability has emotionally affected their life.

I think the difficulties I am trying to describe here are all related to a range of communication problems because as an addition to speech difficulties and trying to make my indistinct voice understood, sometimes the families of disabled people feel alone too, simply because they are regarded as "different" and perhaps because of their caring roles, they need to work to a very different timescale compared to others. Their interests and need to form fun friendships though, remains unchanged.

There is no doubt whatsoever, of course, that regardless of their difficulties, certainly during my young days, the corridors of Victoria School chimed with giggles and cheeky threats like, "Oi, I'll get you for that, you just wait", and just simply wall-to-wall fun. How many people who have been through the process of being educated in an ordinary school, surrounded by so-called "normal" kids possess the happy childhood memory of growing up in an environment like that?

Another very positive attribute, which I think is probably more prevalent amongst the younger children, is that they very quickly learn to identify with, not only each other's difficulties but their many wonderful achievements and newfound abilities too which, certainly from my perspective, grew to be one of the greatest sources of encouragement to further my skills. Let's face it, how could I let anyone beat me? Well O.K., there was that tiny embarrassing incident with the school nurse, but even she had to slightly succumb to except my dogged determination.

Throughout my life, I know that it has always been one of Mom's major goals that my upbringing should be as normal as possible and so she has always tried to treat me as much like my siblings as my disability has allowed.

It was coming up to my 6th birthday and Mom decided to organize a birthday party for me so, not wanting to miss anyone out, she composed a letter to my teacher requesting a list of all the children in my class. She thought there would probably be about a dozen in all, so she set to work to devise a plan.

She realised it was going to be quite a feat to find something suitable to engage so many disabled children for two hours, each with limited abilities but, still being as resolute as ever, she decided that this was to be her next project.

The first thing she did, of course, was to tell her plans to Nan and Auntie, who both concluded that this was a lovely idea, so they arranged to meet up one morning when we had all gone to school, to discuss what needed to be done.

Being the first time they had entertained such a large group of special needs children, however, it was important to organize some simple activities in which they could all join in. Mom decided to invite one or two of the nursery nurses from school too, as they would have a greater understanding of what each child needed particularly as, like me, quite a number of them would require assistance in feeding.

I have to say that I now look back on many of Victoria School's team of mischievous nursery nurses with a great deal of affection and respect. At times, theirs can't have been an easy job, but they were all renowned for their lovely sense of humour and they seemed to be able to inject instant fun into any situation which the children were finding difficult. Over the years though, for reasons which are probably better known to themselves, these mischievous characters formulated a far greater array of nicknames for me than the kids and collectively, they have called me anything from Myrtle, Flash Gordon, Fish Face, to Scraggy Legs and indeed any other outlandish obscenity they could lay their tongues too, so considering all that, did they really deserve to be on my guest list? Um, I think that one is very debatable.

Well, the day of my birthday party finally arrived and by this time, Nan had been hard at work on the sewing machine again, designing two special party dresses for my sister and me, together of course, with a very elegant new trouser suit for my cousin as he had to look the part too.

Mom was up and ready by 7:15 am, as there was so much that needed to be prepared.

Like me, my sister was very excited at the prospect of having a party, so she was awake early too and promptly appeared at the kitchen door to see what was happening. She probably regretted this action pretty soon though as, before she had hardly appeared, Mom made her sit and pump up about three bags of balloons. Great stuff – that's the way to keep her quiet!

I mentioned at the opening of my story, that Mom has always had a great flair when it comes to cake decorating and designing my birthday cakes was no exception, as it was at these occasions when this magnificent talent really did shine. Not just for my first party but spanning over a few years she has cleverly moulded many lovely shapes for me, broadly ranging from sugar-crafted caterpillars, cats on cushions, a Bugs Bunny cake, a cake like a vinyl record, covered in liquorice, my Miss Piggy cake and in fact, it's very difficult to think up a shape she hasn't made out of fondant icing and so in this field, I think I can conclude that once again, Mom's utter brilliance, really did take the cake.

This delightful originality didn't just stop there either, as similar to how she had gone in search of suitable toys for me, for several weeks Mom had been collecting books on children's party food and she would regularly glean even more inspiration from weekly magazines, so in the end, I think I can confidently say that this year, there were going to be a few surprises for everyone.

Of course, at any small child's birthday celebration, a popular treat is often a plate of cheese and pineapple chunks skewered on cocktail sticks just haphazardly arranged on a paper doily, but was that good enough for my mom?

"Oh no, it wasn't!"

This is "Mom" we are talking about here and she laughed at the stupid old doily routine because she didn't just want to give me that.

I had to keep my birthday cake under close observation, not only to ensure that my sister hadn't scratched a lump out of the icing and turned the gaping hole towards the back of the table to conceal the embarrassing truth from my mates, but there was a crocodile on the party cloth, his shape being cleverly sculpted from a cucumber.

There was a large wedge sliced out at one end, which aptly served as his huge, open jaws and the cavity was crowded with ferocious-looking almond teeth. The crafty crocodile lay motionless, stealthily eyeing up the cake, until he was sure that no-one was looking, as at any minute now, he would be ready to start circling it.

The crocodile was furious and seeking revenge, as Mom had gruesomely speared him all across his back with the cheese and pineapples on sticks and as if this wasn't enough to bring out the reptile in him, she had also fixed his bloodshot, Glacé cherry eyes to his face with another small piece of broken cocktail stick so by that time the crocodile's enraged pupils had been reduced down to the size of currants while he quietly contemplated what to do. His almond teeth were gnashing together, but luckily, the cheese and pineapples were a popular snack with the children, so in the end, he was just left wearing a satisfied smile.

By this time, I think Mom had got the message that it would be a sensible move to steer well away from the blancmange rabbit idea, so instead, she created a field of green jelly topped with sheep fashioned from pear halves, or were they pigs? Sorry, but I don't think I ought to start that one off again as I remember that my sister, my cousin and I would regularly get into a heated debate as to what type of animals were actually grazing. I think the only safe conclusion to draw here, is that they were probably pigs wearing woolly cardigans.

With tea now done, after spending the next quarter of an hour stuffing the dirty paper plates, cups and screwed up serviettes into a bin bag, Nan decided that it would be an appropriate opportunity to start dishing out the balloons. The children who lived across the road were always amongst my guests too, so all those who could walk used to join in the task of ensuring everyone had a balloon and in several cases, they would simply tie the balloon strings around a convenient point on my friends' wheelchairs.

However, at a party like mine, it never took long for at least one balloon to go up and suddenly we'd hear a loud bang, but that would be nothing compared with the shrill scream which followed, sometimes carrying on into a period of several minutes, as it became commonplace for one of the children to become spooked by the unexpected noise. One of the adults would then have to immediately dive into the circle, carrying an alternative type of party novelty, such as a yo-yo or a small writing pad with a few wax crayons but preferably this time it had to be a toy with the flawless capacity to remain silent.

This minor blip was soon forgotten as just after there came an unexpected knock on the door and I looked up perplexed, wondering who it could possibly be.

Just then, a clown came bustling through the lounge door wearing an orange curly wig, a big floppy suit and a bowler hat with a felt flower springing from the top.

"Hello boys and girls", he said, "my name is Mr Hi-Tiddley-Hi-Fi. Now let me see, where's Sonya?"

I excitedly waved my hand in the air and all my friends were now shrieking with laughter and pointing at me to verify my whereabouts.

"So you're the birthday girl today, are you? Your mom tells me that you're six today Sonya, is that right?", he asked.

"Yes", I nodded.

The clown then stepped towards one of the nursery nurses and briskly ruffled her hair.

"Well I don't know what's gone wrong with your hair today", he said, "but it's messier than mine."

He then proceeded to open up a large, black and silver chest and he was tottering back and forth, setting up an array of curious-looking props.

"Would you like to meet one of my friends now, boys and girls?", was his next question.

"Yeeeeeeaaaaaahhhhh", we all screamed in unison and at this, I heard my dad chuckling in the background.

Dad had just come in, as he had been taking another delivery in his lorry again and he stood in the kitchen doorway, surveying the cheery proceedings. He was happy to see what Mom had achieved again but now scanned the lounge, looking for a spare seat but they were all taken by the numerous people who had decided to stay to help. At this he just remained standing, leaning against the wall, munching on the butterfly cake which he had sneaked from the buffet.

"My friend is very shy", the clown continued, "so if you really want to meet him, you're going to have to give him some encouragement and say the magic words, because then he will know that I'm looking for him again and he won't be frightened."

At this, he produced a big fat magic wand and with a quick flick of the wrist, a purple silk banner unrolled, hemmed at the bottom with gold fringes. At first, I couldn't make out the funny word embroidered in gold lettering across the centre but, when the clown said what it was, all became clear.

"Can you remember what my name is, boys and girls? I expect you can, but just in case your teachers forget it, I've written it down".

The banner read, "Hi-Tiddley-Hi-Fi".

"O.K. then, get ready, on the count of three...1...2...2 and a bit...3", the clown continued.

Right on cue, my friends all yelled out, "Hi-Tiddley-Hi-Fi" and even those who couldn't quite manage to get all their words out made one humungous hullabaloo.

Just above the lid of the chest now emerged a thick, tangled mass of orange fur. Two large, bulbous eyes followed and then out sprang an enormous, raggedy-looking orang-utan.

He stared into the sea of children, almost as if he was sinking into a mesmerized daze and then he sharply jumped back with a startled shudder.

"Aaaarrrggghhh, who's all that lot out there?", he wailed.

"It's OK", the clown replied, "it's only the boys and girls. We've come to entertain them all today because it's Sonya's birthday, so don't be silly now and just be friendly, or her mom just might throw us out before we've done the show. I warned you about this before we got here, didn't I? Play me up and you'll just have to make do with black bananas for supper as they won't pay us."

"He hates black bananas, boys and girls, so I think he's got a special song to sing for you now. This is his favourite song and he always settles down when he's performed his party piece."

The orang-utan then had a closer look at us and he obviously came round to the idea that we all looked pretty harmless so, after taking an enormous gulp to clear his throat, he proceeded to jiggle his long floppy arms above his head and gleefully warble one of my favourite Jungle Book classics:-

"Now I'm the king of the swingers
Oh, the jungle VIP
I've reached the top and had to stop
And that's what's been botherin' me
I wanna be a man, man-cub
And stroll right into town
And be just like the other men
I'm tired of monkeyin' around!"

At this point, the magician momentarily intercepted by saying, "If any of you know the words, perhaps you would like to sing along, boys' and girls'."

"Oh, oobee doo
I wanna be like you
I wanna walk like you
Talk like you, too
You'll see it's true
An ape like me
Can learn to be human too".

The orang-utan was really getting into the groove now and he was excitedly leaping from one side of the lounge to the other.

When the song was done, the clown said, "I think my friend is getting a bit sleepy now after all that excitement so he says he is ready to go back in his box and have a nap. Do you want to wave goodbye?"

We all bid him farewell and Mr Hi-Tiddley-Hi-Fi carefully folded the orang-utan's floppy limbs back into the huge trunk, laying him comfortably amidst its red, satin-lined interior and he closed the heavy lid.

"Right", he said, "has anyone got a £10 note I can borrow?", he asked, looking around the room.

Granddad reached over our heads and handed the money to the clown.

"Thank you, sir, that is very kind. I'll use that in the pub on my way back", he replied.

Seconds later, however, he had ripped Granddad's money into tatters and I turned around, looking vexed. If the money had been provided by anyone else in the room, especially if it had been a contribution of my cousin's pocket money, I would have been doubled over with hysteria at this point, but in my opinion, to do this with my granddad's money was just about as serious as things could get.

Mr Hi-Tiddley-Hi-Fi must have seen the look of sheer dismay wash over my face at this stage, as a torrent of pitiful excuses now began to pour from his droopy, red lips.

"Sorry about that sir. Please don't get angry, at least not today. I have been trying to be my old happy self as I know it's Sonya's birthday and everything", he said, "but to be honest, I've had a terrible job on the way down here, in fact, it's lucky we got here in one piece because the orang-utan escaped as he thought I was going to sell him off to The Monkey House at Dudley Zoo and he insisted upon perching in the middle of the dashboard, so that he could keep checking up where we were going. I'm telling you, what with having to calm him down and also wearing this silly outfit, I am sure to be pulled over by the police on the way back."

At this, resting on a dining chair, Mr Hi-Tiddley-Hi-Fi pulled out a red, spotted handkerchief from his trouser pocket, and he began to sob.

"Oh look children", he said after a few minutes, "even the spots have run off my magic hanky, as they don't know what to do either. Dear, dear, everything is going all wrong now. What can we do next?", he pondered, now rummaging to the bottom of the chest again.

"Anyway", he said, now mopping his big, red nose on his handkerchief, "the show must go on."

He then pulled out a large, red square of silk and he stepped towards three rectangular, black boxes which he had placed on tall stands, across the front of the radiator.

Next, he lifted the box from the first stand to reveal a black and white, wooden cut-out of a rabbit, smartly donned in a dinner jacket, bow tie and a magician's top hat. He then gave us a quick peek underneath the second box, but that one was completely empty and so was the third and final box.

"Now what I'm going to do, is to give the box on the left three sharp taps on its side and if you can just help me again boys and girls, by shouting out the magic words, the rabbit is going to go hop-hop-hopping right into the middle box but you will all have to be sure to join in or the trick won't work and I will have wasted all my time setting all this up for you."

He scanned the audience now, wearing a glum expression and the room erupted again, as we all shouted, "Aaaaaarrrrrgggghhhhh!"

"Get ready now", he prompted.

"Hi-Tiddley-Hi-Fi", we roared again and just as the magician had stated, after three strikes of the magic wand, sure enough, the rabbit had vanished from the stand on the left and had now taken up residence in the centre box.

"You all did a very good job there", the clown said, "I told you it would work if you all joined in. How would you like one last try?, because you are all so clever, I'm sure with just a little more effort, we could get the rabbit all the way to the last box."

Just as I thought he was ready to draw the trick to an end, Mr Hi-Tiddley-Hi-Fi gave a huge sneeze and at this, his hat fell off, landing right in my friend's lap.

"Hey, I saw that", he said to Lisa, "I'll have to keep a close watch on you, or you'll be trying to steal my money next."

For the final time, my friends and I all repeated the magic words, "Hi-Tiddley-Hi-Fi", and just as expected, the rabbit had been magically transported into the third and final box.

At this point, a few of the children were beginning to fidget and like me, they were probably beginning to think, "O.K., we've already been through all this stupid rigmarole once, so doesn't it get any better?"

I think the clown also started to detect the pockets of restlessness, but then, at the eleventh hour, he suddenly said, "Oh look, children, I think the rabbit has a note for us. Can you see the corner of it just poking out from underneath the rabbit's bow tie?".

At this, he suddenly banged the wooden rabbit with his magic wand and now we witnessed the most impressive trick of all. There came a huge billow of grey smoke and when it cleared, the black and white woodcut had completely vanished from sight and in its place, sat a beautiful live rabbit, contently scratching behind one ear with his back leg.

The clown picked up the rabbit to show him around the audience, but as he did so, the piece of paper the rabbit had been guarding, floated down on the carpet. Mr Hi-Tiddley-Hi-Fi slowly unfolded it and it was, of course, my granddad's £10 note and it was as crisp and fresh as if it had just rolled off The Royal Mint. The rabbit had been sitting on it for safekeeping all the time.

I was totally flabbergasted and I threw my floppy head right back again, rolling in laughter. This was the outcome I had been waiting for all along and at least now, the next time I visited my grandparents' house,

I would know who to tell when I heard the merry jingle of the ice cream man coming down the road.

"Well, my show is almost done now boys and girls", the clown said, "so I hope you all have a really lovely day and you all enjoy the rest of Sonya's party. I'll tell you what though, just to finish off, would you like me to make you some balloon animals?"

It goes without saying, of course, so there are no prizes for guessing how the children responded to this Their squeals of sheer delight practically shook the house off the hill and so without further quandary, the clown began to twist and bend the elongated balloons into a broad array of comical creatures.

I then glanced up to catch my nan just pottering in the background and as ever, just by the expression on her face, I knew precisely what she was thinking. "Oh no, please not the balloon scenario again, we've only just recuperated from the last fiasco."

Thankfully though, Nan's qualms did not come to fruition and soon the children were bouncing a broad array of balloon animals around the lounge.

Everyone had thoroughly enjoyed the show. It had turned out to be the best idea Mom could have employed, but there was still a little more time before my school pals would have to head for home, so to round the day off nicely, my mom had prepared a few party games.

We all shuffled around a little, rearranging ourselves as best we could, to form a circle. It was time to play Pass the Parcel.

Of course, my sister didn't want to join in: all she could do at first was to stand there sniggering, probably thinking, "Oh great, this one is going to be fun", but Mom soon put a stop to that and she put her in charge of stopping and starting the tape recorder at appropriate intervals.

Before my guests had arrived, I had sorted out a range of my favourite tapes, so all she had to do, was to play them.

There was nothing really out of the ordinary about this pursuit, but all the adults chipped in again, being on hand to provide appropriate assistance in loosening the sticky tape so that we could all peel a layer of newspaper from the parcel. Mom, Auntie and my grandparents also paid close attention to proceedings, pointing or meaningfully clearing their throats, to indicate when my sister should stop the music, hence ensuring that each child was given a fair turn. I was sitting next to my cousin, who, at times, was my No.1 rival, so I used to heatedly snatch the package from his grasp, as quickly as I was able, to make sure that whoever had the privilege of undoing the final wrapper, if I had anything to do with it, it most certainly wasn't going to be him.

In the end, though, the little girl who was sitting three places to my right, unwrapped a box of Maltesers, so although I had partially got my wish, the ultimate treat hadn't landed in my lap either but, considering who was manning the tape recorder, this inevitable outcome had obviously been clinched right from the onset, hadn't it, Sis'?

It had been a very long, but lovely day and by this time, a few of the parents who had decided to leave their mischievous offspring to their own devices were now starting to filter back in.

Just to wrap the day's proceedings up in style, however, there was just time for one final activity and that was to engage in two or three rounds of, "Pin the Tail on the Donkey".

Well, the first thing to comment on here, of course, is that I have enjoyed many pleasant days at the beach, but I have never witnessed a donkey trudging across the sand whose leg contour matched this one. Perhaps I have just holidayed in the wrong places and my parents have come across a different breed to me. I just don't know, but it could make interesting Internet research in the future to see if I could stumble upon an equine breed who exhibited a comparable profile.

Anyway, devoid of the blindfold, this always being either fashioned from a headscarf or one of Dad's ties, we could just about decipher the correct end to which to fix the tail.

However, when it was my turn to fumble around and haphazardly stick the donkey's tail on, all that I could hear in the background was the constant onslaught of cackling and mockery coming from my sister and my cousin, both taking immense delight in letting me know that the location of my attempt was so far away from the desired target, that I might as well just give up at that moment and go to bed. I was useless.

I soon learnt, however, that this was all a big prank and my estimation was, in fact, very precise, but I was being teased as usual and they were trying to purposely guide my hand in completely the wrong direction.

In a similar way to which Pass the Parcel had been supervised, many of the grownups took their turn in giving assistance and upon taking off the blindfold, my friends screamed in delight, all being convinced that their attempt was the best.

Yes, following my birthday parties there was always a lot of debris to clear away, but when catering for any small child's party, completely irrespective of whether they are disabled or not, the messy aftermath of it all is never any different. Often lapsing into the next week, there is nothing out of the ordinary about suddenly unearthing the odd serviette which has been concealed underneath a cushion on the settee or the remnants of a party popper that landed somewhere obscure and so failed to be stuffed into the bin bag when the tidying up was done. I think the chaos which is left behind is simply the gratification that a lovely time has been had by all.

Taking various things into account though and looking back on some of these experiences through the eyes of an adult, I now realise that the occasions of my early birthday parties meant a great deal more than just celebrating the passing of another year.

For me, the first thing that comes to mind is that each passing year signified greater progress in my development. Also, up until this point, my friends from school had never been invited to a birthday party before, but everyone had such a lovely time, that from then on, I started to receive invitations all the time and we were all soon transformed into real little party animals. Nan always designed my lovely, pretty dresses, so she became my very own, personal fashion designer.

I had now settled well in school, I had loads of friends, my communication skills were getting better all the time, in fact, in my own way, I was having an absolute ball.

The message I think I have been trying to convey here is intended for the families of disabled children. Some days it is completely normal to feel sad and question why your little one has had to encounter the difficulties they have, but if you look a little closer, you won't just see the joys of a normal childhood, but the happiness you will see in your very special child will be even greater.

Be proud and take joy from their every new achievement as God has chosen you to do a fascinating, important and very special job.

6

Life's Balances

The major theme which we looked at in my last chapter was how young parents and families must feel when they suddenly find themselves responsible for bringing up a disabled child. I then shared with you all the fun and frolics of my early birthday parties and the enormous sense of joy and satisfaction which was felt by everyone after enjoying such a lovely day.

This is describing two very opposite emotional extremes and following Mom's initial apprehension of how she could entertain so many disabled children, in the end all the hard work had paid off and it had made for a very special and memorable occasion. I have always greatly admired Mom for this character and I know I keep saying this, but she is a truly extraordinary lady. She was born under Libra, the zodiac sign symbolized by the set of scales, but it was probably just as well, as it seemed that she had quite a task ahead in perfecting my art of balance.

Of course, any good mother has a special and unparalleled love for her child, but particularly during the early days, it is perfectly natural for all young moms to be looking out for the usual developmental milestones such as talking, crawling and walking. For me, however, any improvements were still only very small and gradual and as far as my mobility was concerned, my ability to walk or to gingerly totter around under my own steam simply hadn't materialized at all.

However I'm not too sure how old I was, but it always makes me smile that Mom once managed to obtain just one photo of me, proudly standing unaided, propped up against the wall of the house. I think I must have been around six and I was attractively, (or "not") modelling my brightly coloured sunglasses, a flowery sunhat, all finished off with my yellow little girl's handbag slung over one shoulder. I probably wouldn't have won any prizes for my fashion sense but at the time, it was still another great achievement.

Anyway, during the 1970s, (as I'm sure anyone in my age range or older will recall), would enjoy some really lovely summers and back in the day, just like any other little girl enjoying the sunshine, I used to love to sit on the front lawn picking clumps of daisies, buttercups and dandelion clocks, (albeit minus their stalks), for Mom. In fact, now I come to think of it, I also used to pick dandelion leaves to feed to our animals, Winnie and Sandy: our guinea pig duo and also, Bobby, the pet tortoise.

Mom often used to send my sister out to keep an eye on me while she was swaying back and forth on her swing, but I remember feeling a little disgruntled really because I wanted a ride too. However, all my dreams were soon dashed again, as I was often told, "well, it's no good you asking to go on the swing Sonya as you will just fall backwards and bash your brains out and then it will be a 9 9 9 job."

I think I used to quietly wonder why I wasn't allowed to ride on my sister's lap, but then switching my over-active imagination back to what I would have looked like if my little brain had been splattered all over Dad's neatly mowed lawn provided the perfect imagery required to turn me off that stupid notion anyway and so, as ever, I needed something else to do to quell my brewing boredom.

Much like most small children, one outdoor activity which I always loved was to play with my sandpit. Nowadays, of course, there is nothing unusual about this: the creative development of new sand toys has come a long way since then. However, it will probably sound a little strange, but Mom hit upon the cunning notion that the old, yellowing baby bath which was stashed at the back of the garage would be just the thing to transform into a little garden sandpit for me. She managed to obtain a small bag of sand from a local builders' yard and so, from here on in, I used to have a real blast, squatted on the picnic rug making my mud pies and sandcastles. At last, Mom had found the perfect solution to coax me out of my disappointment of being unable to ride on my sister's big swing.

As you can imagine though, I think my jolly sand play set quite a scene, probably making a disturbing impact upon both close neighbours and on the steady stream of visitors or delivery people who would come trudging unwittingly up the hill. To make my seaside scene even more comical, most of the time it would also be complemented by my merry humming along to the songs of Dumbo or The Aristocats on my cassette recorder. I think I can conclude that I was really some weird kid.

Anyway, I loved making sandcastles so just a little later Mom said she was going to give me a real treat and take me for my very first trip to the seaside.

In those days, I think this became quite easy, as Dad developed another work base just outside Weston-Super-Mare, so all the family would often enjoy a day on the beach, while my dad went off to work.

Where I have been concerned, nothing turned out to be too straightforward though and, as Mom soon found out, one of the next problems she had to address was how she could stabilize me safely on the beach so that I could enjoy building my sandcastles.

My balance was still quite poor and so every thirty seconds I'd topple forward into the sand, landing flat on my face. I'd then be dragged up into a sitting position again by either Mom or Nan: they would take it in turns to rush to my aid armed with a handkerchief to brush the sand out of my face, but I never ceased to emerge without bellowing as if I was being murdered, resembling some sort of sand yeti.

As time passed though, Mom employed two imaginative tactics in her ardent endeavour to solve this problem. Firstly, she used to dig out a great big pit in the sand, sit me right in it and then she covered me right up to my waist in tightly compressed sand, hence holding me in a secure sitting position.

On an alternative occasion, she also bought me a very low, inflatable chair from a stall which sold beach accessories. I am unsure now which of these methods proved the most effective, but like everyone else, Mom was determined that I was going to enjoy a day at the beach.

The adults in the family would take it in turns to assist me in perfecting the art of building sandcastles, but it didn't take long for my cousin to start deliberately trying to land me up to my neck in trouble again, as he introduced me to the hazardous, but far more exciting activity of hollowing out a great big hole. Sometimes I think the main objective of this was to see how far down we had to burrow before reaching the layer of thick, oily sludge at the bottom. Knowing my cousin as I do though, it was probably just his cheeky ploy to ensure that I definitely did, plunge right into the hole.

Whenever this happened, as it inevitably always did, I would start to scream. My bottom would be sticking up in the air and I hadn't a hope in hell of pulling myself out, but really, I guess it couldn't have been that painful, as I was always keen to have another try.

"Now look what a state you're in", Nan scolded me, "it's no use you trying to copy him, as you know very well you haven't got enough balance. I don't know!", she continued, but at least she'd identified who had instigated the problem in the first place.

It had been entirely my cousin's fault again, of course, as left to my own devices, I would never have dreamt up this silly game.

Anyway, before I had a chance to dig myself into an even deeper hole, Nan announced that everyone should gather around the cars again, as it was now time for lunch.

In fact, the subject of food has just triggered another amusing memory concerning Nan because when she was coaxing me to eat my sand-dusted cheese and pickle sandwiches, she would often say, "If you don't hurry up and eat your dinner, one of these seagulls will swoop down and steal it. I have just seen one of them watching. Can you see him strutting across the sea wall? Well, he's got his beady eye on your sandwich and he is preparing to attack, so come on, get a move on now."

My nan was full of these kinds of stories; she was a lovely character but she never failed to construct some catastrophic consequence of what was sure to occur if you did not heed her wise advice.

Just before teatime on Friday evening our cars were finally packed again and smiling, Mom handed in the chalet keys at the camp shop filled with a lovely sense of satisfaction.

Being my first taste of the seaside just a week ago she hadn't really known what to expect again. How would I cope at the beach? Maybe just like my early Christmases, it would all prove too much for my little mind to adjust to again?

Happily though, this wasn't the case at all and following the initial difficulty of how Mom could stabilize me on the beach, I loved building sandcastles and regardless of my physical problems which have always been so clear to the outside world, Mom could see that I was no different to any other little girl who wanted to play in the sunshine.

Following the weekend it was time to return to school again and my first lesson of the new term was scheduled in the art department. Our class had recently been studying the decorative architecture of ancient buildings and we had been encouraged to notice the differences in present-day architecture as opposed to the more primitive but highly decorative construction work of yesteryear. Following a little research in the History Section of the library, I decided to do a pencil sketch of the Taj Mahal: a white marble mausoleum, which stands by the river, in the Indian city of Agra.

The art teacher neatly suggested that to create the desired mosaic effect, perhaps I should cover my entire drawing with glued down squares of wallpaper, achieving a similar representation of its old stonework.

As you can imagine, my attempts to stick down the first few pieces created anything but a pretty sight, well, that is with the lone exception of the papier-mâché squares which had firmly adhered themselves to the hem of my art overall. Ten minutes into my lesson, however, I thought I was beginning to devise the most effective method of targeting the paper and my artwork seemed to be finally taking shape, but then, as everyone knows, opposites attract and for me, a feeling of satisfaction always seems to entice grave disaster.

"Hello Sonya", my speech therapist greeted me, "so what are you up to today?"

SPLAT!! I had been so engrossed in trying to manoeuvre the next piece of paper into an appropriate position without sticking the entire design to my soggy sleeves that her arrival had gone unnoticed and the sudden sound of a different tone of voice, was all that it took, for me to completely lose the plot.

I just can't seem to get the hang of the complex business of multi-tasking, let alone a task which involves me and the use of a devilishly sticky substance like glue.

I then desperately fought a completely fruitless battle to regain some kind of control, but everyone could see it was far too late for that. The plastic glue spatula had now firmly adhered itself to the cuff of my art apron and dangled like a lone peg from a washing line. If you think that is bad, however, for me this small fact didn't even scrape the surface, as the biggest nightmare of all, was the fact that my cream trousers, - the ones which Nan had only made a few weeks before on the sewing machine, - were completely ruined. There was just no way I would ever be able to wear them again in this atrocious state, so similar to the paper tiles in my mosaic pattern, the only thing my new trousers were fit for now, was to be cut into squares and used as old rags to clean Mom's windows. Just how was I going to sweet-talk my way out of this one?

Despite this small hiccup, however, my design had almost reached completion now and I had certainly managed to capture the required mosaic effect, as my final graphic resulted in being an exclusive mishmash of wallpaper, head hair and crescents of broken fingernails. Maybe I should have patented the technique: my masterpieces could have been highly sought after, particularly in today's climate when most people seem to go that extra mile to ensure they only buy goods crafted from purely natural products.

Thankfully, however, the class's accompanying nursery nurse promptly came to my rescue armed with a flannel and a bowl of hot, soapy water, so I soon looked decent again and I started to make my way along the maze of corridors, heading for the small speech therapy room, concealed in a quiet corner of Lower School.

The interior of the Speech Therapy Room was sparsely furnished, just containing the therapist's desk and chair, a low, wooden stool and a full-length wall mirror which was flanked on both sides by two vertical handrails.

On most occasions, I would remain in my wheelchair throughout the session, but sometimes the lady suggested that I should come out of my chair, transferring onto the stool.

For people who suffer from Cerebral Palsy, this touches on another very interesting, but strangely effective technique which seems to somehow slightly minimize the involuntary movements pertaining to the condition as immobilizing one part of the body can sometimes heighten the ability in a different area, so in this instance gripping onto the handrails proved instrumental in maximizing the control of my speech pattern.

Unfortunately though, having a sense of humour like mine, it was never too much farther into the proceedings when all control was lost again as the first task I was given was to run through what the therapist regarded as my warm-up exercises which were simply to practice my pronunciation of all the major sound groups used in the clear formation of spoken language. I began by practicing some single letter sounds like "t, t, t, s, s, s, l, l..." and similarly, I'd then have to repeat a collection of equally stupid vowel sounds:- "eeeee, oooo, aaaarrr", I said to my reflection in the mirror.

If the Deputy Headmaster happened to be walking down the corridor, showing a group of important visitors around the school, from outside, it probably sounded like I was either in the middle of my annual check-up with the school dentist or being ruthlessly caned for the inexcusable wrongdoing of another of my disorderly classmates.

My speech therapist would tell me that looking in the mirror should help to enhance the tone of my voice, as observing my different mouth expressions would assist me in expelling my words with greater clarity and poise. This is just one paltry reason you see, why I have grown to be so ladylike.

Being honest, however, the pitch of my voice was probably all over the place but there was one thing I knew for sure: there was little wrong with the technique of her sales pitch and now I heard the bloodcurdling clunk I had been dreading for the last ten minutes and the shiny clasps on her briefcase sprang open.

"Go on Miss", I thought, "surprise me and select something different for a pleasant change, please", but either my powers of telepathy hadn't worked, or she had simply chosen to ignore them, because just as expected, she retrieved the small plastic bag of wooden spatulas, which was always tightly fastened by one of those coloured, wire twisty things: the kind of small, inanimate object that my grandparents always had tucked away in the back of the cupboard, just in case of a fitting emergency. I'd inwardly cringe at this point, now watching as the lady finally retrieved a thick, wooden spatula because I knew from bitter experience where it was heading. Yes, to probe inside my mouth, of course.

The spatulas always tasted repulsive, giving me a similar dry taste that you may experience after licking about five hundred stamps to stick on the envelopes of your Christmas cards.

The next hour, (which, to me always felt more like six), would then be spent with me practising pronouncing a hideous array of sounds, words and tongue twisters like, "Lorraine licked her lemony lollipop and it tasted lovely". If you hadn't realised, this was a typical kind of sentence which would be devised to perfect my pronunciation of the letter "L" and every time the therapist concluded that my effort hadn't sounded quite right, I would have to repeat it again, this time accompanied by a few more nippy prods in the tongue with the spatula.

At last, the session came to an end and by this time I was not only on the brink of a severe panic attack after finally being set free from that claustrophobic, boiling hot room, which was little bigger than a telephone booth, but my tongue felt like it had been permanently welded to the roof of my mouth as I was now suffering from a chronic state of dehydration from the clinical taste of the spatula, so I decided to take a brief detour here, passing the girls' bathroom, to take a refreshing drink at the water fountain. The Tuck Shop wouldn't have been a bad idea so that I could have purchased a tube of sweets or something, but this only operated through the lunch hour.

By the time I arrived back in class, the school day was almost done, so my form teacher suggested that I should spend the last three-quarters of an hour finishing off my latest English essay as it was due to be handed in on Friday.

The final bell rang and as usual, my friends and I did our best to arrange ourselves in a line leading to the class doorway. I gazed down at my mucky trousers again, taking a heavy sigh. "Here we go", I thought, "I'm really gonna be in for it now when Mom sees this."

Anyway, I had almost reached the entrance hall and I could see one of my regular taxi drivers pacing up and down the last corridor, scruffily adorned in an oil-stained, tweed coat, his facial features masked in a huge swirl of cigar smoke, when I remembered just at the last minute that Mom had instructed me to collect another batch of raffle tickets, so I doubled back again, now heading for the school office. At least I wanted to be able to go home having done one thing right.

The school raffle was held annually and over the years, my granddad built up quite a reputation for his great success in ticket sales, as being an employee of a local and well-known car manufacturer, his colleagues became accustomed to the draw to such a degree in fact, that on some occasions Granddad's friends started to enquire after their books of raffle tickets even before they had been issued and they always managed to scoop a broad range of beautiful prizes too. In fact one year, the school held a cheese and wine party and the Deputy Headmaster presented Granddad with a special gift, just to express the school's sincere thanks for his superb effort.

At last, it was time to head home, so I made my way to the entrance, where my taxi was waiting just outside the nurses' room.

Our journey home was fairly quiet, as most of the children would be weary after their long day, so we would often just chill out to the radio, or quietly chatter amongst ourselves about the day's events.

A few years later, however, the school physiotherapists began to introduce me and several other children to our first power chairs and so it was decided that it would be easier to transport us by a tail-lift bus so that we could travel in comfort and stay in our wheelchairs.

As far as travelling in this type of vehicle with a group of mischievous, disabled children is concerned, I think there is only someone like me who could describe the kind of amusing but imaginative games which the children devised to combat their boredom and to pass away the time.

In work and play kids like us had to develop a certain degree of craftiness and the very important skill to be able to make adaptations to our worlds so that if we couldn't achieve something via the usual, conventional way, then we usually managed to succeed by exploring an alternative route.

For instance, although I could never quite figure out why, most of my travelling companions seemed to develop a strange desire to pass one small object from one child to the next, so this task turned out a bit like re-enacting a unique and a rather bizarre version of playing Pass The Parcel again, only this time, it was performed on the move.

We would wait for a convenient pause in our journey, such as when the traffic lights were on red, or until we came to a standstill at a busy junction, as this would normally allow just enough time to fling whatever we had that day, across to the next nearest passenger. This menagerie of missiles would vary greatly but, depending on what the children were carrying, these assorted objects could range from anything from sweets, or their empty wrappers, to pens, pencils, erasers, to sticky lumps of half-chewed, chewing gum or any other accumulated piece of useless rubbish. With time, this game gained yet another ridiculous twist, as now, one of the kids came by a huge loop of string, which was just long enough to span around the whole perimeter of the van and so, being equally distributed between everyone, the lads devised the ridiculous notion of hanging a pen from it, circulating it from one child to another, like a lone clothes peg, swinging from a bizarre rotary line.

At the front of the van, just behind the driver's cab, there were sometimes two more little boys who were slightly more able, so they occupied ordinary seats and observing all that was going on, they boisterously chipped in with a continual onslaught of both positive and negative comments, cheering on the progress of the game.

Trips home from school were seldom quiet and uneventful, but the children's amusing antics served to shorten the ride and soon I arrived home.

My wheelchair proceeded to skid down the steep drive, but Mom grabbed me back just in time to prevent me from crashing into Dad's car and scraping all the paint off the door.

"Just look at the state of your trousers", Mom loudly exclaimed, "what on earth have you been doing?...it'll be a miracle if that comes out in the wash and you haven't had them for five minutes. I don't know what Nan is going to say."

I lowered my gaze and gulped, feeling even more guilty following the poignant reminder that Nan had only made them for me just a few weeks beforehand.

"Oh, by the way, Mom", I said, now trying to deflect her attention onto a different matter, "I almost forgot to tell you, but I've got the first batch of raffle tickets in my bag."

"Alright", Mom said, "I'd better ring and tell Granddad."

When Mom had finished her phone call, she said, "Come over here, Mommy's got something exciting to tell you."

"What is it then, Mom?" I squealed, "can we go back to the seaside tomorrow?"

"Err...no, not quite that soon, although I'm sure we can one day", Mom replied, "but I think you will like my surprise even better than that."

"Uh", I said, as I really couldn't guess what Mom was talking about.

"How would you like a new baby brother or sister?" Mom asked.

"What, to live here?" I said, "wow Mom, that sounds good."

I was still only about six and little more than a baby myself, so probably not really getting the point, I just went back to eating my cheese and tomato pizza.

Just after finishing tea, I heard the back door open and as usual, that provoked some excitement, as Granddad walked in.

He smiled and bending down next to where I was sitting, in front of the fire, he said, "Oh, I see you're on the bottom shelf again. What are you doing today then?" (When talking to me, "the bottom shelf" was an amusing phrase which my granddad often used instead of saying, "the floor").

"I'm drawing, Granddad", I replied.

He looked closer and chuckled because he now observed that I wasn't using one of my colouring books, but I'd decided to imaginatively doodle over that night's newspaper and it hadn't even been opened yet. I used to scour the whole thing for pictures of faces, embellishing each one with oddly-shaped spectacles, beards and moustaches, or an equally ridiculous range of facial blemishes such as moles, zits, cold sores, rotten teeth and strange hairstyles.

"I doubt if Dad will be too chuffed at that when he gets home from work", Granddad said.

"Oh well", I thought slyly, "if I can get away unscathed with the trouser escapade, then I'm sure a few musketeer beards won't make that much difference, whether the paper's been read or not."

And so in this chapter, together with my comical recollection of my earliest memories by the sea, I have tried to convey various ways in which achieving the correct balance has played an important role in my life.

From the great joys of building my first sandcastles to toppling the gluepot, to pulling weird faces at myself as I practiced my speech, all these things in many different ways have encouraged me to perfect my art of balance, but quite what to make of this baby who was supposedly coming to stay in our house, I really didn't know. I just hoped it would like playing the same games as I did – in fact, it would be quite interesting to see if it was going to be allowed a ride on the swing, or if it was just me who was banned. I didn't know what to expect as I was still only a tot myself, but when weighing everything up in my inquisitive little mind, I decided that becoming a big sister was going to be the most exciting tip of the scales ever.

7

From My Sunflower To A Sweet Rose

Wednesday morning dawned again: halfway through another week and arriving at school, I couldn't quite remember where I was meant to be for my first lesson, so I pulled my wheelchair into the side of the corridor to consult my timetable... at least it had started out being a timetable until the unmentionable episode last week when I'd placed it on the table whilst eating my lunch. I dropped my spoon, so it was barely legible now, after being completely stippled with the sorry aftermath of my baked bean juice. Oh well, I could still read it, - just about.

"That's just typical", I grimaced, realizing that it was my day to be stationed in the area known as The Resources Centre. This meant me having another long trek today right to the other end of the building. The sun was searing through the school windows as usual: in midsummer the heat of the main corridors could get very oppressive, so I used to feel like I was trudging through an enormous greenhouse.

I noted my first port of call of the day was science and this term, my class had spent most of our time working outside in the small quadrangle where we had been sowing a batch of cress and sunflower seeds.

We were specially equipped with large raised gardens so that there was ample space for all the children in the class to position their wheelchairs around its parameter, each having a small portion of soil to work with.

Soon armed with a packet of seeds, I set to work, my first task being to hollow out a patch of soil with the trowel. As I was about to find out though, spreading my seeds evenly didn't go quite as easily as anticipated, as before I had barely started, the entire contents of the packet came cascading out in one huge mound. "Oh well", I slyly concluded to myself, "Sir can see for himself now that my gardening

103

efforts are a complete joke, so maybe he'll realise after this escapade, that the only thing I can do with plants is to feed them to the animals...I don't know, Mom and Nan would have this sewn up in seconds." I angled a glance in the direction of the class clock..."there's still a long time to go before the dinner bell", I inwardly sighed.

Eventually, though, my sorry deed was done and now the teacher began to circulate again, walking around to check on our progress and also distributing some labels bearing our names. The class had decided to hold a contest to see whose sunflower grew the tallest, each week plotting our all-important measurements on a wall graph.

At first, I remember feeling quite despondent as my ridiculous specimen seemed to be wilting more than it was progressing but, after a few more weeks, my sunflower became the penultimate one to come into flower, although, unlike Mom, I still don't think I would ever describe myself as being blessed with green fingers.

In the early years, the Resources Centre had originally served as being our old hall, but just a little while after I started school, a large, new extension was added, which was then transformed into the modern Lower School building, hence giving rise to some lovely new facilities.

Victoria School doubled in size: the hall was relocated into the new building and its predecessor was partitioned off, now being transformed into our Resources Centre, which mainly consisted of three specialized teaching areas, with the art and textiles classes sitting directly opposite to where I'd been working this morning, in the science and human biology department.

Lower School was also home to the large, heated swimming pool, which sat next to the newly equipped physiotherapy room and so together with the apparatus in the P.E. hall, it was clear right from the start that the staff really planned on giving us all a rigorous workout now.

Another major specialist area was Planned Dependence, which consisted of an indoor sandpit and the Soft Play Room, this being exclusively dedicated to some of my personal, favourite children, who sadly, were too disabled to join lessons. Ideally equipped with foam mats and comfy bean bags, this well-designed area gave a great environment for relaxation and play, whilst right in the midst of it all, stood our three, very cheery, carer-assisted bathrooms.

Of course, working as a special school toileting assistant isn't the easiest of jobs: its physical aspect is both repetitive and demanding because, by the time they had shut one kid up who came through the large, sliding doors, jiggling up and down, screaming, "Quick, I'm dying for a wee Miss", the next dozen children had joined the trailing conga, each parroting the same thing, - and yes, I freely admit that I was often another one.

Many of the youngsters in Planned Dependence also demonstrated their own, unique forms of chatter, provoking an odd combination of amusement and sadness, although upon hearing their calls, most people would feel compelled to respond.

One story in particular, which seldom fails to make me smile, is that the school was once putting on our annual nativity play and as often occurred, my family arrived early, allowing them the privilege of front row seats.

I didn't witness this, but as I have been told, one little girl unpredictably stepped forward right to the edge of the wooden stage and she called out, "Where's my momma? I want my momma", now shielding her gaze and scanning around the hall in sincere earnest.

Upon hearing this story, of course, I instantly guessed the child who had done this, as when paying my visits to the bathroom each day; this is just one example of the funny phrases I became so accustomed to hearing. As usual though, during this particular performance, it was my nan who offered up her bubbly response, "She's coming, my darling".

I will tell you more about our amazingly colourful and multi-faceted drama productions a little later but, despite the tedium of powdering all those little noses, life working in this department was seldom dull.

Anyway, around this time it wasn't just our plants that were experiencing a new spurt of growth, as my skinny, little legs were getting lankier too. The footrests on my wheelchair had been lowered as far as possible to accommodate a child of my size, but the inhabitants of the physiotherapy department were now starting to express concerns that they felt I was demonstrating a poor sitting posture.

In the narrowing eyes of those fastidious physio's, I was seen to be "sitting with a bad list", contrary to some of my friends, who, utilizing an extensive range of walking aids were unlawfully alleged to be "walking with a bad gait". Consequently, according to the views being expressed by the occupants of the Physiotherapy Department, there wasn't a kid in the school devoid of the tendency to lean towards one category or the other.

They concurred that it was now a good time to introduce me to my first power chair, as it would remove the difficult task of trying to self-propel my manual wheelchair, instead providing me with far greater mobility – a very useful commodity, particularly when my desired destination was the girls' bathroom.

In the early days, it took a little time for me to become competent at getting around in my power chair: I have chipped wallpaper and plaster from quite a few walls but, just like the use of my specially adapted typewriter, the ability to move around independently is something that has really transformed my life.

Well, as I'm sure you can see from all these reminiscences, I recall Victoria as being a very happy place: its high-spirited corridors forever chiming with giggles but, probably much like in other schools, the merriment was never as heightened as in the month of December.

Christmastime at Victoria was always very special and something I am so glad I could be a part of. Of course, I am still yet to meet a child who doesn't love all the sparkle and magic but, at a school like mine, it was a time when the teachers seemed to bring their creative skills to the fore, uniting the whole school together in fun and the festivity of the season.

I think one of the earliest of these jolly memories, (although I'm not too sure of my age at the time), is of one of my first school parties. The staff had set out the large, round buffet tables in the hall, deliciously laden with all the usual kind of treats: there were jelly and blancmange, chocolate biscuits and cakes and heaps of assorted sweets. We played games and sang carols but, as you may expect, just like at any other young child's Christmas party, the highlight and the main event of the day, which everyone looked forward to was the traditional visit from the guy who wore the fur-trimmed coat – in fact, he'd probably spent so much money on his plush red suit, that he couldn't even afford a razor.

I remember keeping my place in the queue, (I was probably only in Class Two or Three) and as it drew nearer to my turn, I could hear Santa having the same conversation with each child, going something like, "Have you been good this year?" and, "What would you like for Christmas?" The children in front of me continued to squeal their excited requests. Their little faces were alight with wonderment and joy and finally, it came to my turn.

Peering into his baggy hood, however, I could instantly see that I was sitting face to face with the deputy headmaster, so I replied, "Well, I want a game of Kerplunk, Mr. Davis."

"Sssshhhh", the deputy head mused, briefly nodding towards the line of pupils still trailing behind me, "this lot still believe."

I never could shut up but I remember desperately trying to stifle my sniggers, as, at least for now, it seemed that my innocent friends had fallen for the same old end-of-year chestnut again.

We all had a great time: soon it was home time and as my taxi ascended our steep hill, I was a little taken by surprise to find that Mom wasn't stood in her usual place, but today, my nan was waiting to greet me.

"Oh, hello Nan", I called as the taxi driver began to open the door, "where's Mom?"

"Come on", Nan said, as she pushed me up the ramp and into the hall, "we must hurry up, the phone's ringing."

"Yes", Nan said, answering the phone, "oh that's great, thank you, dear".

Soon the conversation had ended and Nan's face lit with joy, as she told me, "Sonya, you've got a lovely, new baby sister. Mom and the baby are both fine. Isn't that a lovely surprise?"

I was delighted, and I think my first response probably went something like, "so when can I see her, Nan? ... I can't wait to hold her on my lap."

"Oh I'm sure there'll be lots of chances for you to play with her", my nan laughed, "but she will be very tiny for a while, so you'll have to be very quiet."

I think I probably studied on this for a few moments and then changing the subject I said, "Nan, do you know where Mom's put the baby's caterpillar? We must get it ready for her."

Just like most small children, as soon as I heard Mom was having the baby, I decided I wanted to make some kind of special welcome gift, so I had spent many hours sitting on the floor again, crafting my sister a toy caterpillar out of pompoms.

At the time this seemed like a reasonably presentable first offering. It was going to be so exciting and all I could dream of right now was what my sister may look like, what songs I could teach her and how I may get on with my all-new and captivating role of big sister.

For me, it was just an amazing adventure. I probably felt like a princess in a fairytale who was getting another special little friend to play with for Christmas.

In my innocence, I was not only unaware of the fragility of this new life but neither had I any comprehension of the serious level of emotions my mom must have gone through as she prepared herself to be admitted into hospital.

Mom has since shared with me her fully understandable anguish which manifested as soon as she arrived in the maternity unit and her earnest and immediate appeal that she must, without error, be allowed to stay on the general ward right up until my sister was born to avoid the stark and sickening isolation which had been so very present and detrimental at the dawn of my life.

Praise be to the Lord though, all went well this time and my sister carried on the typical family trademark of being crowned with a plentiful amount of thick, black hair. Mom and my little sister returned home on Christmas Eve and the house was brimming with joy and all those beautiful smells we all associate with a dreamlike festive period, these being a combination of fresh pine needles, the turkey gently crisping in the oven, the cinnamon candles which stood lined up like toy soldiers above the fireplace, but the sweetest smell of all, of course, was the idyllic and tranquil aroma of a beautiful, healthy baby girl.

8

Let's Get Physical

Like all older siblings I guess, I felt a great sense of pride as I wasn't the baby anymore and at last, promoted to my new all-important role of "big sister", one of the first things I wanted to know was what I could do to help so that I felt at the heart of all the chaos. To begin with, I remember being delegated two special jobs. Firstly, Mom used to place my sister on the dining table and as she gurgled at me from her changing mat, my task was to alert Mom as quickly as possible at the first signs that she may cry, or as time progressed and she began to get a little more mobile, I had to be especially attentive to prevent her from tumbling onto the floor.

This was, unmistakably, one of the happiest points in my life and even at my young age, I would look into her tiny face in sheer wonder, convinced that she was trying her best to convey a special message to me and considering she has now grown into such a bright, articulate young lady, I still believe she probably was.

A further duty which I loved to do was to help to rock my sister off to sleep. When I was born, new babies were still being transported in the very large, old-fashioned type of pram, but unlike the wide choice of convertible pushchairs which is available today, my sister was bought a carrycot and transporter, which, for the early 1970s, was the most modern form of baby equipment on the market.

Gently pushing her carrycot back and forth across the carpet, I began to sing a sweet lullaby, as it was now my turn to look after the baby.

I found it so funny to watch her wrinkle her nose and blow bubbles at me and in the beginning I think I kind of expected that this was going to be the whole story and my sister would remain a docile, little pink thing who was just going to pull funny faces at me for the rest of her life. However, I think she was secretly sniggering at my innocence, for being a Christmas baby, she had obviously shot a glance at my Advent Calendar, but she wasn't just interested in decorating the tree, but much more fittingly, she was looking forward to the advent of when she could start decorating me.

As I have said, the days were very long and busy for Mom, but as you can imagine, each new dawn yielded its charismatic blend of magic and mayhem. She ardently strived to keep our routine to a tight schedule and despite all our endless attempts to confuse matters and cause complete pandemonium in every sense imaginable, Mom's unstoppable genius always shone through.

Many outside professionals still weren't convinced however and as time went on, poor Mom continued to be bombarded by a constant and steady stream of health visitors and medical professionals, each one convinced they would turn up one day to find us in the midst of some kind of domestic crisis. It was plain for Mom to see that they had all quite simply decided that, due to my disability, there was no way that Mom would continue to cope with all the daily duties of running a home, alongside meeting the needs of all three of her girls. To them, our happy family life probably just seemed like an atomic bomb on the verge of imminent explosion.

Well, all I can impart here is that nothing could have veered further from reality.

The fantastic mother of three, continued as ever, to illustrate her true radiance just as she still tenaciously does today and in my opinion, my little sister has always been precisely what life needed.

Time to move on a little further now and soon it was Saturday again, my favourite day of the week, (Sunday was pretty cool too, as it also omitted the deadly duty of school's monotonous treadmill) and although I haven't mentioned it for a while, Saturday afternoon was always regarded as a particularly fun time for the whole family, as not only could we all see each other again and share our latest tales at my grandparent's house, but my nan had been hard at work in the kitchen again, thumbing through her worn and much-loved pile of cookery books preparing for us another of her magnificent and flavoursome feasts. Of course, she tried to include all of our special favourites and I'll never know where she found them but Nan always seemed to have something new for us to try too.   In fact, in my opinion, there is simply no other fitting description for it, other than to say that Nan's baking can be epitomized perfectly in the lyrics of the Mary Poppins classic, "Truly Scrumptious".

Auntie always came too and tagging three steps behind her, as she ambled along the front path was that roguish, lethal combination of hilarity and fun, as you may have already guessed, - my cousin.

"Here we go again", I thought, "the scrumptious peace is about to be truly shattered now".

If I'm honest though, his presence did have its uses occasionally, in particular on those days when Nan had prepared a trifle for tea. After engaging in our weekly competitive debate over which one of us had the largest amount of grated cheese and pickle on our sandwich, the serving of the raspberry trifle neatly creamed over our childish banter, as my nan simply shared out two helpings between us, his preference being the creamy topping, which left the luscious layer of fruit jelly behind for me. For once, a ready-made solution was at hand.

With teatime done, having sat through the next corny instalment of The Basil Brush Show and listening to his ridiculous "Boom boom" catchphrase over so many times that it was continually vibrating in my ears, my cousin was looking as bemused as I felt, so he suggested that perhaps we should now make a swift exit into the hall, where we could chill out and reflect at length over exactly whose ludicrous idea it had been to view such a useless programme in the first place. Well, I think I'd better leave that one to the imagination, but it most certainly wasn't mine.

It was somewhere around this time, that I first began to develop a keen interest in the current music scene, but to begin with, I just had two favourite pop groups: my first preference being those clean-cut, high-spirited, Scottish boys who jumped around the stage sporting their white and tartan flares, The Bay City Rollers and as embarrassing as it may be, I was also "Wombling Freely" along to the cheerful songs of Orinoco, Tomsk and Great Uncle Bulgaria.

Soon the popularity of the boy band from Edinburgh had swept the country and it was now that I started to accumulate my first collection of pop music memorabilia. In no time at all, my bedroom walls were completely plastered with Bay City Roller posters; Mom started to buy me a weekly pop magazine as I enjoyed gathering their latest photographs and news articles to stick in my scrapbook but worst of all, I even wanted to look like them. On her travels, Nan bought me a big, floppy, tartan cap and it was during one of her regular shopping trips to stock up on fruit and vegetables at Dudley Market, that she also stumbled across a ream of tartan fabric. "Can I have three yards of this tartan please?", Nan asked the lady on the stall and then wandering around to the other side, her next discovery was a small card wound in black fringing. "Oh look", she continued, "this is just the thing to use as edging on a Roller scarf. I don't know", Nan giggled, "the things I do for this little madam".

The next school week began and I was really looking forward to Thursday night's showing of Top of the Pops, as it had been announced on the radio that The Rollers new single was now steadily climbing the charts and that they were billed to make their first live performance.

"Oh Mom, I hope Nan's got my scarf ready by then", I said.

Well, just how she pulled it off, I will never know, but Nan did manage to have my funky, new outfit all stitched up just in time, so I sat leaning against Mom's armchair, fully clad in my new tartan trouser suit, a silly flat cap, whilst gleefully brandishing my red, checked scarf above my head, munching on cheese and onion crisps for supper. Oh no, what a picture.

Anyway, still staying on the topic of dodgy gear, it was around the same time that I also agreed to take up my next new activity, as courteously suggested by the lady who lived opposite. She has always been another great encouragement and having two children of her own, she was forever interested in my ongoing progress. Back then, she would often give me a cheery wave as I played in the garden, but on this particular day, she descended the steep staircase leading to her driveway and briskly came across the road to speak to Mom.

At the time she acted as District Commissioner for the Dudley Brownie and Guide group and she said, "I was speaking to my friend who runs The Brownies, and we wondered if Sonya may like to join? I'm sure she would like it and I thought it would just be something a bit different for her. What do you think?" she asked Mom.

"Oh yes", Mom agreed without hesitation, "that sounds lovely for her", and so our friend went on to explain that the next meeting was scheduled on Tuesday evening, in an old hall, just past the petrol station.

The neighbour said she would pass the message on to the Brown Owl and with the arrangements finalized, soon it was time to head towards town, to go and meet the Brownies for the first time. Of course, I was a little nervous, particularly as I was going to meet new people and I expected that no-one would be able to tell what I was saying again.

However as I soon learnt, both the girls and Brown Owl were all lovely and attending the meetings in my large buggy, I don't think I've ever had so many children in one go squabbling over whose turn it was to push me. Being designated this task seemed to be such a privilege, I think Brown Owl almost needed to draw up a weekly rota. It was great to feel so welcome, and during our races the brownies thoroughly enjoyed themselves, scurrying up and down the hall with me in the driving seat, issuing my instructions.

Well after a few weeks', I was still having such a brilliant time, that I decided to finally make my pledge, now enrolling to become an official Brownie. I'm not too sure now whether my enrolment night fell somewhere around Christmas, but I seem to have some kind of obscure recollection that the Brownie enrolment was tagged onto the end of another special event, maybe a Christmas concert or something.

Anyway, at last, my big moment arrived, so Brown Owl pushed my buggy into the centre of the room and once again, the horrifying spotlight was turned on me. She was a lovely girl, so she gave me a brief introduction and then fully clad in a brown, tea-cosy like hat, topped with a silly pompom, being almost as monotonous as my lamenting rendition of Ding Dong Merrily On High, I began to warble my way through my Brownie Promise:-

114

"I promise I will do my best,
To do my duty to God,
To serve The Queen,
To help other people,
And to keep The Brownie Guide Law".

Half an hour later, the Brown Owl asked, "So what's The Brownie Guide Law again, Sonya?"

"To lend a hand", I grinned.

Following this, I loved my time as a little Brownie: the girls were all so kind to me and it was always great fun to join in with all the songs and games. For me, I think it also gave a new sense of independence, to feel that, at last, I was able to be accepted and to make more friends within my local community.

Without a doubt though, I think one of the most memorable occasions of all, just has to be on that grand day when I joined together with not only my Brownie pack but also the local Girl Guides, Cubs and Scouts and we collectively paraded through the streets of Dudley, heading for a special service, held at Top Church. I remember someone had to push my buggy again and I was given the great privilege of carrying the flag for the Brownies.

I think I stayed in Brownies for about three years altogether and upon joining, I was assigned to the "Gnome" group. There were about four different groups, which as far as I can remember, they were named something like Gnomes, Imps, Sprites and Elves. Time flashed by, and soon I had just reached ten: I was too old to be a Brownie now, and so my Brown Owl suggested that perhaps I may like to move on to her Guide Group instead. Well, I did go along to try it, but I think I felt that I just didn't fit in, as some of their activities were a little too difficult for me, but looking back now, I am so glad I joined the Brownies as it provided me with a wonderful opportunity to socialize with local children of my own age.

Well anyway, reverting to family matters again, my cousin was still persistently laughing at me: I'd been trying to explain that my sisters had been up to their old tricks again, but it was no use telling him, as he just thought everything was one big joke.

Happily, times were soon to change, as midway through September, as the leaves of 1974 were turning to the auburn shades of autumn, my auntie had another lovely baby boy and much to my great delight, it was at last time for my older cousin to find out what having an inquisitive little sibling in the house was all about.

It didn't take long, however, for my new found complacency to backfire at me, full in the face, as the two little ones simply concurred to join forces and on Saturdays there was no other course of action available to my older cousin now, other than to surrender, stop poking fun at my expense and shut both me and him in the hall, assembling a varied assortment of cushions, dining chairs, Nan's wire magazine rack, or whatever else we could lay our hands to, in our frantic attempt, for at least the next thirty seconds, to construct a toddler-free zone.

Occasionally, although these instances were extremely rare, our efforts did show signs of paying dividends, but just as we had resumed our play, the perilous pair were quick to ascertain that all that was required was a little sorrowful pleading with one of the adults that they both solemnly vowed to be very good children, if only they could be granted the very great privilege of being able to join us.

Wryly, my youngest cousin attempted to camouflage that he was holding confidential meetings with my little sister by sprouting a chaotic mass of blonde curls, but now that these two little ones had come to join the blend, it became as plain as day, that if they had anything to do with it, from now on, life was just going to be one big game.

For me, I feel that my generation of the family has greatly enriched life with a terrific sense of fun and for this, I feel very blessed by them all.

The weeks hummed on and in what seemed like no time at all, my sister had reached the age of fourteen months. My dad hadn't long come in from work and he was sitting in his armchair, just having perused that evening's T.V. page in the newspaper, which had pleased him somewhat, neatly observing that the next episode of Star Trek would be showing in half an hour. Dad loved watching Dr Spock.

Mom sat opposite, and during the last few days, my baby sister had learnt to totter around on her feet. She was almost walking, now just needing a little more confidence, to finally free her of the need of having to grip onto the furniture for added stability.

"Come on", Dad urged her excitedly, "walk to Daddy, come on now".

A moment later, the whole household erupted with hoots of joy, as my sister didn't just walk into Dad's outstretched arms – she ran.

Oh boy, was I in trouble now!

Right from the start, it was plain to see that my sister had oodles of energy and I really couldn't guess what she would do next but my little friend had one unchanging characteristic only and that was whatever I decided to do, she made it quite clear that she was going to have a hand in proceedings too and, if you really want me to lay things on the line here, she concluded that she was not only intent upon helping me, she was going to demonstrate her all new and improved way of doing things. My sister would often come from behind me and just look at me as if to say, "Well, what are you waiting for then?" and so she concluded that she would not just show me once, but again and again and again and then maybe, just maybe, her dippy big sister would finally get the message one day.

Staying with the theme of my sister's endearing little, repetitive treadmills, she often appointed me the role of customer, having to pay a visit to her market stall, lined with artificial tins and plastic fruit and vegetables. At first, just to be sure I was going to play and swallow her carefully calculated bait, she suitably hoodwinked me into believing that just a single trip to her cardboard shop would suffice. Unfortunately, it didn't take long before all those plastic pennies began to drop and grim reality hit home that I'd just been unwittingly lured into a six-hour drama exercise, playing a wide-ranging throng of customers, each of whom displayed increasing levels of desperation and eccentricity as time rolled on.

Life, at least for a spell, seemed fine. I was showing steady progress in my lessons, I was developing a keen interest in science and my teachers were particularly pleased that I was attaining steady marks for my English assignments.

However it was around this time that family life was once again thrown into a time of total disbelief and uncertainty, as my dear auntie was tragically diagnosed with Multiple Sclerosis, but really, this is how I remember her most, as I was still, of course, only a young child.

I think it seems appropriate to embark upon this part of my tale with yet another one of my Nan's loved and most memorable anecdotes and I'm sure many families like mine will easily identify with this too. She often said, "Our problems are obvious, but you don't know what other people are going home to."

Well, what a magical piece of philosophy that was. Just how did she come up with that one? At first glance, this may appear to be only a simple sentence, (and I've only just realised it myself), but this is precisely the meaning which I wanted to convey in the title of this story, "Mixed Blessings". I was hoping at some point I would chance upon a reasonably sensible explanation of how I arrived at this choice, but amidst our sadness, the Lord's gentle hand provided. Auntie continued to demonstrate her wonderful sense of humour and as far as our family shopping excursions were concerned, now with two people being pushed along in wheelchairs, plus two, tussling toddlers in a twin buggy, does it come as any surprise that everyone we met systematically began to clear our path? I remember feeling that I was a small part of a very special "family statement", or a significant "presence" and compared with today's more modern trend of domestic unrest, I'm so glad of the privilege of holding such a lovely memory.

We never seemed short of new things to laugh at and life was so busy, with a new twist of fate to deal with from one minute to the next, that we simply hadn't time to worry.

Every three seconds or so, my little sister would groan from the pushchair, "Mom, tell him, he's kicking me".

"No I haven't", my cousin rebuffed, "she was grabbing my foot and she wouldn't let go. Naaaaaannn, just sort her out".

Five minutes later, my older cousin, who was regularly required to push one of us up the hill would wince, "This one's getting too heavy now. Does anyone want to swap over? Oh Nan, can't we call into that shop again and get some pop?"
There was certainly no time for anyone to ever feel bored.

Anyway, one day Mom was casually browsing through the newspaper, sipping her mid-morning cup of tea, when she spotted in the centre pages a small advert, reporting that there was to be a faith healing meeting taking place at Bingley Hall in Birmingham. It stated that there was going to be a visiting minister praying for the sick and so as you may guess, she immediately telephoned Nan again and without hesitation, it was concluded that both Auntie and I should be taken. They both agreed that there was nothing to lose.

I think I would have probably been around the age of nine or ten at this point, so I just accepted it as just another day out and I didn't really know what to expect.

On the whole, however, I find the subject of faith healing rather an unusual phenomenon: it seems to summon a varied range of physical and emotional effect which, although I can't be sure what is going on, I think the idea of it can raise a few more very interesting questions as to what extent the power of belief can change what we can achieve, (and here I am referring to not only the belief in the healing power of the Lord but also a belief in newfound or increased physical abilities) and exactly what it is that is really governing these changes?

Some people may say that a degree of excitement is merely induced by the collective, euphoric atmosphere created by being in a large crowd. I mean, if you don't react in general agreement with the other 600 people who are in the room, you may look a bit weird, right? Personally though, when discussing the topic of healing, particularly in relation to severely disabled people, I believe that the real strength can be drawn from the power of belief and developing a more positive outlook on life.

On this occasion, however, there were several hundred people packed into the hall, but soon both Auntie and I were pushed to the front, finding a convenient spot to park our wheelchairs.

After thanking everyone for attending, the minister who was convening the meeting set the very high-spirited proceedings in motion with what was soon to become everyone's favourite Pentecostal chorus, "This Is The Day".

Next, it was time to move on to the main event, which had drawn my family to attend in the first place and everyone who required prayer for healing was requested to head towards the stage.

Of course, in my innocence, I was expecting people to just share a brief time of prayer with the preacher and then I thought they would quietly saunter back to their seats as if nothing had occurred. This, however, wasn't the case at all and so, as you can imagine, it came as something of a shock to a ten-year-old, to witness that, quite unexpectedly, many of the people in front of me started to fall backwards onto the floor as if they had become unconscious. In contrast, a bizarre range of missiles began to be thrown through the air including walking sticks and arm crutches. Various walking frames were being cast aside and I think there was probably a couple of old ladies handbags in there too, so as my position in the queue advanced ever nearer to the preacher, I recall thinking, "I'd better start ducking in a minute, or I'm going to be clipped around the ear with something".

Waiting in a queue like that, particularly for a first-timer, I have to admit that I did want to believe that there was some divine presence in that building which was in some way going to have a big and lasting effect upon the physical problems of either myself or Auntie, but I think I can conclude that, at least from the emotional aspect, it was a very encouraging and uplifting occasion for us all.

From time to time, the topic of Faith Healing and its mysterious effects has been hotly debated not only within my family, but it has also periodically been analyzed as a topic on television. Personally, I tend to hold the belief that, although I feel it would be very wrong to give sick people false hope of a complete cure, I also think that even if they don't receive healing during this lifetime, certainly from the views expressed by my own family, it is still clear that the positively-charged atmosphere of the meeting served us well in lightening our hearts and drawing us ever nearer to God.

This type of meeting can also be strongly likened to the well-known, Roman Catholic tradition of embarking upon a pilgrimage to Lourdes. I think it is simply a very human desire to go in search of cures for any type of disability or sickness, whether it be with the use of conventional medicines, faith healing, or, of course, it is now becoming more popular to seek a more natural and holistic approach.

Anyway, it was here that we met another very dear friend, who, at the time, turned out to be the pastor of Dudley Pentecostal Church. We were asked to fill out a form, stating our names and addresses and he came forward to introduce himself and to invite us to his church and from the time of our very first attendance, we were greeted with such kindness and abundant friendliness, we all knew, that this was where the Lord had wanted to lead us.

This lively venue then became my family church for many happy years and, for me in particular, all I can say is that the pastor's great ministry and making friends with such a nice family was a true inspiration, - and in only a few short weeks, the pastor could certainly raise a fair share of stifled giggles from me.

Well, soon we had learnt some great choruses, the family seemed to acquire a new-found peace and much of the burden which had existed before simply dispersed, and the pastor was always tremendously supportive and interested in my progress at school.

On the home front, my social life now seemed to be blossoming, but after another Sunday evening service at the Pentecost, all too soon another weekend had passed and once again, it was time to head back to school.

Just like in any school I guess, our lessons and the activities we participated tended to alternate, varying from one term to the next, but staying consistent with other members of the family, there was one subject often pencilled into my weekly schedule, which I really loathed with a blood-curdling and gut-wrenching venom.

I mean, in my opinion, I was a very good kid and surely most of my teachers would have to admit that I would studiously plod on with just about any task I was given, irrespective of the level of difficulty, but I'd love to know exactly what evil deed I was supposed to have committed, serious enough to be timetabled to participate in P.E.?

As far as I was concerned, the only "educational" snippet I ever gleaned from that lesson is that I couldn't "physically" do it, having explored the topic from every conceivable angle. Anyhow, just to stack up some evidence and maybe yield a little more light on just why, at the first sight of our P.E. apparatus, the only thing pole vaulting was the contents of my stomach, let's just raise with you a few of my sorest points.

If I am being lenient, I suppose my efforts in "so-called" basketball weren't too bad. I have used the phrase "so-called" because unlike most of the boys, who boasted far stronger arms than me, I could never join in with the main game as the basket was set far too high up on its wall bracket and neither could I keep up with the rapid pace of the match. Instead though, as usual, Sir came up with the suitable alternative, that perhaps I could practice throwing a football and aim it into the bin, which, in my opinion, was probably the best place for it.

"Come on, Sonya", he urged, "keep your head up and propel the ball forward. That shouldn't be too difficult, even for you. Throw it in the bucket."

After about three or four attempts and completely missing the target each time, I just rolled my eyes, sighed and grumbled, "Oh well, I don't think this is working, is it Sir? and anyway, each time I lift the ball,

I not only can't aim, but I keep scraping my chin on the football and the surface is really rough. I'm just rubbish, Sir."

I was simply being honest, although by now I think I'd figured out that playing sports just wasn't for girls', - and especially not for a girl like me – and as usual, the only goal I had any interest in scoring, was the final one of the day, heading through the doors and on to my awaiting school transport – "YES!"

It wasn't much farther into proceedings that I began to learn my real lesson, and sorely admitting my despondency, soon it wasn't just my eyes that were rolling, - but my whole being had gone into a complete spin.

I'd noticed that for the last ten minutes or so, the class nursery nurse had been helping the P.E. teacher to rearrange some of the gym equipment: they'd set out some wooden benches. There were several beanbags of different colours, which I presumed were probably going to be featured in some sort of relay race and right in the centre there was a red, open-ended, plastic barrel lying on its side. It was plain, omitting to be adorned with any graphic, it came void of a skull and cross bones symbol. It was empty, containing no venomous snakes or spiders, so upon my initial inspection, I thought it looked like any other barrel, - pretty boring and presenting no apparent threat.

"O.K.", the teacher announced from the centre of the hall, "everyone who can, I'd like you to get out of your wheelchairs onto the mats and let's see how you can get on with my assault course."

"Oh no", I thought, "this is gonna be fun."

Anyway, with minimal assistance, one of the first tasks I had to tackle was to try to haul myself along the wooden P.E. bench, gradually slithering from one end to the other, whilst lying on my stomach, as I desperately clung onto its polished surface.

As you can imagine though, this task soon proved a tad too adventurous. I could grapple no longer and just moments later my sticky palms skidded off and I found myself dangling upside down, with my face pushed into the foam mat.

"Good effort", the teacher continued to shout in encouragement, but next...flop, my legs had finally decided to join the rest of my body, as I grazed my left knee, now lying face down, inhaling air into my tired lungs, perspiring like a defeated boxer.

Next, it was over to the tall, wooden gym bars: at least from my viewpoint, this seemed to yield the simplest objective of all, as the only thing which needed to be accomplished was to throw three beanbags through the bars. It didn't matter how high we managed to drive the coloured beanbags into the air, as long as it landed on the other side of the bars, but the higher and more impressive our shots, the greater our final score.

This task seemed relatively simple compared to others: well at least my yellow beanbag had reached its intended landing place and amassing a total score of two out of a possible twelve was quite an achievement for me.

"Alright", my instructor finally announced, "well done, I think you have worked up enough sweat on that now, Sonya, so if you could just finish off by crawling through that red barrel over there, I think we can call it a day and you can get back into your wheelchair."

"Well here goes then", I silently grimaced, "at least it's almost time to go", as I now inwardly, (or so I thought), prepared myself for my final task and soon, on hands and knees, I entered into, what I soon learnt was, "The Barrel of Hell."

I managed to crawl halfway in, but then, without warning, I completely lost my balance, now slamming my full body weight into the side of the open-ended barrel and then I began to roll and scream and bellow... "GET ME OUT, SIR, JUST GET ME OUT...AAARRGH, I'M STUCK... PLEASE STOP ME...HELP".

It's impossible to tell exactly how the ratio of my emotions were apportioned between panic, hysteria, humiliation and fear, but to any

124

astonished witnesses, I must have looked like a 30-stone hamster, wildly revolving inside an unstoppable wheel, rolling on for an eternity, but the whole predicament was all done and dusted in a few short moments, as my teacher simply grabbed me firmly around my ankles and dragged me out. Back in the day though, it was never too difficult to send me into a complete spin.

Anyway, staying with the subject of putting me through my paces, it was just a few months later, that I was invited to participate in my next sporting event.

Of course, much like in any school, it became customary, just before the summer break, for all our families and friends to be invited to cheer us along on Sports Day. This yearly event usually took place in either the hall or the playground, but this year, it was set to be particularly special, as just a few pupils from Victoria had been chosen to attend a day of disabled sports, which had been scheduled to take place at a large sports stadium, in Wolverhampton.

My P.E. teacher said that if I was interested, I would be a suitable candidate to compete in the Power Chair event, which would either be an ordinary race, or a slightly more difficult challenge which was to weave my way in and out of different obstacles in the Wheelchair Slalom. He decided to set up a special trial course in the playground so that any pupils who were interested could practice during the lunch break.

Many disabled schools in the surrounding area were taking part and we were extremely lucky that when the big day arrived, the sun shone beautifully and there wasn't a grey cloud in sight.

My family soon took up a suitable spot in the spectators' gallery and meanwhile, the pupils from the various special schools, were allocated an appropriately coloured team badge and then the young competitors who were to participate in the first running race positioned themselves at the starting line.

At last, the whistle blew and the children were off: my team with only one thing in their sight – to raise that big, silver winners cup as a proud tribute to all the hard work by both teachers and pupils alike at

Victoria School. The cheers from the crowd erupted as the children ran around the circuit and the P.E. teacher stood in the wings fanatically yelling a continual onslaught of both criticism and praise. Other teachers were now gathered at the finish line, busying themselves to pour out much-needed cups of orange squash, for all the winners – because you see, all the competitors were looked upon as winners, as they may not have been the first to cross that Finish line, but just in taking part, they had each accomplished another wonderful achievement.

Next it was my turn, and the moment I had been inwardly dreading all morning was finally here as it was time for me to make a complete idiot of myself again in the Powerchair slalom, and just to make me feel even worse, I hadn't escaped from the badge queue yet, let alone joined my team and all I could hear was my sisters and cousins shrieking with laughter. I was sweating from every orifice even before the horrendously embarrassing episode had started and the only thing I wanted, as usual, was to just go home.

The rules for the slalom were very rigid, as some of the tasks had to be performed whilst driving forwards and other obstacles had to be approached in a backwards direction, so we had an instructor to explain each task as we went along. The spaces in which I had to gingerly manoeuvre were very narrow, only just giving enough room for the standard width of a wheelchair, so I didn't do brilliantly and was later awarded a third place, silver medal, but as usual, the only event I had been eagerly awaiting all day was the home run, in Mom's car – especially if it meant calling into the local chip shop on the way back, because after all that exertion, I was absolutely famished.

Like many things though, looking back on this through the eyes of an adult, I can now see that events like this one have all been enormously beneficial in refining the control of my hands.

I am almost ready to move towards my teenage years now, but I hope that the collection of stories I chose to convey in this chapter have gone a little further in unveiling how the labyrinth of my sometimes perplexing and multi-faceted character has slowly evolved.

I don't think it is ever really possible to fully comprehend, or find the ideal answer as to why illness or hardships befall us, but along the way, we have also had the very great privilege of meeting some really lovely people. Life moved steadily on again and even the two babies had stayed out of peril for the last ten minutes, so maybe my efforts on Sports Day had given them something to think about after all? Well, I could only live in hope, but I dread to ponder just what they are plotting to spring upon me next? Oh no, it seems like they've even acquired baby telepathic skills now because here they come again and I'm about to be whacked around the head by the two stuffed Humpty Dumpty puppets which Nan's just made for them on the sewing machine.

"Naaaaaan, what did you do that for?" I think it seems appropriate to finish my chapter here and in fact, by the look on their faces, I'd better make a run for it.

9

Teen Trends 'N' Cultures

If one day there are any of my school teachers from Victoria sitting curled in a comfy armchair reading this memoir, then you may be thinking one of the things I have heard so many times from my mom. She often says to me, "It's quite amazing how much information you have been able to recall after all these years". Well, maybe it signifies that you must have done something right with me? or perhaps I have just been some kind of living sponge and I am dredging up all this old stuff from the hidden dusty depths of my mind?, or, although it sits a little less comfortably, I suppose the final possibility could be that I am hitting middle age and this is the onset of some sort of crisis that I've heard soft murmurs of? I don't think I'll even go there, to be honest, so I'd better just stop waffling and continue with my story, or I'll be forgetting what I wanted to say next...

Luckily these days my beautiful band of lively nieces and nephews keep me very young at heart, but first let's see what I can recall as we slowly proceed towards my teens while I tried to avoid being sent to the Head for speeding in the corridor.

Predictably, of course, the closing years as a pupil at Victoria bought with them another range of very different and amusing memories, but first "Oh no, pleeeaaassseee, who's grassed me up now?..."

Well, I began to get the distinct impression that one of the nursery nurses was to blame, or maybe the trouble was rising from that private little hideout which was tucked away in between the girls' and boys' toilets where the jolly group of toileting assistants used to gather to boil the kettle and top themselves up with custard creams in readiness for their next chain-pulling session. In fact, it probably was them, because I can actually recall this event with some considerable clarity now and on the day in question the main one who probably stands out as being the most likely culprit, did look a tad more flushed than usual.

Oh yuck and as for the school cleaner, I don't know what's the matter with her today either, as it looks like she's abandoned her mop and bucket right outside the girls' bathroom. Never mind, I expect she will remember where she left it eventually and anyway, today I have far more important matters to deal with as, according to this silly little rumour, apparently it has been alleged that I have been witnessed dawdling in the dinner queue, just so that I could spy on the new, attractive brood of cadets, dressed in their smart tan-coloured uniforms. I mean, can you seriously imagine ME doing that? I was now almost fourteen and all I can recall is waiting to see if there were any seconds to be had of the Chocolate Brick pudding (which, incidentally, was aptly named as such because we practically required a pneumatic road drill to break it). Just how anyone could have mistaken this as anything more sinister, I really can't imagine.

However, by then it would have proved a completely futile mission to try and sidestep these allegations as one of the boys had just taken great delight in informing me that they were even talking about me in the Physiotherapy Department and I knew it must be true because, within the next couple of days, I was urgently beckoned down there as obviously the senior physiotherapist just wanted to inquire exactly what had been happening, so that she could issue a suitable punishment.

"Sonya Hill", she bellowed sternly from the far end of the corridor, "I've got something to ask you."

I rolled my eyes in cynical anticipation. "Oh no, wait for it", I inwardly scoffed, "I'm really in for it now and if by some minuscule chance that my suspicions are wrong, then if they're going to suggest that I participate in yet more strenuous physical exercise then the answer is a firm and categorical "No". I haven't even recovered from the delights of Sports Day yet".

Anyway, when I reached the corridor's end I'm sure the sickly expression on my face must have said it all. The physiotherapist knew she'd got me and so the agony rolled on as she now beckoned me further to enter into her private interior office which was completely closed off from the main treatment room. I didn't know what was coming next, but the one thing I knew for sure was that whatever IT was today, IT was going to be BAD.

The tension in my churning stomach rose and I felt the beads of sweat beginning to surface on my brow, for instinct was telling me that, quite aside from the incident in the dinner hall, she was so disgruntled with my sitting position that she was about to issue me with a straight jacket, right there and then.

Taking into account the things I had achieved in the last few weeks though, I would have thought she had every reason to be pleased with me. "Just what did she expect of me?" I mean, I had already vowed, (albeit foolishly), to brave the toxicity of the swimming pool on the following Monday even though this would probably leave me suffering from borderline hyperthermia and a chronic sore throat.

When you enter into the private domain of a physiotherapist it's a bit like going for an audition to play the part of a real-life episode of Mr Benn. You go in as yourself, wearing your own regular gear, having no need, (in my opinion), to accessorize but then shortly re-emerge with weirdly-shaped pieces of foam protruding from everywhere. I realise now, of course, that she was just trying to help me but when viewed through the eyes of a child who just wanted to feel as normal as possible, I used to think things like, "Oh, for heaven's sake, Miss, I only need a lick of green paint down my back and I would be completely transformed into a Ninja Turtle. What's going on now?"

At long last, however, after emptying her Darth Vader mug of the last few dregs of coffee, which by now had probably gone stone cold, she smiled and reached for the riding hat that had been obscured behind some boxes of different aids at the side of her desk.

She then went on to explain to me that she had located a riding school not too far away and she was in the early stages of compiling a list of pupils who may be interested in participating so she asked, "Would you like to join my horse-riding group? Of course, there won't be a space every week as there are quite a few pupils who have put their names down already, but I think we will be able to fit you in about once every two to three weeks, that is if this idea meets with your approval, Sonya?"

Of course, I was absolutely delighted and my huge, cheesy grin said it all now spreading almost as widely as my best friend's acne and so, from hereon in, I became a regular participant in the riding group.

I could hardly wait to get home that day to tell everyone of my good fortune and I pleaded with Mom that I should have a new riding hat as soon as possible: this being particularly relevant, as we had also been issued with an important newsletter stating that there was a severe infestation of nits sweeping the school, strengthening my line of attack considerably that if Mom hadn't bought me my own headgear by my very first riding lesson, then I was sure to be the next casualty - "Yes!".

She telephoned Nan to tell her of my news and as usual, they put their heads together and by the weekend I had my new riding hat lined with shiny orange satin.

Soon the day to go horse riding had arrived, so I made my way outside where some of the other children had already started to be loaded and clamped into the school ambulance. With everyone finally settled and strapped in securely, our trip began.

I still have a very clear memory that on my first arrival at the riding school, it only seemed to be a small place. As our ambulance passed through the entrance gates, the majority of the interior space was taken up by a muddy, square car park which was flanked on opposing sides by two rows of stables and then, just beyond the car park sat the main riding arena where most of our riding lesson would be taking place.

Apart from a small gap which allowed entrance in and out, the arena was bordered by felled tree trunks and its interior ground was covered in rough compost which looked like a combination of soil and trodden down bits of tree bark.

First of all, we were introduced to the main riding instructor and then I observed that each of the awaiting horses was accompanied by two horsy assistants, all especially dressed for the occasion, sporting the traditional range of cream jodhpurs, quilted body warmers, hairnets and silk headscarves. The sky was blue and the atmosphere was perfect, well, that is, if you don't mind all those rich countryside aromas, but Mom has always been insistent that it is very healthy.

Next, it was time to get into the saddle; this took quite a while, but to make it a little easier to help us onto horseback, there was a high concrete platform the sides of which were graduated to form a ramp. With a wheelchair positioned on its pinnacle, the horses used to be lead up to one side: its simple objective being to raise us to saddle-height, greatly lessening the lifting distance required to mount the horses. Here we were also issued with a special safety belt featuring sturdy leather handles on each side which were firmly held by the riding assistants to aid our stability and balance.

Our riding lesson soon kicked off with a gentle warm-up exercise, usually consisting of two or three steady circuits of the riding arena and after the initial stage of familiarizing ourselves with the horses, we were encouraged to let go of the reins with one hand, so that we could point out various parts of the horse's majestic body and bridle.

I think our riding saddles were pretty standard in design, but I've just remembered that sometimes I used special reins known as ladder reins which were purposely designed for disabled riders with limited hand dexterity. As the name suggests, these reins were constructed exactly like a ladder because, instead of having a single loop of rein to hold, they consisted of several shorter additional pieces of rein which formed a ladder-like structure, simply providing several different points for us to attain a comfortable grasp.

"Now let's see how well you can all control your horses", the instructor said.

I was riding Trigger today and just to add a little more competitive intrigue, we were separated into three teams and our next task was to complete two lengths of the riding arena, carefully steering the horse first one way and then the other, zigzagging through a line of coloured poles which were topped with a small cup. We were in turn required to retrieve one cup each, then cantering back to the start. One point would be deducted from the team's overall score if we should drop the cup to the ground. I managed to finish this time without error, but I was glad when my turn was over, as my right foot had slipped out of the stirrup and I was clinging onto the reins with all the strength I could muster.

My friends and I had soon settled into the lesson, (especially David, who sat two horses in front of me, because he hadn't stopped laughing yet), so the instructor decided we now seemed competent enough to leave the confinements of the riding school, as it was time for a spot of local sightseeing.

As I recall, there were two options available to us here. The instructor was always keen that we should familiarize ourselves with the sensation of riding across a variety of different terrains so sometimes we would make our way in single file, through the large brown gate, going into the adjacent field, or if my friends and I had really given an impressive performance in the first part of our lesson, we would go for a breezy trot along the narrow, country lanes, often searching for fallen conkers or sycamore seeds on our way. We all enjoyed the summer sun, but leaving behind the safe confinements of the riding school, also gave way to the hazards of the traffic and we would often be required to pull our horses towards the roadside hedge, allowing for a car or the farmer's tractor to pass.

I used to love my horse riding days and as we gained in confidence we were given the opportunity to compete against pupils from another school for disabled children in a gymkhana, but if my recollections are correct here, I think the pupils from Victoria School cantered away smugly, being awarded the highest number of rosettes, but our opponents did put on a jolly good show too, (claps and boos all round).

After this, every few weeks it was time to go riding again and just as another small activity, we were given the task of learning the correct terms for the different parts of the horse's anatomy and so, especially when we had another test coming up, I would go down to the physio each dinnertime and study the equine diagram which was displayed just to the right of the nurses' room.

Well, time was moving swiftly on again and I think this brings us roughly up to the beginning of the 1980s and just like every new decade, it saw the rise of its own very distinctive phase in teen culture, symbolized for me by a bold range of new hobbies, music and fashion.

My Bay City Roller cassettes had long since been mangled up and discarded in sheer disgust and the only sounds being filtered through the radio stations which I now considered to be groovy and cool were coming from bands like Adam And The Ants, Spandau Ballet, Blondie and not forgetting, the group which had forever been my favourite of all time, fronted by the incredible musical genius Freddie Mercury, it was, of course, Queen.

I loved the sounds of all these great artists, but for me, I always regarded Queen as being particularly special, as rising to fame in the very early seventies and having consecutive hits in every subsequent decade up until and going into the twenty-first century, I think Queen's fantastic catalogue of timeless hits has seemed to compose a complete musical history of most of my days.

Similarly, around the same time, a new craze arrived on the high street. It became an overnight success and it even held the potential to keep a multi-faceted character like my older cousin from chattering for two whole consecutive minutes, so it was clear I was going to want one, just to analyze and try to replicate its apparent mesmerizing properties. The modern new gadget I am referring to is, of course, the Rubik's Cube and its prototype was invented in 1974, by the Hungarian sculpture and professor of architecture, Ernö Rubik.

It soon became clear that the Rubik's cube held great potential for me. From a very young age, I've always shown great interest in solving puzzles, this probably being another characteristic which came into being through spending so many enjoyable hours in Granddad's great company, but the rugged design of the cube proved fantastic for me to grip and so I found it an excellent device to further extend the abilities in my hands.

The 3x3 cube, however, was merely the beginning as within only a short space of time we saw quite a conundrum of perplexing new twisty brainteasers being advertised both on the television and in the windows of most high street toy shops. I think another of my favourites was the Rubik's Snake puzzle and I remember I would sit for many happy hours in front of the fire trying to manipulate the snake into quite an amusing but greatly varied collection of strange shapes. For the benefit of people who weren't around in those days, or haven't ever seen one, the snake was constructed rather like a chain of Lego bricks which were all linked together and threaded on a very thick and strong length of elastic. These individual bricks could then be rotated, bending the snake this way and that and within only a short space of time, I'd learnt to craft it into the shape of a monkey, a puppy dog, and a snail carrying its spiralled shell, but the task which I found the most challenging of all, and it took me many hours of arduous practice before refining this skill, was to gently manipulate it into a two-coloured sphere.

Creating a ball was an incredibly long-winded and tricky business for me and my concentration would only need to be broken for a fleeting moment by something as simple as if Mom suddenly emerged from the kitchen to inquire if I was ready for a drink, or my dad rushing in from his day's journey in his lorry and my fist would immediately smash right into the heart of my delicately-constructed ball and so the last three quarters of an hour of concentration would prove completely fruitless. After a moment's disappointment, however, which would often be accompanied by Mom coming up to me to inquire if there was anything at all she could do to promptly assist me to rebuild my model to its original state, I would simply giggle and say, "Oh well Mom, I will make this ball again before today is over" and when a newfound determination like mine is firmly clicked into place, there was absolutely no way I was going to mess it up a second time.

Looking back, there were quite a few interesting developments going on in the early eighties, but for me, the most special one of all of them, arrived in mid-April of 1982, when I became an auntie for the first time and my older sister gave birth to my beautiful baby niece.

I have a distinct recollection that in this year we enjoyed a really glorious summer. The weather was sweltering day after day, so my sister would go to great lengths to keep the baby cool and I think she had soon modelled every design of pink, yellow and flowery sunhat in town.

I was almost fifteen by this time and right from the start, I have always loved being an auntie. I think this side of my personality derived from having such a special relationship with my own auntie and holding so many happy childhood memories, of innocent laughter and having so much fun.

As I'm sure everyone knows, when new babies arrive on the scene they snuggle down with their bottle and just as you think they are about to drift off into a nice peaceful two-hour nap, someone coughs or sneezes on the other side of the room, (and in our house, this offending character has nearly always been me), but that is all it takes to spring their little eyelids wide open, their wrinkly hands raise above their heads and they cease drinking, now shooting an initial fretful glance at their mothers' as if to say, "Well I don't know what is going on Mom, but I don't particularly fancy being eaten for dinner yet because I've only just arrived, so PLEASE JUST DO SOMETHING!". Thankfully however the initial awkwardness often disperses within the first few minutes of meeting me and as long as I don't cross their next forbidden boundary of breathing too deeply, let alone committing the unearthly sin of trying to talk to them, their tiny poise then diverts to phase two, which in baby language is probably equivocal to, "Oh well, goodness knows what you're up to Auntie, but I love that shiny power light on your wheelchair and if you don't turn it off in the next three seconds, I'm going to send you crashing right into the T.V. set. Do I make myself clear, Auntie Sonya?" Finally, however, a new tranquility seemed to wash over my niece's lovely face, she closed her eyes and began to giggle and blow her milk bubbles.

Now let's see, what else was going on back then?

Oh yes, time for another day in the classroom and this morning I knew I had nothing pressing to do, so I thought it would be a good chance to work on my current English assignment. We had been given the task of compiling an argumentative piece about how the lifestyles and roles of men and women had changed and evolved during the last century: a pretty simple topic when you weigh up all the pros and cons, because these days women just get all their own way - no argument.

The second lesson pencilled into the day's schedule was maths which never equated to one of my favourite subjects and I'd spotted that the teacher had been angling me a few strange glances all morning, but what the theorems of Pythagoras had got to do with me was really beyond my comprehension.

The cool thing about maths, however, was that at least the teacher had recently shown enough common sense to issue me with a large buttoned calculator, but who cared about stupid equations and theorems, because I'd just figured out that if you turned the calculator round so that the LED display was upside down, you could spell out words: this was even more amusing in the steadfast knowledge that the kid sitting next to me couldn't even work out what my numerical message said.

Upon reflection, I sometimes find it a little surprising that I seemed to have a relatively good understanding of numeracy and when a little later I came to sit my end of school CSE exams, surprisingly, mathematics was the subject in which I attained my best grade.

From a physical point of view, talking in terms of the difficulties I experienced in handwriting, I always found it a struggle to present my arithmetic in a form which could be interpreted by the teachers. Of course in my very early infancy I was totally unable to hold a pencil and so for much of my school life my only option when it came to maths, was to present my work on the typewriter. I did, just about cope with this, although as the years passed, I began to feel that it seemed to be taking me longer to concentrate on lining up my figures than it did to work out my answers. In hindsight, I think that had the technology have been available, this would probably have been a perfect time to introduce me to using a spreadsheet package but I was still a newcomer to the world of computers and so this solution wasn't yet an option. Observing my difficulties, the maths teacher soon suggested that maybe I should attempt to comply with the conventional method and produce my assignments by hand, as over time he assured me that he thought it would gradually become easier, so optimistically he handed me a brand new maths book and I sat there for the next ten minutes deeply inhaling the smell of its glue-like newness and contemplating if I dare scrawl an inscription in the front cover declaring that I loved Adam Ant, or maybe I should make it slightly more subtle and just doodle a swirl of marching ants?... No perhaps not, because it looks as if the class nursery nurse is doing her rounds again and coming to check on my progress, so I'd better at least try to look engaged.

"Oi Miss", a voice rose from the next table, "Tell him, he's flicking the rubber and it's only just missed whacking me in the head". The rest of the class momentarily erupted in riotous giggles so the teacher promptly stepped forward to jot down our next equation on the blackboard in an attempt to quell the brewing squabble.

Today's maths lesson was almost ready to draw to a close when there was a brief tap on the door and another teacher poked his head in, requesting me to go along to his office, as he said he had some new gadget that he thought may interest me.

The Sequal Trust has donated a very nifty piece of kit for us to try out", he told me, "and due to your dexterity problems Sonya, I thought it may be just the thing to help you."

I smiled, as I was fully accustomed to the computer teacher's sense of humour by now and I knew he was deliberately trying to keep the conversation going all the way down the corridor, simply to avoid disclosing what he was actually talking about.

As it happened though, our consultation was to prove to be a very valuable one, for it was now that I was introduced to my next innovative aid: this time in the form of an electric page turner.

This had the general appearance of a regular upright bookstand, but it was additionally fitted with two very thick and strong pieces of elastic which were used to slide inside the cover of a book, securing it firmly in place. With my book positioned, there was also a small remote control which had two large buttons. Sitting on the floor, it seemed to be the easiest for me to operate these switches with my knees and so upon the press of the right button, a small metal stick topped with a wheel was driven across the page which I wanted to turn. Reaching the edge of the book, the continuous rotation of the wheel was precisely what was required to gently flip the next page on top of this revolving mechanism

138

and then all that was needed was to drive the page back in the opposite direction and I was ready to read on.

The idea behind this device was in essence, a very simple one, but my page turner provided a great new way to enjoy my love of literature and all without the need to restore my pages with Sellotape.

Well, that was another awkward glitch which had been superbly solved with the wonderful use of technology. It seems that my journey into the fabulously diverse and amazing world of computers is set to be a very wide-ranging and complex one but, just before we fully launch right into cyberspace, it was also at a similar point in time that I was given the opportunity to try out another very practical little device which, this time, came in the form of a communication aid, known as a Canon Communicator. I found this to be such an enormous help at the time, as particularly now, as I was heading into my adolescence, I remember feeling terribly self-conscious about my continuing speech difficulties as it not only causes great embarrassment on my part when I am unable to make myself understood, but I know it is very frustrating for the people I am struggling to converse with too.

I remember that my new machine used to be either fastened around my knee or the arm of my wheelchair with a Velcro strap, but one of the most valuable lessons which I picked up on at a very young age, is that in my position, you have to adapt things or situations to best suit your needs and so relaying my ridiculous messages on the calculator lost all its appeal as now I had suddenly gained the further advantage of being able to print them out on a very thin reel of ticker-tape.

The continual emergence of new technology was set to make a tremendous impact in what I would go on to achieve in the years to follow, but now, before I had hardly realised it, another action-packed year at Victoria School had sped by. The long summer holiday was in sight and on the last Tuesday of term our families and friends were once again invited to come along to join the fun, this time at our annual summer fete.

My days with my fellow classmates were gradually drawing to a close, but events involving our families were always terrific fun and on this occasion, the assistance of Mom, Nan and my older sister were soon enlisted in serving tea and cakes from the hatch of the school canteen.

A few hours into the proceedings however, I started looking a bit miffed, grumbling that there seemed little point in hanging around the kitchen a moment longer as it was just dead boring. There was nothing for us to do now as we'd eaten all the food we could manage and the only rancid remains didn't even look fit for consumption by the school's pet rabbits.

Of course, Auntie had come along too and she was sitting in the sun just outside the kitchen, quietly surveying and listening to all that was going on.

"Oh, listen to you", she laughed, "you are having a lovely day out, why are you complaining that you're bored, you little monkey?"

However, before our disgruntled lament had time to spiral completely out of control, it was Granddad who once more stepped in and came to our rescue pointing out that we were all becoming a little too boisterous now and he said that he'd just spotted that the headmaster was starting to circulate so, in an attempt to calm things down a little, he inquired, "O.K. then, who fancy's going for a walk around? I think you're getting in the way a bit and anyway we haven't seen what's going on in the other parts of the school yet."

I was mobile in my electric wheelchair, so it was decided to take my auntie for a wander too, as it wasn't much fun for her either, having to just sit in the sun with the heat of large, boiling kettles wafting towards her.

"Why don't we have a go on the tombola stall?" I suggested. My cousin shot me a wary glance as plainly he wasn't too keen on this notion, reasoning that we would probably do much better to go inside and make our way down to the hall as the wheelchair dancing group was scheduled to perform in ten minutes.

Under enormous duress, I was disastrously timetabled to participate in this unspeakable activity for a little while but overall my effort was completely useless and I can only describe myself as having four left wheels. It was enjoyable to be a spectator however and when entertaining at a social occasion, the back of each wheelchair would bear a special velvet tabard creatively stitched with a golden wheel logo. Our wheelchair dancing group went under the name of "Wheels & Co.", so this was also embroidered around the parameter of the design.

I remember that over quite some time the class staged quite an assortment of dance routines and as you may expect the children had soon learnt to perform their very own unique version of The Hokey Cokey. This could be quite an amusing feat at times as one of its objectives was for each dancer to maintain sufficient control of their chair to prevent a major crash of footrests which would then come completely adrift, joining the increasing heap of redundant metal in the centre of the circle.

Another entertaining variation was that some of the dances were presented in the style of Morris dancing and for this the children were kitted out with wrist bands each decorated with silver bells and colourful flowing ribbons.

Our summer fair is another lovely example of one of the school's much-enjoyed family events and it was a great way of boosting funds too, which the children at Victoria never had any problem in exhausting, particularly when it came to consuming bottles of orange squash.

As you can probably see, travelling along life's path with Cerebral Palsy has been quite a varied one and I have certainly participated in a diverse blend of activities. I've shared with you my enormous joy of becoming an auntie, my lovely horse-riding days out in the countryside and I also unveiled my first tentative steps into the wonderful and multi-faceted world of using technology.

Futuristically, this was set to make the biggest impact upon the many interests and skills that I steadily began to develop and upon which I continue to draw on today.

I was developing into quite a charismatic young teenager. The wallpaper in my bedroom was now totally obscured by posters of Adam

And The Ants and John Travolta and I'd now started complaining that I was fed up of crawling around on the floor as my gaudy knee patches looked a right mess, particularly when I was trying to pluck up the courage to casually introduce myself to those cadets but if my best of intentions turned pear-shaped, I could blame my interest onto my best friend because she would never know anyway.

Hitting my teens was once again, set to bring forth another special blend of madness and mayhem although I think I've done enough work for one term. Soon, however, it was time for the six-week summer holiday, and this year was going to be particularly exciting as Nan had promised to take me to visit her sister in Brixham, Devon.

Brixham is a very pretty fishing village and one of its main features, which I loved to visit was its busy harbour, with its wide variety of fishing boats gliding in and out to sea. In 1851 Brixham had one of the largest fishing fleets in the United Kingdom but this has now dwindled and although it is still in existence, it now operates on a far smaller scale.

It was great fun to see my distant cousins again: there were so many lovely things to do and places to visit, but I always remember that one particularly memorable trip we did was the day my great auntie suggested we pay a visit to Buckfast Abbey.

The abbey consists of several buildings which, when they are looked upon collectively, have been arranged in the formation of a cross, with its church at the core. This spot is where its monks gather to share a time of prayer and is thought to be a sacred location, where God dwells.

Like most places which disabled people tend to come across from time to time, certain areas could only be reached by going down a steep flight of steps so as my great auntie had visited many times before, she offered to take me for a walk around on the ground level, freeing Mom to explore the basement.

What neither Mom nor I realised though, was that my great auntie had a secret, ulterior motive in mind in sending Mom away, as in her absence Auntie stealthily proceeded to soak me in Holy Water, in the hopes that its healing properties would in some way have a beneficial effect on me.

Well it was a lovely thought, and I'm sure it did me no harm but just then Mom returned a little earlier than expected only to find Auntie mopping up the remaining evidence with her hanky.

Baby me

Early Years

Loving my garden ...

Will my sister play?

Meet My Family...

My lovely Mom – My best friend EVER!

Dad & Auntie – Laughing at me as usual

My niece – Living it up at my 50th birthday party

My Saturday tea with Nan, Mom & Granddad

Life Goes On...

Two photos sporting those silly hats...

And *still* I SMILE

Enjoying the sun at Brean with Grandad

Looking out to sea again with Nan

My last trip to Dudley Zoo – Taken within the ruins of Dudley Castle

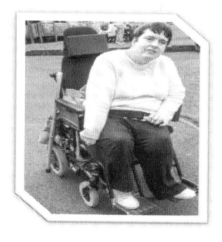

Just starting out on the BBC Micro.

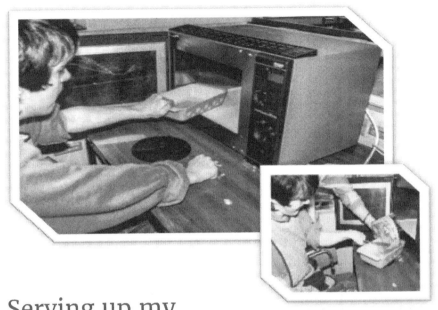

Serving up my
dish of the day at Dudley College

Me & Mom –
Enjoying life
in Scotland
at our
local bistro

Me, Mom and my nephew celebrating my 50th birthday party kindly hosted by our parish church

Here is my lovely birthday cake – one of the many gifts from friends at church

Tobias, deriving from the Greek version of the old Hebrew name, Toviyah, meaning *"God is good"*. *What a beautiful boy!*

10

It Ain't What I Do
It's The Way That I Do It

Have you ever glanced back to your teenage years and thought, "You know what...it was all a bit like a weird, emotional jumble sale", as back in the day, I couldn't really foresee into my future at all, but peering through the eyes of a high-spirited young girl this was the only clear picture I thought I could see.

Well, I don't know whether most people go through a similar phase, but during my adolescence some of my ideas regarding what I was going to do for the rest of my life seemed to me like a foregone conclusion. I think the kind of thing I am talking about can probably be best described as that young, excited uncertainty which is commonly defined these days as the wannabe age and as is reflected by most weekend prime time television it seems that a huge proportion of today's young people dream of or wannabe a member of the next boy or girl pop band. I always knew that this wasn't to be my destiny, of course, I can't even stand to listen to myself warbling in the shower, but at this age I decided I was either going to carry out typing duties for Dad, being paid by a bottomless supply of ice-cream and sweets or become an author of some kind. I think I'd realised that I was probably going to change a little in facial features, but for me, the mere concept of finally shaking myself free from the shackles of lessons and never having to sit through yet another dreary, afternoon assembly just seemed to leave every pore of my being oozing with a glorious sense of total, unadulterated paradise.

One clear message which I seemed to be getting from everyone around me, however, was that if I wished to achieve anything at all constructive in the future, then I was going to have to put in even more time and effort, pushing my physical boundaries to their absolute limit.

The school physiotherapist advised us that the next few years would be quite a mystery tour for everyone and that physically my teenage days could potentially bring with it a considerable improvement in my abilities as I was now entering a key stage in my development. Indeed, I remember that around this time a small number of other children did start to walk independently for the very first time.

Setting myself goals, having positive amounts of both self-motivation and encouragement from others has been rewarded with the steady growth of new skills, all of which is important of course but I'm starting to speculate on whether the long road to recovery from a severe brain injury requires something more than that but, before I try to respond to this question in too much depth, at Victoria School there seemed to be no peace for the wicked. My physiotherapist decided that I'd done enough horsing around for one week and before I could set my sights on that forthcoming disco, the only thing I was going to "get down to" was some serious exercise.

It was Monday morning again. The driver of my school transport had just unloaded me from the yellow, tail-lift vehicle and I was just about to make the usual long trail through the school to arrive at my classroom in Upper School when I was stopped in my tracks by the head swimming pool attendant.

"Stay right where you are Sonya", she called, "you are down for another swimming lesson today and I know you've been saying that you've had a sore throat for the last three weeks but surely you feel better by now? So how about it, are you ready to brave the water?"

I peered hesitantly through the steamy, wired mesh of the pool windows, listening to the muffled instructions as the pool attendants assisted one child after another in and out of the dazzling water.

"O.K. then Miss, I suppose I'll go in, just for you", I teased, even though inwardly the notion of sliding into that pool and glugging down three-quarters of its disinfected contents filled me with an indescribable mix of nausea, dread and horror, "but I'll have to go and take my stuff to class first", I added.

Anyway, it didn't take too long just to make sure my daily attendance had been recorded on the class register and to take my duffel coat to the cloakroom, so then I retraced my journey and headed down to Lower School's indoor swimming pool.

I suppose, at least upon my first glance, the water did look quite inviting, but as I was soon to discover that was only because I hadn't yet got into it. I loitered around for a few more moments, listening to the strange, distorted echoes and watching the children floating out of the plastic chair on wheels, their shimmering bodies becoming weightless.

"That looks easy enough", I thought and so I continued around the next corner in search of the girls' changing room.

"How did I get myself into this one?" I mused, now hurrying to find a convenient empty square of space.

Well, I couldn't have sidestepped it for much longer or I would really have got it in the neck I suppose and even Mom had packed my swimming gear this morning. It was fastened to the back of my wheelchair in my waterproof barrel bag, so I might as well just get on with it. My heart sank though merely at the thought of being engulfed into those evil, echoing ripples of the pool and this was all it took to put a dampener on what could otherwise have turned out to be a potentially decent day.

I slid out of my wheelchair onto my knees and proceeded to undo my swimming bag to see what weird-looking gear Mom had blessed me with today.

My swimming costume was nothing out of the ordinary. It was just two different tones of blue and, upon closer scrutiny, I saw that Mom had remembered to stitch on my ten metres badge which had been proudly awarded to me during a morning assembly about three weeks ago. "Oh, what...?" I said aloud, in sheer disbelief. My friend, who was sitting on a wooden bench looked up to see what all the commotion was about and I now retrieved from my bag, the most hideous monstrosity I'd ever seen. Crumpled beneath a thick, pink bath sheet, I slowly unfolded a terribly attractive, blue swimming cap but worst of all was that it was neatly crowned with a big floppy rubber daisy.

This was just way beyond my greatest nightmares. I then thought that Mom must have intended this as a gift to my little sister and, perhaps she'd inadvertently put it in with my stuff in error. Surely she didn't really expect me to emerge from the changing room wearing this thing?

Ready for my swim, I then poked my head, complete with rubber daisy, around the curtain in the hopes that one of the swimming teachers would be in a generous humour today and bring me a chair instead of making me crawl to the edge of the pool. Inevitably, of course, the lack of a vacant wheelchair would only result in me feeling completely shattered and was it necessary to put me through all that hassle, even before I got my big toe wet?

Anyway, soon I reached the water's edge where, stabilizing myself by gripping onto the teacher's shoulders, I plunged straight in.

We would often get the lesson underway with what for me was the relatively easy task of pulling myself around the pool's parameter, kicking my spindly legs and gripping onto the metal rail for balance. The handrail only extended along three sides of the swimming pool, the fourth being occupied by the slippery ramp, where other pupils were constantly being assisted in and out and so when I came to the end, I would then be asked to repeat the exercise, this time retracing my route.

"Yet another completely wasted journey", I whispered to the girl bobbing up and down next to me, who was pitifully expected to carry out the same tiresome drill.

Of course, in a special school like Victoria, being in the pool presented another ideal opportunity to concentrate further on our exercise regime and to practice some more physiotherapy, or was it just another excuse for those treacherous physiotherapists to torture me? I have never quite been sure.

Next, I would have to wade through the water going from one side of the pool to the other, gripping onto one of the swimming attendants for added stability. Sometimes this exercise would also be accompanied by having to blow a small plastic float across the surface of the pool. I remember that the floats were yellow on one side and white on the other, so the teachers imaginatively used to refer to them as fried eggs.

They did, of course, attempt to teach me to swim but, for me, my most striking achievement was when I managed to float on my back without sinking. This attained me my first and only swimming badge, as I kept my composure long enough to complete two lengths which, in our small pool, equated to a distance of ten metres.

After my swimming lesson, I was always pretty tired from all that physical exertion, so I slowly made my way back to class.

I chose to take the slightly quicker way today, hurrying past the small kitchenette in Planned Dependence, crashing head-on into the two sets of double doors as they had all slammed shut when I was abruptly intercepted by one of my best friends. She just seemed to appear, now charging towards me, bearing a huge grin.

"Guess what?" she said, "Sir has been doing the rounds and he says he's putting a computer class together. It's going to be held in a little room in Lower School, you know the one just past the hall, but there's only room for him to take three of us at a time and I thought you could ask to be in my group? What do you say?"

"Yes, that sounds cool to me", I agreed, "so let's go and find him quickly before all the places are taken."

We hadn't gone too far when we met, what looked from a distance like a huge cardboard box which had miraculously sprouted human arms and legs and from the blue multi-lingual text and graphic which was displayed on its side, I could see that it contained a new computer monitor. It then became clear, of course, that we'd found exactly who we were seeking.

"Sir, sir", I called, "I just want to ask...er...I've heard that you are going to start a computer class and I wondered if there was any chance that you could fit me in at all?"

"And me, sir", my friend chipped in from behind in her chirpy Irish tone, "perhaps we could both do the lesson together?"

"O.K. then", he nodded, flicking through a tattered diary retrieved from his inside jacket pocket. "You'll have to check that it fits in with your timetable but I can take you on Friday afternoon if that suits?"

"What do we have on Friday?" I asked my friend, but before she had a chance to offer a reply, I said, "Oh, half of that time should overlap with assembly anyway, so that's ok. Please, can we start this week Sir?" I enquired.

The teacher smiled at our eagerness. "I'll see you at one thirty", he nodded, "no later."

Pleased with the deal, I saw that the time was ticking along fast and I would have to hurry now or I would be late for my next lesson, which was textiles, this being held in The Resources Centre, just through the door from the cookery department.

Spanning over a few years, I enjoyed participating in a very broad range of creative projects in this lesson and from a physical point of view, I think many of these activities were particularly useful to further promote my fine finger movements.

One particularly enjoyable activity which I recall is that it was during this lesson in which I first practiced the art of cross-stitch.

After rummaging in the back of the storage cupboard, the teacher made her way around to where I sat at the table and she said, "I know you won't be able to manage an ordinary needle Sonya, but I thought you could have a try with this one. What do you think?"

This was one of those rare occasions when for a few moments words simply failed me and even the class's biggest chatterbox could only issue three responses – to sit, stare and gulp.

The long, pointed implement she held before me looked more like the sharp end of a medieval dagger than an embroidery needle but, on second thoughts, at Victoria, it had probably been purchased by the nurse to administer her lethal brew which she had lovingly concocted for wannabe malingerers – as let's face it, anything could arise from those dark catacombs of the nurses' station.

"I'd better watch my jugular here", I thought, "or is that what this spike is really intended for?"

Putting my initial qualms aside, however, it took me a little while to best refine a method of manipulating a sewing needle. At first, I think my biggest dilemma was actually how I was going to push the needle through one side of my embroidery to the other, as I still only had the use of one hand.

In the end, though, I realised that the perfect solution was sitting on the desk right in front of me, in the shape of a Dycem Non-Slip Mat, which is a great use for people like me, who have problems manipulating objects with their hands, as it is designed to prevent things from sliding on a tabletop.

The simple idea of the mat complimented the intricacies of embroidery with ease, as when I had pushed the needle through the cross-stitch mesh, my crafty tip was to completely sink the needle into the mat's rubber surface, as this not only served as an ideal safety precaution but gently pulling on my design, it also proved to be the perfect method of achieving a stitch.

After just a few weeks of practise, I was able to create two or three different styles of stitching, so I decided to pursue this activity as a new hobby and although it took me a very long time, I remember designing a picture of a Grenadier Guard adorned in his traditional red uniform and Busby and I also based another cross-stitch project upon my scenic memories of a large fishing boat moored at Brixham harbour.

My love of embroidery was probably further fuelled by spending many pleasurable hours at my nan's side, watching her as she repaired and designed new outfits at the sewing machine.

For many years she had worked in a small factory earning a living as a seamstress, but previous to this, during WWII, she had even helped to make aircraft, but I suppose most ladies had to offer whatever skills they had in those days.

Nan's creative stitching had also come to the fore in 1977, when the whole country had regally united, hosting many street parties and social gatherings in its patriotic efforts to celebrate the Queen's Silver Jubilee.

I don't know where she came by them now, but on her travels, probably whilst during a trip to one of the local markets, Nan located a stall which sold large sheets of plastic; it stocked a wide selection of hues and so in her usual friendly tone, Nan inquired, "Could I have six sheets of this plastic please? I'll take the red, white and blue, that's two of each, I think that should be just about right", she continued, as she rummaged in her purse, slowly gathering the correct change.

This then gave way to another very enjoyable Saturday afternoon for me, as after everyone had chipped in cutting out the triangular plastic buntings, Nan positioned my wheelchair next to her sewing machine delegating me the special task of handing her the coloured buntings as she alternately stitched them along a large span of fabric tape.

The buntings looked great nailed across our roofs: I think most of the neighbours simply displayed Union Jacks in their windows but, as ever, Nan's effort outshone them all.

Anyway, back to school and my form teacher suggested that perhaps it would be a good idea to finish off the comprehension exercise which I'd been given on Tuesday, so I went over to retrieve it from my small drawer where I kept my books. Personally, I felt that this was quite a neat idea as, despite its tedium, at least its completion would lighten my impending homework load.

With my head in the clouds, most likely lost in another daydream about the leg shape of the cadet I now seriously fancied, I was suddenly shaken back to the trials of reality: my cardboard folder containing my

English assignments had split down one side as I tried to lift it out of the drawer and if I wasn't really careful then the whole lot was heading for the floor and I don't think the nursery nurse would have been too thrilled at the prospect of having to re-order all these papers. She hadn't recuperated from the last fiasco yet, as only about a quarter of an hour earlier, one of the boys had neatly smashed a whole bottle of milk, its jagged shards of glass spreading as far as the door.

"Everyone move back", she had screamed, "or one of you lot are going to puncture your wheelchair tyres next."

The class fell silent, that is, all except for a small pocket of stifled sniggers which rose from the table by the window, but the nursery nurse was still busy squeezing out her mop and, even if she had heard them, I suspect she was just too weary to offer a reply.

Just as the pandemonium had died down, however, there was a light tap on the classroom door: it was the senior physiotherapist and she requested for me to join her.

Chatting to me as we made our way through the winding labyrinth of corridors, she explained that she was launching a new type of exercise class, which was specifically aimed at pupils who suffered from Cerebral Palsy and she felt that it may be of great benefit to me.

Of course, a healthy measure of exercise always plays an integral role in the development of any child, but for someone with Cerebral Palsy, there were just a few more essential ingredients which still needed to be explored. The new exercise programme was known by the term "Peto", so-called after the Hungarian founder of Conductive Education, Professor Andras Peto.

I did a little research of my own on the subject of Peto and the first fact my Internet search engine uncovered, which I thought a little ironic from my point of view, is that Andras Peto, died in 1967, this being the year of my birth and then I further noted that the first Peto Institute was built in Budapest in 1984, which likewise correlates with my final year at Victoria School. I simply found it quite interesting that both years seem to mark these significant points in my life.

To many people, my description of our daily Peto sessions will probably just sound like any other exercise routine but as it was specifically designed for the treatment of patients who have suffered brain damage, its real concept is a little more complex.

Peto is a strict form of physiotherapy which employs a balanced combination of both relaxation and exercise.

Each Peto session usually ran for around half an hour a day, being squeezed into our routine just before the lunchtime bell and one of its most significant aspects was the use of specially designed wooden tables and chairs that didn't just serve as furniture, but they were also employed as multi-purpose pieces of exercise equipment.

Their design, in my opinion, was extremely intelligently thought out. The tables were low with thick-set legs, but the most important feature was that instead of consisting of a solid tabletop, they were comprised of evenly spaced wooden plinths, ideal for the children to obtain a firm grip with one hand giving the freedom to perform a desired task with the other. It is quite amazing how beneficial it seems to be to stabilise a redundant hand as, strange as it may seem, this does appear to increase the dexterity in the hand which is being used.

The Peto chairs were also fabricated on a similar theme, basically consisting of a low stool, with the addition of chair backs which were constructed like the rungs of a small ladder, providing a useful aid in standing and kneeling exercises.

As well as moving our arms and legs and having the benefit from the physiotherapy point of view, I think another important aspect here, particularly for people who have suffered a brain injury, is to take a little time to focus upon the action you are intending to take, even before you do it. To a degree, I suppose people could say that everyone has to do this, simply to ensure that you perform a task correctly, but for able-bodied people the dexterity which is required is automatically pre-empted by the brilliant subconscious abilities of the brain so, in addition to trying to increase the physical strength in our muscles, Peto was very much focused upon concentration and relaxation.

Another helpful tip which seems to be broadly employed by most people with Cerebral Palsy, is that rather than trying to carry out a big task which may prove problematic, it is often easier to break things down into several smaller steps, always keeping one important objective in sight – to succeed.

Anyway, in the Peto class, it wasn't long before we all knew the daily drill off by heart, so if you think that you have had a hard time probably having attended an ordinary school and being made to chant your times tables until you've got a chronic case of laryngitis, then, believe me, that is precisely nothing compared with having to fulfil the bizarre poetic requirements of a Peto instructor.

One of the skills the leading physiotherapist said we had to accomplish was to correct our disgustingly poor deportment, which in layperson's terms, simply means to sit up straight, and so as an attempt to address this matter we would take up our positions around the Peto table and clutching onto one of the plinths together we said the following bizarre little rhyme:- (and whoever was responsible for thinking this one up, I think they must truly have lost the plot.)   In unison, trying desperately to avoid making direct eye contact with the child sitting opposite me, so that I could at least, attempt to keep a suitably convincing straight face, the daily drill began, not forgetting, of course, to simultaneously execute the all-important actions:-

"I am sitting on my stool,
My head is in the middle,
My arms are straight,
My back is straight,
My bottom is back,
My feet are flat,
Arrr. Mmm."

This is only a short, simple rhyme, but even the ordering of each line illustrated the important principle that to achieve what was considered to be an ideal sitting position, it was necessary to realign all the different parts of the body, from our heads right down to our feet. The last line was simply another speech therapy exercise, as these are particularly important sounds to accomplish when trying to form spoken words.

By implementing these simple rules, we were taught to attempt to minimize the unwanted effects of spastic, involuntary movements and perform our everyday tasks with far greater precision and accuracy.

The effort the children made, with their heads held high and smiles on their little faces, clearly illustrated that although many of them endured even greater mobility and coordination problems than I did, their great senses of humour shone through as always and I remember that many of my friends would often give a cheeky headshake in disapproval, trying to cajole each other into having to repeat their work all over again as their performance was simply useless.

My recollections of Peto are now complete and although we have looked in some detail at the clear physiotherapy benefits, I thought it would also be good to bring to mind the important role that simple exercise and relaxation techniques have to play in the treatment of people with Cerebral Palsy, also being of benefit to people with a whole range of other disabilities too. The exercise element is of great use to strengthen weak muscles while the addition of employing steady breathing techniques and other forms of relaxation, especially when whispering a joke in the ear of a friend sitting next to you, can all be wonderfully instrumental in relieving muscle tension and stress, which in turn goes a long way in minimizing the frustrating and sometimes painful effects of spasticity.

The meticulous physiotherapy programme shaped in the late sixties by Professor Peto gives another excellent example of how important the role of a special school is in providing the best treatment for disabled children.

Just as one brief and final point, however, it seems to be believed by most disability professionals that it is during these early years of development when Cerebral Palsy patients are most likely to show increases in physical ability levels. However, I think I can conclude from my own experience, that it is important to understand that the human brain is the most complex and extraordinary organ in our bodies and although it seems extremely unlikely that people can ever make a full recovery from this type of injury, I firmly believe the combination of muscle relaxation and the repetitive physical patterning which is taught in the Peto programme or, perhaps a session of hydrotherapy, has been proven to be of tremendous benefit for people of all ages.

Well soon it was time to make my long journey home again and today I wasn't sorry to hear that last bell as I felt really tired after all that exertion. The afternoon sun was so hot and all I wanted to do was to get back, find out what was on offer for tea and to relax in front of the T.V.

"Let's see", I pondered quietly, "I wonder what's on tonight? Oh yes, I remember now, it's Happy Days. I'll have to hurry up and make sure Mom turns the right side on as soon as I get home because if my little sister starts watching the cartoons again, that will be the end of that idea".

I had almost reached the school entrance when my best friend gave me a brisk prod in my left shoulder, keenly urging me to look in the opposite direction.

"Oh for heaven sake", I grumbled, "don't you ever think about anything else?", now realizing that she was just drawing my attention to the fact that three of the new cadets were just making their way down the corridor.

"On second thoughts", I secretly thought to myself, "The one at the back isn't too bad; I wonder what his name is?"

My friend, at this point, was doubled in two, almost rolling out of her wheelchair in mirth.

"Be quiet you idiot", I grimaced, "or you're gonna make us both look completely stupid, you've just got to act natural. Do you think you can manage that, if only for two minutes in a row?"

I shook my head in weary dismay.

I could be a little reticent as a young girl and I would often try to conceal my true feelings as a means of compensating for the shrill giggles and over-excitability of the others. This dude, however smitten, was determined to play it cool, - well at least for now and I continued through the front entrance and onto my awaiting bus.

Anyway, soon another week was drawing to its close and I'd been looking forward to Friday afternoon for the last few days as not only did it mark the end of another busy week but I was also booked in to try my hand for the very first time at using a computer.

In those days, still being at the onset of the 1980s, we started to see the steady emergence of a few different brands of early computer and if my memory is serving me correctly here, I think the school purchased an early Apple machine, but in the opening few minutes of the lesson, I settled myself in front of the **BBC B Microcomputer** and switched on the monitor. A white cursor blinked at me as if inviting me to input my first command and although I didn't realise it at the time, that old **BBC** machine was about to take me through a mysterious virtual doorway which would lead me to an all-new and captivating way of life.

Up until now, I had always produced my written work on a typewriter, so I was thinking, "This thing had better be pretty durable, because if anyone's gonna wreck it, then I know it's going to be me" and as usual, just as I had expected, within the first thirty seconds, I had perilously hit the Escape key and the screen had changed from blue to black, now displaying some weird kind of text that I couldn't even read.

The teacher just chuckled and upon the brisk tap of just one key, he instantly restored the **VDU** to its original state. "Trust you", he sighed comically, "you've got all those keys on the keyboard which accidentally hitting them would have taken no effect whatsoever, but you just had to find the Escape button. We're sure going to have some fun teaching **YOU**."

My first task, of course, just like anyone else who is just starting out in the field of computing, was to familiarize myself with all the different pieces of hardware. We were given a few introductory sheets to read through together with some very simple exercises.

However, still being accustomed to using an electric typewriter and only having the capacity to type in a very particular fashion just with the use of my left thumb, it only took a few short moments to realise that I'd now hit upon the first problem.

"I'm never gonna be able to master this Sir", I groaned, "the keyboard is too flat, so there's nothing for me to rest my fingers on and my hand is just flying everywhere like the sails on a windmill. I think I'll just go home, as this simply isn't working".

The teacher nodded thoughtfully, heading for the small, adjoining storeroom and so, during his absence, I decided to have another go with the mouse and try to activate the icon which led to the word processor.

In those days, as I'm sure lots of people out there will recall, we had to get to grips with a real gem of an application called, "Wordwise". In my opinion, its very name was probably a subtle clue to the fact that if you possessed a shred of "wisdom" at all, (which, alas, I didn't), then you would have steered clear of this program. Just why I had to be clever and activate that silly little icon I will never know, but that was all it took and upon his return, my teacher exclaimed, "Oh that's good Sonya, I see you've found the word processor. Maybe I will start you off with that next week. What do you think?"...

"However, first", he continued, "let's try this" and as I watched he proceeded to fix a long, white box to the keyboard, securing it just above the top row of keys with a few large blobs of Blu Tack.

The general idea of the box did seem to work and so the final solution we tested, was to employ the aid of a keyguard.

Nevertheless, just like anything to do with me, as expected, the final piece of the puzzle can never slot into place without a final amusing twist. The keyguard was expected to give the perfect solution except that when tested, the circumference of the holes through which to access the keys was too small to accommodate my thumb and consequently I kept getting it stuck. In fact, at one stage, I gingerly escaped becoming the school's first left thumb amputee, but that's rather a sore point now.

My first I.T. lesson had turned out to be a lengthy but thought-provoking process and by the end of the lesson, it seemed that at last, we had arrived at the perfect solution.

Simply by chance, we found that the Perspex top of the keyguard was completely detachable and could be lifted off, leaving behind a wooden, open-topped box which contained the computer keyboard. Just like the cardboard box which we had tried earlier, the simple aid of the box, minus the inserted keyguard, was the perfect light support needed to propel me into the wonderful world of technology.

"Oh look", I sniggered to my friend sitting next to me, "after all that bother it looks like Sir has had enough for one week. I think he's gone back to his office to have a cigarette. Anyway, did you do that exercise we were supposed to do?"

"No mate", she replied, "you must be joking. I typed the first paragraph and then the word processor froze up and all I could get to work then was a game called Bomber but I don't know how I am supposed to land this aeroplane".

"Oh yeah", I jibed, "I bet you REALLY tried. Well, I've worked hard this afternoon, even if YOU haven't. C'mon, let's just go home"...

For me, along with the many special friends with whom I was privileged enough to share my time at Victoria School, our goals in life have been greatly shaped by our individual physical challenges which for some unknown reason, life has dealt us.

Our school timetable had to be adjusted and carefully fine-tuned every step of the way not only to meet our enormously mixed educational abilities but to enhance our many independence variants too.

Just a few weeks in, after the early dilemma of how I was going to operate the computer, my abilities in this field were going from strength to strength. I was composing letters to friends on the word processor, I had taught myself to draw and soon I began to lose interest in simply playing the games and I began to buy books to teach me how they were written in Basic, the programming language of the **BBC Micro**.

A vibrant, new era had just burst open before me and although I hadn't fully comprehended it yet, that first computer had just totally transformed what I did and the way that I would do it - forever.

11

<u>Back To The Jungle</u>

Another new term began, marking the close of the long summer in which we'd enjoyed six weeks of glorious almost unbroken sunshine and I returned to school, ready to begin another new term.

I felt very grown-up today as I'd just been informed by the Deputy Headmaster that I'd been selected to advance into the top class which, when Lower School was built, had moved its location into the room originally assigned to the old physio department. According to its name, it was now home to Victoria's lively 16-19 group but, as for me, this was just another rule to which I seemed to be a rare but distinguished exception as I was actually in there from the age of fourteen to seventeen.

It was a large L-shaped classroom and at least when I was a pupil, it seemed to be arranged into three separate areas. The first square area which you came to, as soon as you entered the classroom door, was where I would spend a large proportion of each day being exclusively used to store our various adapted typewriters. I had hardly found my feet in the top class, having just sorted out the best place to stash my belongings, when one of the nursery nurses informed me that this area was known as The Geriatric Suite, of which I was now Assistant Manager and she boldly fastened a sign denoting the fact right above my typewriter. Two other very good friends of mine also shared this space, so they too were granted signs declaring them "The Manager" and "Vice Chairman" of Geriatrics, so it was clear from the start that my final years at school were set to be teeming with fun and good humour.

Passing through the central archway which led out of Geriatrics and into the main classroom was where most of the day's lessons took place. This archway had little significance other than being a distinct structural feature of the room or at least, that is, until the month of December when, with Christmas fast approaching, the nursery nurses took enormous delight in hanging a large sprig of mistletoe from the centre cheekily declaring that it was now a new class rule that whoever passed under the mistletoe would have to be kissed.

Well, as you can probably imagine, my classmates and I then went to enormous lengths to avoid being caught under what we now aptly named, "The Great Arch Of Doom" and in sheer desperation, some of my friends even tried to bash the festive clump to the floor by waving their crutches above their heads but to no avail, of course, as for most of them it was just a smidgen too high. The only other possible options we were then left with were to either dodge to one side, not actually passing directly under it, or just simply to try to avoid using this area altogether, at least until the staff were busily brewing their next cup of tea. The class kettle and teabags were always kept in the last section of the room furnished as the multi-purpose kitchen and sitting area, so it didn't take long to work out that when our nursery nurses were engaged at that end of the class, we were safe.

I'll tell you more about our Christmas festivities in a little while, but first, let's get back to lessons.

Contrary to most other classes, the majority of which were staffed by just a singular teacher and its accompanying nursery nurse, Top Class was inhabited over time by quite a repertoire of different people, but the most astonishing fact in this respect was that when our mathematics and P.E. tutor decided to give up his post, his job vacancy was soon refilled by a new guy of exactly the same name.

Life in residence in Victoria's 16-19 group could certainly never be described as being uneventful and the remainder of my schooldays were spent with another fantastic and very memorable bunch of youngsters, many of whom I still regard as some of the best of my school friends. Those young guys were certainly full of life and despite being located in a relatively quiet part of the school, only sharing our corridor with the room used for woodwork and metalwork, the three years I spent in Top Class were never dull.

"What's going on now?" one of the nursery nurses shouted. "Put that snooker cue down before one of you gets clunked on the head".

During break-times the snooker table became one of our most popular distractions, particularly amongst the lads and to make the game a little more disability-friendly, the school invested in a set of adapted, lightweight snooker cues, which, to facilitate ease of use, each featured a small plastic crescent on its tip, innovatively designed to fit lightly around the cue ball, giving the option of one-handed gameplay.

On the whole though, I don't think taking part in sporting activities was ever one of my strongest points and when one of my P.E. teachers suggested that maybe I would prefer to amuse myself by playing some computer games, rather than participating in the hockey match, then I think that says it all.

It was during my final years at school, however, that I soon embarked upon another great interest and on Monday afternoons the teachers excused me for a spell from the tedium of classwork and I went to help all those lovely little occupants of Victoria's nursery department, which sat next door to Upper School's library.

Just like Planned Dependence, the nursery always boasted a smashing atmosphere and only after a few short weeks, the children grew accustomed to my visits and on arrival I had to wait at the door to be let in, while the staff inside joined forces in moving a giggling throng of toddlers back towards the large toy mound, enabling my safe entry.

By this time, the school had started to take children in as early as two years of age, so some of them were little more than babies.

My role in the nursery didn't amount to much really. I simply spent most of my time circulating, chatting to the children and trying to assist them in whatever activities they wished to do. Watching their young play was always a great joy and it seemed that the children were just as fascinated by my presence as I was with them, as each week I was always kindly welcomed by a sea of cheeky smiles. For me, I think the experience bought back memories of my early years, reaffirming that their joining Victoria School would continue to assure them of the best possible treatment and encouragement suited to their individual needs, granting them all the potential to achieve great things.

Their physical difficulties aside, however, I don't understand why disabled children are much different to any other kids They just have slightly more complex needs but they are all incredibly mischievous and simply adorable.

When the weather was warm and sunny it was always great fun to join them in their outdoor games. This took place in the nursery's small playground, offering the standard range of swings, a slide, some little cars and bicycles, but as you can imagine, many of them preferred to go for the messier option of playing with the sand and water.

Of course, it was very necessary both on a daily basis and also when there was a school event taking place in the hall, for the nursery assistants to be able to quickly and safely transport the little ones from one end of the school to the other and there were never enough pairs of hands to push all those little wheelchairs and buggies. Soon, however, Victoria's staff came up with just the thing, which proved simply perfect to solve another little glitch.

It was now that the school invested in a large wooden cart featuring low benching around its interior, which was ideal to seat the nursery children, being of particular advantage to those with none or only limited walking ability, providing an excellent means of transportation around the school.

Each week I continued to help in the nursery until my schooldays ended. So in my latter years, this is certainly reminiscent of my most enjoyable times.

Anyway, I will have to hurry back to class again now because, as long as there is nothing more pressing about to be slotted into my agenda, (referring in particular, to all those frequent ominous visits from The

Physio Department), I decided that the last hour before home time would be a perfect opportunity for a little more exam revision.

There seemed to be so much information to get into my head and, even worse, I only had a few short months now in which to do it. I was also filled with growing concern that the examining boards would not agree to grant me suitable time concessions and I would never produce enough work to attain acceptable grades.

The preliminary plan was soon in place in readiness for the following spring so at least, for now, all I had to do was to work my way through my never-ceasing mound of dreary homework.

My time in Top Class wasn't all about hard work however as there were always plenty of fun activities going on too and it was during my closing few years as a pupil, that Victoria School devised what became another of its very grand and colourful traditions.

In any school the build-up to the festive period often brings with it exciting preparations towards some sort of nativity play. I think everyone goes through this don't they?, although I don't actually remember acting out a specific part in the Christmas story. I think it was enough for me just trying to stop my carol sheet from falling on the floor. Most of the time, I think I must have been a lone stargazer or something, making sure that the three wise men took the correct dusty path which lead the way to Bethlehem.

I never wanted a major role in anything as the untold humiliation of having to make a public spectacle of myself just really freaks me out so you can imagine my relief when one year I was assigned the role of a tree. Although I can't be certain now, I think on that occasion we may have based our drama production on the popular children's tale of The Lion, The Witch and The Wardrobe and it probably took the teachers all of their time to talk me out of hiding amongst the clothes.

However, I concluded that at least having to play the part of a tree probably wouldn't amount to much and I quelled my stage fright with the resolve that maybe I could remain partially camouflaged by my leaves. Upon a time of gentle reflection, I am now convinced that this latest casting was all down to those nursery nurses again as they were alleged to have been circulating the story that I was now completely barking mad. Luckily for me though, it seemed that I'd managed to get to the root of the problem just at the perfect timing, so they did have to turn over a new leaf for a while.

After the first few practice runs, my next notion was that, if I could just manage to keep really still, then my whereabouts onstage would go unnoticed, naturally blending into the dully-painted eastern backdrop, which provided a welcome cool shelter for the weary camels.

Like most schools, we would similarly put on some kind of a jolly presentation every Christmas and on another occasion, my teacher decided that she'd had quite enough of my acting coy and that I wasn't going to be allowed to spend another season simply sitting there, looking starry-eyed, and this year she promised she was going to set me a real festive challenge.

Again, slightly wavering from the traditional story of the birth of baby Jesus and setting the familiar scene in the stable, it was decided that this year the whole of Victoria School would be joining forces, collectively performing in what turned out to be the first of quite a repertoire of our phenomenal and much-loved Christmas pantomimes.

Amidst its initial planning stage, the teachers proposed that it would be good for the complete show to be based upon a common theme and one of the first most popular ideas was to craft something out of the incredible artistry of Walt Disney.

Many imaginative possibilities were now spread before us and after much deliberation, it was soon unanimously agreed amongst all the teenagers in Top Class, that we should forge our own spoof version of Jungle Book.

The first most important task, of course, was to decide upon the characters we would like to play and I'm sure you can imagine the resounding whoops of joy when it was suggested that the maths teacher would also be swinging into action, munching on rotten bananas and dressed in a gorilla suit.

Anyway, rehearsals and preparations were soon fully underway and in the end, it was agreed that I should open our act, dressed all in grey, sporting two enormous paper ears, in my comical portrayal of Colonel Hathi, the leader of the elephant herd.

I felt physically sick as at last the evening I'd been dreading for the last four weeks had finally arrived and our Christmas performance lay before us.

Upon my return home, Mom said we only had an hour and a half to spare before it would be time to start on our trip back to school again so I couldn't expect anything too fancy for tea. I would just have to manage with a couple of slices of cheese on toast and a piece of Nan's homemade fruit cake. She told me that I'd have to get a move on as I needed my hair washed too and I'll never understand how she managed it, but in less than two hours, Mom had both my little sister and myself fed, washed and changed and for the second time that day, I was on my way back to school being closely trailed, as ever, by Nan and Granddad in their orange Allegro.

Well, by the time we arrived, cars and adapted wheelchair vehicles were everywhere, lined nose to tail all along the grass verges and there were no vacant spaces at all by Lower School so I suggested that perhaps it would be easier to venture a little farther up the hill to use the old entrance.

"There's always loads more room there, Mom", I said.

I decided to slightly sidestep the minor detail that this would also result in my being dropped off directly outside Top Class, leaving everyone else to walk right to the other end of the building but for me, the plan was a good one.

Tonight we had been scheduled to perform in the grand finale so there was plenty of time to prepare and, in the meantime, one of the nursery nurses had provided some bottles of fizzy pop and a selection of savoury nibbles, as it was clear to see that it was going to be a very long night.

The next two hours and twenty minutes, however, seemed to just blur into a dreamlike nothingness and before we hardly knew it, the Head of Upper School, who had been given the task of making sure that the production ran without a hitch, poked his head around the door. "O.K.", he said, "I suggest that you start making your way down in about five minutes. We are currently on Act 11" and then pointing towards the row of spent pop bottles which now lined every work surface, he laughed, "Well, I am presuming, of course, that at least one of you can still count."

"Come here, quick Miss", I winged, "I need some more hair clips, cos me ears are falling off."

Soon I was on my way and I was just passing the girls' loos in Lower School, when I heard someone yell, "Oh no Sonya Hill, what do you think you look like now?"

As if it wasn't bad enough having to listen to the constant friction of my huge paper elephant's ears rubbing against my shoulders, three of the cadets stood huddled in the doorway leading to Planned Dependence, all with one thing and one thing only in their sights – to cause me paramount humiliation and embarrassment.

"Alright, the show's over", I giggled, and I tried to move on as quickly as possible.

The teachers were now slowly moving down the line, giving out instructions and making the last-minute adjustments. Finally, after about another quarter of an hour of gradually easing my way through what seemed like a never-ending trail of wheelchairs and walking apparatus, I reached the ramp leading onto the stage and I was ready to face my final curtain.

I saw that the penultimate group of pupils were being assisted through the side exit of the hall and right on cue, The Elephant March began... "Hup, two three four... Keep it up, two, three, four..." and I shot up the ramp, triumphantly brandishing my trunk as I headed for the piano, the rest of the jungle trailing slowly behind me.

The hall was dimly lit, just suggesting a little atmospheric jungle glow. Out of the corner of my eye I could now see that the hair clips which were meant to be securing my African ears were slowly coming adrift, dropping lower and lower towards my chin. It wasn't too much farther into proceedings, however, when it became clear that this was the least of my worries.

"Just how much more do they expect me to endure?", I thought, as it seemed that I'd been swinging first one arm and then the other in my goofy impersonation of an elephant's trunk for so long, that I felt confident that either one of them was about to drop off or that I was going to end up being stretchered offstage with at least one, if not a duo of frozen shoulders. "How much longer?" I inwardly cringed.

I was in absolute agony now and my concentration was being distracted even further by the constant, stifled chuckles of my sisters and cousins, who all had front row seats situated about four feet away from me, directly parallel to my natural eye-line. I knew that the only slight chance I had now to finish my act, suppress my giggles and to exit the hall still in possession of my all but remaining shred of dignity, was to continue to stare at my imaginary white light blinking at me and boosting my courage from the far corner of the hall.

Finally and not a second too soon, (or, at least in my opinion), I observed my friend who was dressed as Bagheera, the black panther, was just starting her slow descent down the ramp, signalling the end of the show. Being the final pupil to exit, before I reached the makeshift stage curtain, the lights flared up again and I briefly saw the headmaster, as he rushed from where he had been seated at the side of the piano, but, before he had time to embark upon his closing speech, Victoria's hall erupted in cheers of joy, whistles, and a standing ovation.

The success and the overall reaction to our first festive pantomime had been amazing and I think everyone involved not only felt an enormous sense of achievement but the teachers had just identified this as being another excellent opportunity to showcase the children's diverse and varied abilities in the years to come.

Awaiting our return from the classrooms, our family members and friends rounded off their lovely evening with a chat and a tempting spread of light refreshments.

My first term as a lively, young occupant of Victoria School's 16-19 group had gone well and I was enjoying the new sense of independence I had developed in pursuing a wide sphere of personal interests.

Following the show, there was only about a week and a half to go before the end of term and so the pace of lessons gradually began to slow, being replaced by an enjoyable array of more leisurely pursuits such as listening to Christmas carols, participating in our endless rounds of Hangman and generally finding various ways to spread the festive cheer, being forever mindful, of course, to steer very clear of that ominous clump of mistletoe at all costs... oh go on then, I'll admit it just for you, maybe its presence did slip my mind now and again, but I was only trying to prevent those cadets from stealing all our mince pies.

12

When Destiny Calls

With another year's festive celebration behind us, soon it was time to return to school again and for me, from now on, that was going to equate to two things - an ever-increasing pile of exam papers to work through and an even faster growing pile of homework. Hadn't those teachers heard of free time and if only once in a while, couldn't they at least sometimes show me the courtesy of giving me a break? Alas, for the meantime, it seemed not.

After the Christmas holiday, lessons in Top Class became a little more specialized and we were soon divided into smaller groups in preparation for the forthcoming CSE examinations. In accordance with my ability levels, it was decided that the three main subjects which I should now concentrate on were English, Mathematics and Typewriting and so most of the next two years I dedicated to my assignments. My workload seemed inexhaustible and on the days when I wasn't working on my latest essay, I still had the task of either more maths revision or reading another chapter for English Literature. I remember that we had to study a play called, "Hobson's Choice". The two novels we did were, "Lord Of The Flies" by William Golding and "Kes", the intriguing tale of Billy Casper, a young boy who captured and trained a kestrel and finally we also had the task of writing a critical poetry review.

For me, I found English Language was my best subject. I think this is probably why I have so often been accused of being Victoria School's biggest chatterbox but, at first, English Literature seemed far more challenging, being solely reliant upon the possession of a good memory, but when I settled into it, I found the adventures of Kes fairly enjoyable.

In terms of school years, the educational clock was ticking quite rapidly now and, although like me, many of my friends were becoming relatively comfortable and secure in the somewhat monotonous daily drill of the 16-19 group, at some point for everyone this was going to have to change and sooner or later we were all going to have to make plans for our inevitable future.

I expect there may be quite a few young teenagers out there who have a very similar sphere of feelings as I did in that, back then, the future just seemed like a distant blur of confusion. I suddenly seemed to find that I was having different pieces of advice coming from all sides but today the only thing I was bothered about was whether I had remembered to ask Mom to call in the paper shop and get me the magazine I'd seen advertised on television: the one with the centre-page feature about Adam and The Ants, promoting their latest album release. I'd sort everything else out in my own time but if we didn't hurry up and get one, then we'd miss the chance and next week's issue would be out and Adam Ant looked really hot. Oh, the simplicities of teenage life.

Up until this point, my routine of taking my daily trip to school had just become my ordinary way of life. Victoria School had catered for my physical and educational needs superbly and Mom had always had the ongoing assurance that should any problems arise, then the staff were forever close at hand, being keen to listen and an excellent source of help and advice in times of need, so what were we going to do in the years ahead?...

Anyway, time to go back to class now, and I was just driving past the girls' toilets, when..."Oh no, what the...?"

My best friend came charging up towards me but as I soon realised, there was no time to make out what she was babbling about, as there were far more important things to concern myself with. My eardrums had almost reached shattering point now being constantly assaulted by the high-pitched screech of the fire bell.

The English teacher came into view next, running through the double doors which led to the Home Economics Department and then

172

several other people, both staff and pupils, began to emerge from classrooms rapidly filling Upper School's main corridor, all joining forces to frantically fling open the exit to the playground, their anxious voices now screaming as one, "Get out everybody, come on, JUST ALL GET OUT!"

The whole corridor was soon blocked with a jostling sea of wheelchairs, but despite all the chaos, I couldn't help myself from having a quiet snigger, as the voice of a young boy arose from the crowd and he asked innocently, "Have we got a fire, Miss?"

We proceeded to systematically wend our way towards the entrance, all heading for the designated assembly point.

Being in the school environment, I was fully expecting that it would transpire to be just another haphazard fire drill but even I was a little alarmed to find that there was a real fire engine in the playground, surrounded by about half a dozen firemen dressed in their black, waterproof overalls. Two of them had already set to work, unreeling the long buff coloured hosepipe. Another one climbed back in the cab now steering the vehicle forward, coming to a halt again at the edge of the brick sandpit.

"Well, I still can't see any sign of smoke", I said.

"Perhaps it's a pity", one of the boys laughed, "We might have all have been given a week's holiday".

Shortly afterwards, the headmaster arrived on the scene. He congratulated all the staff and pupils for their swift evacuation of the building and then, after welcoming the fire brigade to the school, he quickly handed the rest of the proceedings over to the Chief Fire Officer, who continued to give us a short talk on general fire safety and also a demonstration of how to extinguish fires using a selection of different fire hoses and ladders which were strategically placed along the wall of the school.

At this point we all began to bellow, as two of the fire-fighters started to shoot thick white foam from their fire extinguishers, the majority of which came to rest in a huge bubbling pool in the centre of the playground. The crescendo of mischief and excitement continued to rise and just a second or two later, one cheeky little chap decided he could bear the temptation no more and, appearing from nowhere, he simply raced forward in his wheelchair, screaming with delight and heading straight for the centre of a large pile of foam.

One of the firemen stepped forward, deterring him from going further and with the Fire Safety lesson now drawing to a close, the headmaster appeared again, this time initiating three cheers and a well-merited round of applause.

"Now children", the headmaster instructed, "starting with the front line, if you could all begin to slowly make your way back to your respective classrooms, then I'm sure you can have a closer look at the fire engine on your way passed... but of course", he added as a precautionary afterthought, "be sure not to touch any of the equipment, we don't want any real accidents."

It was almost time for the lunchtime bell, but now, miserable after sitting outside for half an hour and getting covered in frothy foam, I decided to go back to my class via The Tuck Shop. A girl and a boy from Lower School had just started to unpack the boxes of stock, so I treated myself to a bag of cheese and onion crisps. Now all I had to do was to track down a free unsuspecting nursery nurse to feed me.

Anyway soon the lunch break had passed again and my first lesson of the afternoon was originally supposed to be music, but I had agreed with the teacher that this time would be much better spent working through another maths paper, as it was of utmost importance now that I should put in as much revision as possible before the impending exam. I was struggling a little with algebra so I decided to run through a few extra exercises again, free from the additional headache of trying to keep up with the rest of the class.

The maths teacher told me that yesterday he had been in further discussions about some of the physical challenges which would inevitably arise in sitting my exam because it was felt that, although he was fully accustomed to reading my large, sprawling figures, to the eye of an

174

examiner, who would be unfamiliar with my indistinct handwriting, it was going to pose a problem. He told me, however, that it had been agreed that I should carry this out as normal, but also additionally submitting my final answers in the form of a typed document and finally the examination board had also permitted me the aid of a scribe.

Oh dear, what a controversy I was causing again but at last the final details were in place and so, for the next few weeks, my revision seemed ceaseless.

It was at around the same time, that the teachers arranged regular meetings with a visiting careers officer and he was given the task of trying to set up and negotiate college placements in accordance with what the teachers considered as the most suitable option for our individual needs and abilities. They started to encourage me to consider the option of going to residential college, as they knew of one place, in particular, which had extremely good facilities, seeming the ideal choice for me.

Well, as far as I was concerned, in the beginning, having never ventured away from home before, I was dead against the idea. As you can see, I had an extremely happy and contented life; I had always drawn comfort not only from the love and support of the adults in my family but also from the wonderfully unique blend of mayhem and mischief supplied by my generation. To me, the thought of losing this was simply not what I wanted to consider right now so, at least for the meantime, I continued to study for my exams.

We'll look at how this story eventually unfolds for me in a while, but school life continued and for the next few months Top Class also began to venture to a slightly different territory: each Friday, making the short trip by school ambulance necessary, to reach a nearby, comprehensive school.

Having spent all of our lives in a special school, I think this was simply a way of providing us with some experience of integrating with able-bodied youngsters.

During lesson time, we were given the use of the vacant geography room and although we had our own class, the layout of the school had a similar appearance to that of some private hospital wards, with each room running parallel to another, just being separated by two glass partitions which allowed us a clear view of all the goings-on with the pupils across the corridor.

This soon gave way, of course, to a constant source of class disruption and despite the teacher's futile attempts to interest us in the presentation being shown on the projector, I think we spent most of the day holding up scrawled messages on tattered bits of paper or trying to flick pencil and eraser missiles in perfect unison with our equally disruptive and delinquent able-bodied counterparts.

I was still making regular use of my Canon Communicator and this nifty piece of gadgetry came in particularly handy in the playground as, once I had managed to fluff my way out of the initial embarrassment of having a speech impediment, in a desperate attempt to try to deflect the children's attention, I kept them amused by industriously printing out reams of ridiculous jokes and when eventually this novelty began to wane, I harvested a little more redemption by egging on a full-scale paper fight. Yes, this probably seems a total waste of paper, but at least it provided me with a slightly more dignified way to interact and on the whole my brief rendezvous with the teenagers in the local school turned out to be quite amusing.

As I recall, I don't think our geography lesson showed all that much difference in its levels of boredom and interest as it would have done back at Victoria, but at least spending the day in the small comprehensive school provided the chance for us to mix with other teenagers.

Anyway, soon it was April 1983 and my friends and I hadn't a spare moment at all, as just a month later it would be time for our exams to start so most of every day was spent either revising or helping each other to refine our maths skills. The routine became very tiring and now the only recreational time I was allowed was on Monday afternoons, when I continued my work with the nursery children.

"Sir", I said one morning to the maths teacher, "I don't think I'm ever going to do this. I'm just useless at trying to calculate the area of circles and as for this algebra stuff, well, it's as clear as mud".

"Sonya, what are you panicking about?" he asked, "Your marks are well within the expected range so as long as we can get these suitable time concessions in place, then I'm sure you'll be fine. Just have confidence in yourself, O.K.?"

"Oh yeah", I mused, "I'll believe that when it happens. I'll never get all this into my head."

Anyway, the weeks seemed to fly past: soon the morning of my maths exam was upon us, but unlike in an ordinary school, in which it is customary for whole classes to sit their GCSE's together, I recall that only one other boy was joining me, so we were designated the use of a small room in a quiet area of Lower School, where the teachers felt we shouldn't encounter too much disturbance.

I remember popping into Top Class first though, just to hang my cagoule on my peg and to ask one of the nursery nurses for a cup of squash and finally, after meeting up with the other queasy-looking candidate, we made our way down the corridor. As you may guess, when we drew nearer, there was no mistaking where we were supposed to go because the outside of the designated room had already been adorned with a large cardboard sign, which read in bold, black capitals, "QUIET PLEASE!!, EXAM IN PROGRESS."

The room was all but empty, merely containing two small tables and chairs but at first glance, it was obvious which desk was meant for me, as I saw that my typewriter was set up and ready to go.

When at last we were settled, the teacher advised us that we were required to answer three questions from the first section and then another two of the more complex ones printed on the back sheet. "Good luck" he said, "and please try to get at least one right."

The instructions given on the front page of the exam paper stated that we were to be given a maximum of two hours, although I had been awarded an additional time concession, taking into account my physical difficulties and the fact that I also required practical assistance.

Anyway, after skimming through all the questions, I decided to tackle the fractions section first, as this initially looked like the easiest area but unfortunately, by the time I'd managed to line up all my figures on the typewriter, the only fraction which could sum up how I was feeling right now was "frayed nerves over headache".

The assisting nursery nurse was sitting in the corner at this point quietly skimming through her magazine but I decided that my next question would require a Venn diagram: a drawn image of three overlapping circles, so upon my instruction, she pencilled this in for me, using the top of a plastic cup as a guide.

I'd just about finished arranging my numbers in the correct spaces when the accompanying teacher looked up from his desk and instructed us, "O.K., you can stop what you are doing now, that's half time."

"How are you doing?" I asked my friend, "It's worse than I thought."

"I'm just about coping, I think", he frowned, "but the heat in here is killing me."

"Yes", the nursery nurse chipped in, "it's getting far too humid in here now. I'll see if I can open that top window. I think we're all gasping for air."

Despite the heat, it seemed that the second half of the exam seemed to pass much quicker, which may have been attributed to our break so I decided to use the final ten minutes, not just to check through what I'd done, but it was also essential, at this point, to get the nursery nurse to ensure that each piece of work was ordered correctly, also doing a final check that my questions were all clearly numbered.

"Happy?" she asked me, just as the timer sounded, marking the exam's completion.

"As far as I can be", I replied, "just glad it's done, but I think I need a rest now. It's been a very long morning."

Each of the exams I took at Victoria School, not only in Mathematics but Typewriting and English, (both in Literature and Language subject areas) were all administered in a very similar fashion, all being extremely well planned, supported and managed. Yes, of course, being able to attain my first recognized qualifications was for me another great achievement, but unfortunately, in this story, I have still only been able to capture just a very small fragment of the brilliant planning and expertise of all of the involved staff without whom finishing school with any qualifications would never have been a possibility for me at all.

I will always be very proud of my achievements at Victoria School and certainly, with my level of disability, regardless of where I may have been educated, from an academic point of view I don't believe I could have achieved anymore.

I was almost seventeen now and just like my parents, I have always been very self-motivated, possessing a strong resolve to use my capabilities to their fullest potential and even though I had never been away from home before, I arrived back from school one day and in what seemed like a very coy, spur-of-the-moment decision, I drove up to the kitchen doorway where Mom was preparing tea and rather timidly, I said, "Mom, you know this thing about going to residential college?"

"Yes", Mom replied, "what about it?"

"Well, the thing is Mom", I spluttered, "I think I might have had a slight change of heart, Mom...er...what I mean is, I don't know whether it will work or not, but I've decided to apply for an interview Mom and just, give it a go", I gulped, now almost in tears... "I hope you're not angry or sad, Mom. Typically, of course, being the very loving and completely supportive mother she always has been, she immediately came right over to me with outstretched arms and gave me a big hug.

"I'm very proud of you", she said, "and I will always support you in all you want to do, you know that Sonya...but," she added, "if anything goes wrong, then you will always have your home here."

I nodded, solemnly and then simply said, "Thanks Mom."

And so you see, my exams went well, I was going to finish my schooldays with at least, some recognized qualifications. I was tentatively starting to make plans for new challenges and joys which now lay ahead of me and slowly I began preparing myself for my next adventure. Just like any other confident, mischievous young teenager, however, I was still convinced that I knew what my future would bring forth. Or did I? No, of course, I didn't. As always, the days to come were all very mysterious and in the hands of the Lord, but there was at least one steadfast assurance however and that was, if I was planning to bid my final farewell, then particularly after enduring all those gruelling hours of exam revision, the last thing I intended was for my final goodbye to Victoria School to be a quiet one.

13

<u>Get Into The Groove</u>

Early one morning, just a few weeks before Christmas, 1983, an official-looking envelope dropped through the letterbox, coming to rest on the brown, bristled doormat.

For a few moments, I convinced myself that this morning's pile of mail would probably just contain the next quarterly gas bill and a few local advertisements about Dudley, but of course, at the bottom of the pile, Mom had soon found something else.

She tore open the letter and nervously, she delivered the news which I'd been half expecting all along, that I was invited to attend an interview, due to take place on the 10th – 11th of January 1984, which would involve a two-day and overnight stay on the campus of a residential college and then, subject to my exam results, I would most likely be awarded a place.

At this point, I think I had more or less decided that I would just go for a look around, thoroughly hate it and simply return home with my tail between my legs, after reaching a definite decision that it wasn't the place for me. "It was just a matter of time", I told myself, "and if it failed to achieve anything else, then at least it would show the school that I'd had the nerve to try it and perhaps then, my slight, stirring curiosity could, once and for all, be laid to rest."

Anyway, at least for the meantime, Mom said I should try to put all thoughts of the interview out of my mind. Of course, just like any other mother, she has always understood me more than anyone so, aware that I am probably one of the world's biggest worriers, as usual she did her best to put me at ease so that we could all relax and enjoy a peaceful holiday time.

For me, however, this Christmas seemed to take on a very different air.

All the usual anticipation and pleasure which I normally felt both during and in the days running up to the festive period just didn't seem to happen. To a degree, of course, when the event arrived I was routinely pleased with my presents and just like any other year, I enjoyed spending time with the family.

Despite this, however, the one thought which was clinging heaviest on my mind was, as you may imagine, my looming date with destiny.

I did attempt to enjoy the celebrations and to enter into the holiday spirit, albeit mainly because I didn't want to spoil it for everyone else, but of course, every few minutes I found my thoughts were drifting nervously back to the ominous contents of that unmentionable envelope and so, as far as I was concerned, the sooner it was over and put behind me, the better.

The next week seemed to pass by quite uneventfully and it didn't seem long until we were awaiting the final strike of Big Ben, signalling that in the UK, the opening moments of January 1984 had just dawned.

I think I was originally due to return to school before my appointment, but Mom cancelled the bus, as I said that I'd rather just stay at home until "it", or in other words, my interview, was over.

Just a few days later, however, the date circled prominently in bold red biro on the calendar arrived and, desperately trying to take my mind off where I was heading, I grimaced over to the clock to see how much time I had left to aimlessly add things to my overnight bag, most of which I doubted I would require anyway, although I had always been bought up to believe in another old, family proverb, that it is better to be safe than sorry.

Soon our final preparations were underway and after I'd managed to force down most of my usual bowl of cereal, despite fighting an intense and constant desire to just retch it all back again, Mom set to work packing up the car, tightly trying to accommodate my wheelchair, a suitcase each and enough overnight essentials to last us for the next fortnight let alone for just one night. Mom had reserved a room at a nearby hotel for herself so that she hadn't any need to take the long drive home only to repeat the journey to pick me up again on the following day.

Well, my interview took place over thirty years ago now so as you can imagine, some of my memories have become a little scanty, although I must start by saying that at first glance my overall impression was that the college itself seemed very modern and well-equipped. Its male and female dormitory blocks were set in pleasant, grassed surroundings, all being linked by wide, railed paths, which were sheltered by overhead plastic canopies. Their sides were open, however, so, as you can imagine, this passageway could become very chilly, particularly during winter months.

When we arrived, I recall that a member of staff met us in the car park and our first port of call was to head into the main college block where I met up with a small gathering of other nervous-looking prospective students whom I soon learnt had been called in for their interviews and to check out the college on the same day as me.

"Hello", I said to another girl in a wheelchair, who had parked herself just a little further along the corridor, "my name's Sonya".

"Sarah?" she asked.

"No, it's Sonya", I started to say again, but by this time, Mom's comprehension was three steps ahead and realizing the young girl's dilemma in understanding me, she quickly intercepted, saying, "This is Sonya, how are you?"

"Oh I'm fine thanks, I'm Sam, by the way", but then, before our conversation had time to develop further, a door opened and a middle-aged man dressed in a smart, grey pin-striped suit and tie appeared and extending a general invitation to everyone, he said, "Hello, my name's Mr Burton, I'm head of the college. Goodness", he continued, "there's no need to look so terrified", which at the time I automatically assumed to be a comment being exclusively directed at me.

We all then began to make our way, slowly and methodically into the small office.

After just a few minutes everyone was finally settled and I noted that there were about four or five other members of staff present, but it was Mr Burton, who, without further ado, set proceedings underway.

"Well, first, may I extend a very warm welcome to you all."

He then started to gather up a dishevelled pile of papers from the desk, which was situated just in front of about three rows of neatly arranged seats.

"If you could just take a few moments to fill in some details about yourselves, then you will see that over the page, it goes on to give you just a brief outline of the program for the next two days. That will be great and if you have problems in writing, then perhaps your parents could assist", Mr Burton continued in a very efficient and business-like manner.

We filled in the questionnaire without difficulty and then, with the preliminary meeting and introductions out of the way, the next thing I remember is being taken to another part of the college, although I can't be sure now whether we went into a classroom or the hall, but it was in here that we were given some tests to demonstrate our competence in literacy and numeracy.

Not too long afterwards it was lunchtime and so making my way to the dining room which was still on the ground floor, it was the first real chance we had of meeting some of the current students.

The dining room was very spacious, being set out, as you may imagine, in a very similar fashion to any other college canteen: it featured several rows of tables. There was a long handrail spanning the whole width of the serving hatch and then along another wall there was a drinks dispenser and a few other options for people who may prefer a lighter snack. I was quite hungry though today, so decided I would go for the fish and chips, probably to boost my depleting energy levels.

I think most of the remainder of my time, was more or less taken up with a guided tour of the college, observing its different facilities and departments and meeting other members of staff, including teachers, physiotherapists and care assistants.

I have to be honest here, in saying that, overall, my first impression of the college was a good one and my interview seemed to go better than I had originally thought. Everyone seemed very friendly and willing to help and gradually, I found myself thinking that maybe going to residential college was starting to look like a viable solution for me after all.

Looking back, I think putting myself through the process of going for my interview left me experiencing a very different range of emotions to those I had expected. All areas of the college had the impression of being both modern and well-equipped and I think at this stage in life, there still seemed to be many questions regarding what I was going to be able to achieve in the years ahead, particularly with regards to any future employment prospects I may have, so I felt that this needed to be given some serious thought.

In fact, as you have probably guessed by now, even though I had found my college interview a very daunting and tiring experience, setting aside all my initial fears and trepidation, I think I had more or less decided that if I passed the interview process, I would begin the next academic year, enrolling on their Business Studies course. By then, I reasoned with myself, my exams would be over and at that point, I felt that, academically, Victoria School would have completed its mission and as a schoolgirl, I would have achieved all I could.

Well, when I first told Mom and Dad that I was now considering this as perhaps a much more realistic option, their initial reaction as you may imagine, was one of total disbelief and shock. It was such a big leap of faith for me and one which was so far from my usual home-loving character but, as ever, they both showed great compassion and understanding and they promised to support me in whatever I decided to do.

It was just a few days later, when I received another letter, this time stating, as expected, that further to my interview, I had been awarded a place on a Business Studies course, due to commence at the beginning of September and so, with little more discussion, I accepted the offer.

My interview now behind me, of course, at least for the next few months, it was time to get back into some semblance of everyday life and during the remainder of the summer term of 1984 I was still in the throes of working towards my second year of CSE exams, so most of my days were still being consumed by yet more exam revision and coursework.

Life at this stage, I think, all seemed to be about looking ahead and trying to prepare for a greater sense of independence in years still to come and on many occasions, as I was dawdling along Victoria's great labyrinth of corridors, I regularly overheard many amusing mumbles that, maybe I'd been paying more attention to my Peto sessions than they thought, as I did actually seem to be becoming a little less clumsy. Of course, as many people probably find out at some point in life, it is always gratifying to hear that your teachers are pleased with you, but alas, little did they know that my recent surge of improvement wasn't down to them at all, but the complete carpentry genius of Granddad.

Granddad loved his woodwork and, particularly during warm, summer months, he spent many happy hours in his small shed, which was tucked in the corner of the garden almost completely concealed by rose bushes. The interior of this tiny shed was immaculate and despite only comprising of just enough room for him to stand at his tiny workbench, I always viewed the discipline of its neat interior as really quite extraordinary. Its walls were lined with shelves which he had constructed himself from leftover bits of timber and they were neatly laden with tiny boxes of everything you can think of in the way of nails, screws, tacks, elastic bands, buttons and not forgetting, of course, his prized collection of sanded down matchsticks which he had collected to build up the model of the ship he had travelled back from India on, after The Second World War. We all called him Mr Fix-It, as he was brilliant at designing things and if something wasn't quite working in the way that it should be, we all knew whose workbench to take it to.

However, it was during my early teens that Granddad started to consider how he might be able to use this skill to help me. He was always tremendously observant and similar to me in a way, I think he had a very active mind, seeming forever ready for a new puzzle or challenge and particularly when I was within the local vicinity, he was usually given one.

He now really began to become more curious, being particularly interested in how I was using my hands and it was through these subtle observations that my granddad set to work to design and craft for me, a very unique, but simply fascinating collection of wooden tools.

Much like most designers, of course, Granddad's ideas normally started out as just a rough sketch in his notepad: its initial plan being very vague, but it was always great fun to mull over different strategies and as time progressed, these cleverly designed gadgets continued to evolve in their many different shapes and sizes. Granddad's unique, handheld aids, however, had two things in common – they all worked the first time, and they all helped me to achieve their intended tasks, perfectly.

Just a few examples of these small gadgets have included: a rotating stand/box: the inside of the box was designed to house my radio-alarm clock, whilst its top provided a stand to hold my small, portable T.V. The whole thing was then set upon a separate wooden base, enabling me to easily rotate the television and watch it from either my bed or my wheelchair.

Staying with the subject of strange boxes, on another occasion, Granddad also constructed a box which, this time, proposed to take on a very different function.

Spanning many years, as I'm sure my siblings will easily recall, we all passed many an enjoyable hour playing simple card games with Granddad. We amassed quite a repertoire back then and some of our old favourites included Go Fish, Knock-Out, Whist and Rummy. However, slightly later in proceedings, I took up the hobby of teaching myself how to play various forms of Patience and so it didn't take long for me to hit upon Granddad's next project.

"Look at this, Granddad", I said, "it's just ridiculous. I'll never be able to master this; I just can't concentrate because the cards are flying everywhere."

"Is that right?" Granddad replied. "Well show me what you are doing and then I'll have a little think about that one."

I smiled, as this was exactly the response I was hoping for.

Pondering upon the solution that Granddad now came up with still fascinates me to this day and as you have probably deduced by now, this invention certainly didn't lack patience.

If most people had been given this challenge, then I would expect that the common response would be to construct a regular box of suitable dimensions to hold a pack of fifty-two playing cards, which would simply enable the cards to be stored neatly... hey-ho, the job is a good one, but as usual, Granddad had to take his idea just one step farther.

It was his vision to try to create a tool of much greater functionality and so by the time of its completion, this clever device had been completely transformed into something so much more than just a boring old box. So tangible was Granddad's vision of what the precise action of dealing playing cards involved, he managed to nail two broken rubber bands to its inside enabling the cards to slide out easier which, in essence, acted almost like two miniature conveyor belts.

Do I really need to give any other explanatory reason of why we all called him Mr Fix-It?

Time swiftly moved on again: soon another school week was underway and Tuesday would be my full day in The Resources Centre.

I remember that during my last few years at school, as each group in Resources only occupied a small area, it became habitual for the class to be divided so that throughout the year we would all have a chance to take all the available subjects and one of the classes I was timetabled to take just before I left school was Home Economics.

The vast majority of this area was dedicated to the running of two, adjacent cookery classes, which just left one small, additional space used to perform other routine household chores giving rise to quite a range of different topics such as Hygiene, Laundry Skills and Safety in the Home. Being assigned to this study area would often entail having to identify and deal with potential hazards, many of which would be of particular danger for wheelchair users and on other occasions, our money management and budgeting skills were also put to the test.

Well, as you can imagine, I think my H.E. teachers certainly taught me how to identify "hazards" but unfortunately, my biggest problem was I seemed to spend more time being the cause of them as opposed to preventing their occurrence.

Although I'm not too sure of the timing now, I remember that on one particular occasion, our teacher informed us that a little later that day some youngsters from the neighbouring autistic school would be coming to visit and so it would be today's task to prepare for them a few light refreshments.

We were asked to cook lemon biscuits and we decided that we could also offer them a few leftover bottles of orange squash.

After donning a clean apron, rolling up my sleeves and washing my hands, I set to work to prepare the biscuit mixture and I began to scan down the recipe sheet to see what was required.

First, I decided that it didn't sound too bad to combine the flour and butter so assuming I was expected to complete the task by hand, I was just about to plunge straight in, when I noticed the teacher heading towards me armed with a small electric hand whisk.

"Why not try using this, Sonya?" she said, "I think you may find this easier than the messy business of mixing it by hand."

"O.K. Miss", I nodded, "I'll give it a go" and so my H.E. teacher assisted me to guide my whisk in the direction of the mixing bowl, finally plunging it right to the bottom.

This task seemed to go quite well for the first moment or two and so, thinking that I seemed to have satisfactory control of the whisk, the teacher decided to slowly withdraw her assistance, to see if I could manage unaided, but then, seconds after she'd let go my next sticky situation was unleashed.

All in a moment, I lost my balance and my original calm composure was transformed into sheer panic. If the headmaster had been in the habit of dishing out detentions, then I am in little doubt that I would have been the first in the queue that day. My whisk suddenly tilted off at an angle and within seconds my teacher leapt into action, desperately trying to regain control as the mixer blades continued to spin, chaotically splattering my cake mixture everywhere. Eventually, of course, the teacher did manage to retrieve the rotating mixer from me but following that gooey escapade, she advised me that, in future, I would most certainly be sticking to my wooden spoon.

My biscuits (or at least those which I managed to get in the tin), seemed to go down quite well in the end, but as usual, I think I made quite a stir that day.

Time progressed again and there were only a few weeks to go now before the summer holiday of 1984 and just like me, most of the residents of Victoria's 16-19 group were due to leave school, all moving on to different special needs colleges.

At last, our exams were over and the general mood in Top Class became significantly lighter. We were all feeling weary now, following what had seemed like an absolute eternity of nonstop revision and even the teachers agreed that it was time to chill out a little and to plan how we would like to mark our last remaining days at Victoria School.

This suggestion at once sparked off another very bubbly and lively debate, being consistent as you may expect with feedback which would arise from any group of high-spirited teens. We decided that our plans were going to require some careful thought. It would take a while to agree on the final details and to come up with something which would suit all, but there was one thing for sure right from the start - we were going to party and the kids of Victoria's 16-19 leavers group, were going to party in style.

The teachers agreed that we could use some of the funds that we had saved from the petty cash tin, (which, even I must admit was an extremely generous gesture on their part considering that this money, as a rule, was only used to keep them well-stocked in coffee, tea and Bourbon biscuits) and so with notepaper and pencils poised, we all crowded around the table.

"O.K.", one boy began, "we need an all-day party, cos if we don't get things going till the afternoon, for a start we won't be hungry after dinner and unless we start early, all the time will be gone before the party has started and we want plenty of time to have a drink, don't we all agree?"

"Precisely", everyone agreed in unison and then the next five minutes was completely wasted by a typical mix of sarcastic jokes and uncontrollable giggles.

Next, it was my turn to chip in and in a desperate attempt to get proceedings back on track again, I asked, "Do you think it would be cool to hire a D.J. and maybe have a disco, or something?"

As you may expect, this suggestion was an instant hit with everyone and, following a little more deliberation, it was decided that perhaps we could push our luck even further and request to hold two events: our Leavers' Party and then the disco on another day. In fact, if we were particularly nifty with our money I suggested that we could have two events for the price of one? ...or maybe not, judging by the growing frown and worry lines exhibited across the teacher's brow.

I think the nursery nurses were starting to fidget a little too, all turning varying shades of green, as they were probably reflecting upon the amount of washing up they would incur, but before they had time to dwell on it too much, the chairman stealthily changed the subject and announced the next most pressing item on the agenda which was to decide upon what food and drink would be required.

"That was a bit of quick thinking", I sniggered to the girl sitting next to me, "because continuing down the route of a financial debate could've headed for disaster" and at least the mere thought of food had seemed to act as a comfort to all concerned.

Well after a few moments, the overall feeling seemed to be mutual that we needn't run to anything too fussy and that it would be ample to just provide some sandwiches, (maybe cheese and ham), a few different varieties of crisps and then the Chairman suggested that we should take a vote on the most popular choice of desserts and after much deliberation, the suggestions to come out on top, by an overwhelming majority were the Black Forest gateau and a strawberry cheesecake.

And finally... we requested that maybe we should throw in half a dozen bottles of fizzy pop but, at the last minute, one of the nursery nurses came up with the great idea, that just to add an interesting twist, she could, if it met with our approval, make up a fresh fruit punch bowl.

My friends and I all loved the sound of this, but by now, I think the staff had started to perform rough calculations in their heads of how much all this could potentially cost.

"Hurry up", one of the nursery nurses bellowed at the Chairman, "just read out the closing minutes now, cos our arms are going to be as long as an orangutan's by the time we've carried all this shopping from Northfield. Please have a heart, kids."

On that note, I think we had achieved just about all we could reasonably expect. The overall result was a good one, but it was plain to see now that if we had tried to stretch school funds any further, we wouldn't just be leaving school, we would have been thrown out and at this late stage, it would be good to escape free of detention.

"All agreed", we yelled, "Thanks Miss"

Well although many years have passed by since then, I still remember that my final days at Victoria School were a real buzz. When the night of our 16-19 Leavers' disco/party arrived, as usual, the staff did us proud. As requested, they did hire the services of a professional D.J., the hall was decked with balloons and we had handmade curly-whirly streamers draped across the ceiling and just to add to the excitement, during her shopping excursion to Northfield, one nursery nurse returned armed with a plentiful collection of party poppers, crackers, fruit jelly sweets and enough chocolates to fill Victoria School's swimming pool.

However, I expect our school cleaners were probably in need of a few strong cups of coffee when they saw the mess they had to clear up. In fact, now I come to think of it, I don't think they were on their own, as when I arrived home that night, Mom had to brew me something very strong and black too because exactly what had been added to that punch bowl by the end of the day, is something I will never know, although it did taste pretty groovy before I fell asleep on the table.

My years as a carefree little schoolgirl were almost done now but what an incredible journey it had turned out to be being a pupil at Birmingham's Victoria School. No, even after all those years, I don't think I could ever describe myself as a loyal and devoted fan of attending school, but although it grieves me to say so, that nurse was right after all – I was just stubborn. The most fantastic thing of all though, was that by the time I left, all that stubbornness had been brilliantly transformed into a strong desire to achieve – and to achieve my best.

14

<u>Victoria's Last Bell</u>

I would imagine that at some point in life, there comes a time when most people wish to make an impact on something or someone and in fact, I think this was probably one of my main aims in my writing of this book. However now, upon reaching the ripe old age of forty-something or being honest, probably closer to fifty-ish, I think most people with whom I have crossed paths are most likely to agree that I have seldom passed unnoticed. Today however, I was finally going to be saying farewell to the many staff and very special friends at Victoria School forever. The sun was shining, a new day had dawned and just like on any morning, I was still unaware of exactly how things would pan out but there were two things for certain and they were – I was leaving school today and I certainly wasn't planning on going quietly.

However, before I continue, I feel it is probably a good idea to remind you that, at this point, I was still silly and seventeen, but on my last morning at Victoria I decided to be an obedient little pupil as it was so important to put on a good impression, as I prepared to make my final entrance into Top Class...

Just how I had the brass nerve to do it, well, that one still beats me but, to this day, I think my school-leaving get-up stands out as being one of the funniest and most garish pranks I have ever pulled off but it just goes to show the true scale of what all those teachers, nursery nurses, physiotherapists, bathroom assistants and not forgetting, of course, that pesky school nurse, had all truly driven me to.

My best friend had something weird up her sleeve too: she'd been reminding me of the fact all week by pulling strange faces at me, miming and generally gesticulating, but now that I come to think of it, she'd been doing that on a daily basis for most of our school life although by a unique amalgamation of winks, nudges, whispers, sniggers and bizarre hand signals, I knew that she too, planned on having one or two surprises in store.

The night before Mom had advised that it would probably be a good plan to aim to get up maybe just under an hour earlier than usual which would potentially allow her plenty of time to refine my new look, as I wanted to go into school with the air of a mysterious woman about me, or was the final result bearing closer to the appearance of an ugly sister? I have never quite been sure.

Anyway soon I was ready and my usual appearance of a quiet, docile school-girl had, just for today, undergone a total transformation and I was dressed to kill.

In truth, I looked quite a sight, probably being worse than most young girls ever to debut on the set of most long-running soap operas but for my final day at Victoria School, I was going to have a total blast.

"Oh dear, Mom", I chuckled, making my way down the hallway, "what the hell am I doing now?"

"Well, it's a bit late to ask me that no, Sonya", she replied, "I've only done what you asked, so hurry up now the driver is tooting the horn."

"O.K.", I said, "sharp intake of breath, here I go", as I mentally prepared myself to spring forth into the outside world, taking on board the full impact of what I was now, about to let myself in for.

"Arrrggghhh, NO, Sonya Hill", the driver spluttered, "am I really expected to load you on my bus looking like that? You're gonna get me arrested Madam and I've done nothing."

One by one, as I was raised on the tail-lift, the children all began to shriek and whoop with joy, each of them stretching forward as much as possible to obtain a better view.

"Oh no", one lad said, "what do you think you look like and why have you sprayed your hair gold?"

I put my hand behind my head, pouted and sniggered.

My glittery gold hairspray was just for starters. I wore thick, face powder, bright red lipstick, a large painted on beauty-spot on one cheek, a tight, white t-shirt, fishnet stockings and a green lacy garter topped with a plastic daisy. As far as the daisy was concerned, you would have thought that I'd had quite enough of them by now, following all those agonising years of having to wear that hideously unmentionable swimming cap.

It appeared not, however, but as you can imagine, my journey to school that morning was simply brilliant and mind-bogglingly funny; the whole experience probably being comparable to that of being the central character on a float, taking part in some kind of grand street procession or celebrity carnival, except that predictably, the only one drawing attention and making a complete public spectacle of myself, was me. Sitting sideways, right at the back of the bus, also gave me an added advantage putting me in the perfect position to spend the entire journey waving and pulling stupid faces at the vehicles travelling behind us and probably depending on the different personalities and age groups, the resulting feedback I received from the public was very mixed, ranging from the conservative stiff-upper-lipped group, who just wanted, at all costs, to avoid making eye contact with me and overtake our bus as quickly and surreptitiously as possible, to another poor young befuddled guy on a motorbike, who almost swerved straight into a roadside hedge, whilst trying to do a double-take. Either way though, I think the many reactions were all equally funny.

Soon we arrived and as often was the case, by the time we'd done the usual drop-offs at the other schools and managed to escape the long line of traffic queuing outside Victoria, there was only one possible parking space left, just in front of the doors to Top Class.

Of course, I had planned to take my usual route, through the main entrance and up the grey tiled corridor leading to my classroom, but there was no time for that – not today.

As I exited the bus the maths teacher was standing close to the window, brewing his morning mug of tea. He suddenly looked up from the work surface and immediately noticing me as I was lowered on the tail-lift, he bought his mug down so hard it almost shattered and then he leapt through the classroom doors, bouncing towards me with so much speed and energy, he looked as if he had springs suddenly shooting from the soles of his shoes. I know he'd taken a few P.E. lessons over the years, but as a rule, not even Sir moved that quickly.

"SONYA HILL", he bellowed, "you disgusting, little madam...and I always thought you were 'the quiet one'. Come in, let's have a look at you. I just can't believe this", he continued to waffle.

The other staff had also begun to congregate now, all coming to see what the commotion was about, but not long afterwards, my best friend arrived, making her grand entrance: I'd been waiting to see what gear she would roll up in as I knew she was also planning to leave behind a lasting impression. At the same time, we both fell in a heap of hilarity, neither of us able to speak as we both looked equally stupid, but again, it was another great experience to share with one of my best friends. Thinking back, that last day was almost like holding our own, miniature version of, "Stars In Their Eyes", as the first thing I saw was the gradual emergence of a thick mass of billowing multi-coloured ribbons and sporting a black flowing dress, I soon realised that she was dressed as Boy George.

Well, there were no lessons scheduled today so we decided we would like to join each other in making our final tour around Victoria, knocking on every door and paying a special visit into each class and department, although we did make sure that the toilets were all vacant before making our way through the boys' bathroom.

It was an awesome experience, not just in dressing up and seeing the excitement on the children's faces, but for someone like me, who was naturally quite a shy person, especially through my most self-conscious

197

teen phase, I think it was also a clear indication that, at last, the staff at Victoria had succeeded in their mission. I had not only gained an education, my first recognised qualifications and a strong resolve to do my best but despite my Cerebral Palsy, I was now developing into quite a comical and happy little character.

Anyway, my final day continued and by dinnertime, I think we had completed our grand circuit of the school, leaving most of its inhabitants suitably shocked and all looking very scared. Even after creating all that commotion, however, I was still buzzing with adrenaline and excitement and just like a pantomime dame in the throes of performing a big comedy sketch, I abruptly fled out of the doors of Top Class and driving my wheelchair right onto the centre of the island, which stands in between my school and the other special needs schools, I let out one long, ear-splitting bellow – because today, "I could".

"Aaaaaaaaarrrrrrrgggggghhhh", I roared, making such a rebellious din that I alerted the attention of the headmaster from one of the other schools across the road. He came charging over to me, as upon hearing my screams of torture, I expect he thought that I had been wrongly expelled and maybe he had originally intended to offer me a place at his school, although following closer scrutiny of what I was wearing, I think he thought better of it.

"What's all the racket about?" he asked, "are you stuck, or are you sitting there intentionally. Do you make a regular habit of coming to school dressed like that?"

"Umm...", I began, as he had seemed to fire so many questions at me all at once, that I didn't quite know where to begin and all I could do was laugh, although my amusement was only short-lived, soon mutating into a genuinely frightened scream, as my wheelchair began to skid and at one point, (although I don't think I'd better own up to Mom), I think I was balancing on just three wheels.

"I'm leaving school today, Sir", I said.

"I see", he replied, "well, by the look of you, I think you'd better get down off this island, or I fear you'll be leaving via A&E. Go on in now and be careful".

"O.K. thanks", I chuckled, and then, feeling a little red-faced, I started to make my way back inside.

Soon it was time for lunch and after the morning's madness, proceedings seemed to hit a slight lull and the main thing which was scheduled to take place in the afternoon was our final assembly so, expecting this to be a rather more sombre affair, I had bought a change of ordinary clothes with me and considering I'd already narrowly escaped getting into trouble with one headmaster, the thought of upsetting mine, particularly at this late stage, would be just too bad. Even now though, I was still unsure whether I had been seriously reported for chasing those cadets, or was it the firemen? I really can't remember now but I'd been set up so many times I'd lost count, although I had always tried my best to be a good little pupil.

Could I seriously be in trouble now? I deliberated, after all that I'd endured and been through after my diligent and religious completion of all those English essays and maths papers. I'd done my Sports Days, I'd sat my exams, survived swimming lessons, I'd had the inside of my mouth and tongue prodded and re-positioned by the speech therapists sandpaper-textured spatulas and as for the inhabitants of Victoria's physiotherapy department, well, thanks to them, I'd just spent the last thirteen years of my life being helplessly engulfed beneath weirdly-shaped lumps of foam frantically attempting to detect one small gap just about big enough to allow me the meagre admission of oxygen essential to my human existence.

It was amazing though, that just at the very last minute, after all those years of waiting, that kind Sir came rushing to my aid and had it not been my last day, I'm sure that I could have had each member of Victoria's staff duly arrested, simply for their sheer brilliance and kindness towards me.

I slowly made my way back indoors but I think my teachers had probably comprehended my thoughts more than I'd realised, as I now spotted that Top Class had just acquired the addition of a new BBC Micro, which was housed on a trolley, standing in the corner of the class.

"Where's that come from?" I asked, "who's that for?"

"It's yours", my teacher replied and just at that moment, I started to recall that a few weeks earlier, I'd composed a letter to The Sequal Trust, requesting them to provide me with a computer to help me to complete my future college assignments.

As you can imagine, I was absolutely thrilled, but just like any other typical teenager, my next question was, "Has it come with any games, Miss?"

"It's meant for you to work on, Sonya", she chuckled, "but yes, don't worry, I'm sure there is plenty to have fun with too."

"Cool", I replied, now with my usual huge grin rapidly spreading from one ear to the other.

"Well", I taunted my friend, "at least SOMEONE must have been a good girl, but you're getting nothing."

At this, she just giggled and flicked her Boy George plaits in my face.

Shortly afterwards, it was coming up to lunchtime; the morning's mayhem was starting to die down and so I decided I'd better excuse myself from class, just giving me time to pop to the girls' bathroom to make myself look a little more presentable in readiness to attend my final assembly.

Now, for the first time since I had arrived at school, I found myself alone, so I decided to make my way at a very leisurely pace down the corridors, simply taking a little time to assemble a few thoughts and to build up some kind of lasting impression of Victoria School, the one which I knew would probably stay with me forever and I think, up until now, it has.

Most of the children were still busy doing whatever they had to do in their different classrooms and apart from hearing the occasional voice raising as I passed by, the main corridors were perfectly still and quiet and the only one who seemed to be going about their business was me. It was just me now, my only companions being my silent thoughts.

I began to feel almost as if I was floating along. It was as if I was in some kind of a dreamlike state, but maybe subconsciously, I was trying to make sense of the fact that all those classrooms, the playground, the bathrooms, the nurses' room and physiotherapy department, all of which had played such a major role in my world for so many long and happy years, had now very nearly fulfilled their pledge and in all truthfulness, even though I had never seemed to cease making my feelings felt about not wanting to attend school, today I somehow knew that the only memories I was going to be taking away from Victoria School, were all going to be, as they remain today, very, very happy ones.

Its children were known by everyone. Each one being renowned for their lovely sense of humour, their pleasant little jibes, their bravery and humility and their own continuing stories of courage and achievement, but as I look back to those days now, I feel that by far Victoria School's most enduring quality, which for me, just stands out as being the real jewel in its crown, was the children's love, mixed with their complete empathy and understanding for each other's disabilities...but somehow the formula adopted in the running of this school simply worked, and I'm sure to this day, the evidence continues to shine out for all to see.

My time as a little schoolgirl at Victoria, a very special school in Northfield, Birmingham, was at last, about to draw to its conclusion, - and what an experience it had been. However, it was almost time for my life to move in a new direction now, but as I hope the story of my schooldays has been able to convey, there was only one lesson my school failed to teach me and that was how to hold a celebration without style and my final assembly that afternoon was certainly not going to be the exception.

As on any other grand occasion, when at last everyone was settled, our hall was bursting at its seams again with staff and pupils alike and just before the headmaster arrived to deliver the opening message, I remember looking across at all those children and thinking, "Well, my schooldays may be done now, but wow, what a truly amazing and awesome journey it has turned out to be to have the honour of sharing my childhood with all these very special children."

I also have to admit that the majority of those boys and girls had also, in their own unique ways, contributed to giving me my fair share of cheeky pranks and practical jokes to deal with but, as I have tried to illustrate, I feel that one of the greatest strengths which I was able to draw from growing up in an environment like Victoria, was from those children's tremendous sense of courage, togetherness and comradeship.

Well, eventually all the children were settled in the hall and I was squeezed on the end of the row, sitting next to my best friend, which allowed me just enough visibility to see everyone from behind the piano and then the last person to come into the hall was the headmaster, armed with a few notes and some large important-looking envelopes.

"Good afternoon children", he began. "I can see that most of you are looking happy, as you will probably be looking forward to the holidays and I expect you have plenty of exciting things planned to keep you busy during the summer."

By this time, I think my concentration was already starting to waver: my hands became clammy, I would have done anything for a cup of pop and my eyes began to nervously skitter to and fro around the hall, as I continued to fill with a rising feeling of dread and anticipation, now in the awful knowledge that at any moment, the entire school's spotlight would be turned fully on me.

Starting from the other side of the hall from where I sat between my best friend and one other girl, I listened as the headmaster gradually drew nearer to giving a short talk about each of the school leavers, whilst also handing out our End Of School reports.

It is probably very difficult for me now to find suitable words, which adequately describe the tears and emotionally charged atmosphere that filled Victoria School's hall during my concluding half an hour of being a schoolchild. Of course, none of us knew what our futures would hold, but that day, as I have said, I had made my way to school, intending to leave an impression behind me or make a memorable impact. As my final day ended though and that last bell rang, for me, I think I knew that it was Victoria School that had made its tremendously rich and unforgettable impact on me. I had just witnessed and been a very small part of something amazing and also, given the complex problems that my Cerebral Palsy had presented, I don't believe I could have been educated anywhere better.

I can now wholeheartedly say to all the staff at Victoria School, "you knew what you were doing with me, didn't you? and I think you all got it right, and now, as the years seem to be speeding by even faster than I do in my electric wheelchair, I still feel that The Victoria School, in Northfield, Birmingham, was the best place of education for me and for that, I sincerely thank you all."

15

<u>Nothing Ventured – Nothing Gained</u>

Well as I'm sure my story has shown so far, probably in an abundance of colourful ways, my time at Victoria School had turned out to be quite an intriguing and epic journey and I think I have even surprised myself a little too, just in the sheer number and variety of childhood memories I have been able to share.

Just like for anyone else though, I knew I couldn't have continued attending school forever and my days at Victoria had finally drawn to an end and so gradually, in the months and years which were to follow, it was now time for me to start exploring the world in a slightly more adult capacity and I think my going away to residential college was to form my first real lesson in teaching me, exactly, what I was going to need.

First, however, it was time to chill and enjoy my hot summer break of 1984, so I thought the holiday would be put to best use by brushing up on my skills on my new **BBC Micro**. This probably sounds just a tad more impressive than it was, as although I did make some scanty attempt to work out how to set up the printer and practice using my new trackball, whilst trying to get to grips with all the other strange bits and pieces that came bundled with it, more honestly, I think I spent most days playing on its broad range of 8-bit arcade games.

Being one of the first computers to appear on the high street, the BBC Acorn machine represented the most hi-tech computing equipment of the time, almost overnight, seeming to debut as the popular new gadget to sweep the nation.

Very quickly, as you may imagine, reports of my **BBC** had been transmitted down the telephone again and soon my older cousin came on the line, excitedly relaying his urgent message, "Oh, tell Sonya not to worry, I'll soon come up and help her sort it out,...err...will tomorrow be ok, Auntie?...or have we got to go shopping again?...err... I'm free anytime; I presume it must have come with all the disks and instructions?"

"I thought he'd soon be coming to check it out", I sniggered but being honest, I was delighted that he was coming to help.

The **BBC** Micro, with its accompanying software packages and Welcome disk, was in comparison to today's technology, a very simple machine. In those days the most up-to-date computer monitors only had the capacity to display around 64,000 pixels, which resulted in the presentation of very crudely drawn images, their composition clearly visible as a simple culmination of moving coloured dots or pixels.

Simplicity aside, however, the old arcade-style games were still great fun and for the foreseeable future, just like the youngsters of today, I passed many happy hours bent over my keyboard engaged in games like Space Invaders, Pac-Man, Castle Quest, Killer Gorilla and many others, which I'm sure most 80's geeks will recall easily, with equal amounts of warm and fluffy nostalgia.

Of course, the computer was still only in its early infancy really, but it was during that summer, that I began to see that my new **BBC** wasn't just a source of fascination for me and my cousin either. All the other children in the family started to show an interest too and I found it a great joy to involve my young niece. I think she was coming up to three at this point and she always loved to perch at the side of my wheelchair and it posed me quite a challenge to try to decipher exactly which game she was requesting from her amusing little descriptions.

"Auntie, you know that game with the monkey who keeps rolling the footballs and...", she'd typically begin.

I would generally be able to guess at this point, that she was asking to play "Killer Gorilla", but right from those early beginnings, the one thing I have always loved best about using the computer is that it has provided me with a wonderful way to interact with my siblings and the family's children.

Just a few weeks later, however, this was all set to change as I was soon to become a college student, so I remember that I also began to spend time flicking through the glossy pages of my prospectus, trying to envisage what my new lifestyle at college was going to be all about.

I think I was also trying, to little avail, to gently coax Mom and Nan into the belief that everything was cool. Deep down, of course, I was aware that fleeing the nest for the very first time to attend residential college was about to pose my biggest challenge to date, involving a major lifestyle change, but I'd made up my mind and at least for some time to come, it still seemed a realistic option to plan to attain the qualifications necessary for me to pursue some kind of career within the secretarial or business field.

All too soon, my usual six-week, summer break was drawing to an and finally, it seemed that our long period of uncertainty and speculation was about to come to a head and so for the final few days, just like any other student who is about to go away to college or university, I assisted Mom to compile a list of all the things I was going to need.

"Err, have you bought me any pop, Mom?... and um... Is there any biscuits for if I get a bit peckish in my room?... I need to pack my radio as well, cos you know I'll be climbing the walls without my music. Well, that's about all I can think of now", I said, "but anyway, I'll be back at the weekend, so if I need anything else, we can just sort it out later", I continued.

If I'm honest, however, in a weird way, I think I was just hyper now and my mind was starting to work overtime, simply because of the sheer volume of essentials I seemed to need. I was feeling extremely jittery, my legs had turned to jelly, my speech was very unclear, my mouth felt as dry as sandpaper and I just became very tense, feeling generally fearful of what lay ahead.

For me, this was it now, and I've just remembered that my first day fell on a Sunday so that the new students could get settled into our rooms and get our bearings before the courses began.

Much like able-bodied students starting university, my first week at college was probably equivalent to what they regard as "Fresher's Week", comprising of a very busy, jammed-packed schedule of meeting people, attending various talks and workshops and generally learning about different college procedures whilst also trying to find my way around the campus. As new students, of course, it was also important to make appointments with the nurse and the onsite physiotherapist.

Just like at Victoria, at first glance the physio room appeared well-equipped, but I was relieved to see that, at least for now anyway, there didn't seem to be any obvious pieces of foam hanging around, although I felt that as I was booked in to see the senior physio, she was probably just trying to break me in gently.

The college complex itself was much larger than what I'd been used to at Victoria and I've never been much of a navigator so I think I decided that as long as I could find my way between my dormitory, the dining room and every girl's toilet en route, then at least for a start, this would have to do.

As I had requested earlier, I was pleased that I had been given my own, single bedroom. It wasn't overly big, although accessible and fit for purpose, simply containing my bed, a desk and a chair and the washbasin with the small, drawstring wardrobe sat opposite, allowing just enough vacant floor space to comfortably manoeuvre my wheelchair.

The overall size of the dormitory blocks seemed very spacious, although they each merely contained three main essentials: our individual study bedrooms, the carers' station and then a larger communal T.V. and sitting room. As you can imagine, during the day, the dormitories were seldom quiet with its constant surge of busy students and we would also get a fair number of able-bodied youngsters passing through too, coming from another F.E. college sharing the same campus and so, all in all, this gave rise to a very lively and busy atmosphere.

My first week seemed to go quite well but, as I had expected really, I found the experience very tiring and daunting and I slowly began to realise that I was now within this large unknown territory and from hereon in, I think I knew that I was either going to sink or swim. Right from the start, however, which I think has always been part of my nature, I decided it was important for me to try to make a good impression.

Soon, our new timetables were handed out and it didn't take me long to realise that, although I had maybe one or two free periods during the week, my regular working day was about three hours longer to what I'd been used to at school and it also seemed to comprise of a few different subjects too which, at this point, I'd never even heard of although, in due course, I knew I'd be enlightened.

My lifestyle at college had completely changed and my typical day now began at around 7 am, when the first indication I had that it was almost time to get up was usually announced by the light shining in from the corridor outside my room and this was quickly proceeded by the voices and hurried footsteps of several carers who had just arrived to start their daily duties of assisting everyone out of bed.

There was just about an hour to get washed and ready before the latest acceptable time when I could turn up for breakfast. Of course, there were always various nutritious options on offer, but just like in any other busy canteen, it made sense to get in the queue as early as possible so that the food was still freshly cooked and there was plenty of choice of where to sit.

Almost as soon as breakfast was done, the daily routine of lectures was set in motion and it wasn't uncommon for my first class to be held on the second floor but, before I could catch the lift, I'd often have to find one of the carers to push my computer trolley to my required destination and set it up for me.

The Business course on which I enrolled, as I soon began to learn, comprised of several different study areas. As expected, it provided the usual mix of maths, English and Computer Studies, as well as Human Biology, together with a few other subjects which seem to have escaped me now but, as its title suggests, the main aim of my course was to sufficiently develop my computer skills to either find employment with some kind of pre-existing company or alternatively, to embark upon developing a business enterprise of my own. At the time, I still felt that this may have been a reasonably plausible option for me, although I now feel that, with the benefit of later life experiences, my opinions on this subject have changed a little.

I can see now that I was still only seventeen and in those days, in terms of life experiences, some of my views were very young and probably still quite naive. As I have already outlined, I have always tended to be, naturally, quite a nervous person but, as my weeks at college unfolded, I don't think I had the first clue of the levels of both the physical and mental pressures I was soon to find myself under.

Once more, (and I know that now and again I am finding myself straying back to the topic), my journey at residential college seemed like, quite a marked example of how I have had to learn to manage my problems, by trying to strike the right balance. However, have you ever come across a stereotypical, sensitive young teen furnished with enough maturity and emotional depth to understand that one? I really don't think I have and at that age, I know that this description didn't fit me either.

During my time spent in the classroom, I think I was probably giving the overall impression, at least to begin with, that everything was fine and just like everyone else, I had everything ticking along nicely well, perhaps I did get half of that statement right, because it was definitely "ticking", it was just that, inside me, I knew that everything was starting to "tick" like an unexploded bomb.

Probably regretfully in some ways, I found that my course was soon spiralling quite erratically and uncontrollably beyond anything I had dealt with before and the speed of this downward spiral was now just becoming too much.

In general terms, I think I can conclude that quite a large chunk of the problems which I found myself experiencing, were probably attributed to what I can only describe as a rather confusing blend of embarrassment, my poor communication skills and, as has always been a typical trait in my nature, I also began to feel that all my arduous efforts in trying to keep on top of my work were simply failing and I felt I was unbearably letting people down.

Whilst I was going about my daytime lessons, or at least to begin with, the onset of my problems probably went undetected by the teachers, as I was either spending most of the time working silently on my computer, or I was able to contribute quite efficiently to open class discussions.

This was all that was needed, however, for me to primarily create the illusion that everything was fine and I was coping far better than I was, but unfortunately, in reality, this wasn't the case at all as I can now see that many of my problems were initially ensuing within the privacy of my study bedroom.

After my evening meal in the canteen, which would generally finish somewhere around the region of 6 p.m., I'd set off again, making the short journey to reach my room and at this point, I could just about manage to scramble my key into the lock, gaining entrance.

On many days, unless I'd nipped back for a drink break, or to drop off or collect some additional equipment, this would often be the first time I'd been back to my room all day and its usual appearance can only be described as a typical, student bombsite.

It was customary, however, to observe that at some point during the day, the carers had been in to carry out general bed-making and cleaning duties but, only being a small space, it was vital to keep everything within easy reach, so I guess, as most students may agree, some of the mess was just necessary and functional.

My working day of lectures had seemed never-ending, but I was now beginning to see that if I was going to succeed and be able to make a serious and constructive go of my course, I knew that I was going to have to get through my ever-increasing workload, but how I was actually going to do this, I simply didn't know, in fact, even now, I am inwardly starting to cringe at my choice of wording here, because the plain and simple fact was, it was becoming clearer to me with each passing day that my pile of awaiting assignments was growing, never shrinking. I felt that the course simply seemed to contain too many subjects and at times I felt that my room and indeed, almost my whole existence was just totally swamped in paperwork and for the first time, I felt that my course was breaking me.

The number of subjects and the sheer level of work involved soon proved too great for me and as my story clearly explains, I think I was spending too much time trying to give the impression that I was coping with daily college life, when I simply wasn't.

Here, I think I can slightly relate to how Mom has described all those monotonous feeding routines she went through when I was a baby. When I briefly mentioned this slight correlation to her, Mom could relate in some way to what I meant but she also wisely pointed out that her feeding me was a labour of love: my labour of trying to complete all my college assignments was just draining.

Typically, I would come right back from my evening meal and almost as soon as I'd hung my coat up, my resolute conscience would kick in again and instead of being able to unwind and relax, I would immediately reboot my computer and try to grab the first piece of coursework I could lay my hands to, sometimes totally irrespective of when it was due to be handed in.

Abstractly similar to listening to the constant drip of a leaky tap, I was becoming increasingly aware that both the physical and psychological constraints imposed upon me by my Cerebral Palsy were just being pushed to their absolute limits but, if I had been given the same tasks within an environment like Victoria School, just in smaller, more manageable increments, then I'm sure I would have found some of the work easy.

As you have probably guessed, just after a short time, I could see that I wasn't going to be able to settle into life at residential college. I felt constantly agitated and forgetful, as on most nights I was suffering from sleep deprivation or insomnia because it just became impossible for me to relax as I felt responsible not only for producing my work and handing it in on time but also, for my medication and my personal needs.

Just to briefly summarize, as I look back at that time now, I can see that I needed more support in various areas, but I was still only a child really and I couldn't and didn't know how to explain or how to put this into a rational context because, at this point, I think my stress levels were beyond salvage and consequently after what may have seemed like only a short time, I made the decision to leave and return home to my family.

I can understand that this decision was probably a disappointment, not only for the college staff but for my schoolteachers too, as they had all placed so much faith in me although, looking on the bright side, albeit only a brief encounter, I think my journey to residential college had still provided me with different life experiences and perhaps it did go a little way in fuelling the independent opinions which still motivate me today.

However, as I think this tale shows in abundance, I am a family girl at heart. I love the bones of my folks and anyway, almost as soon as I returned home, my little niece was waiting for me again and giggling, she said, "Come on Auntie, where have you been?, can I have another game please?" and just as I had always been promised, the main thing which was waiting for me upon my return was, as ever, an abundance of love, but my next question was, of course, "Well, what am I to do next then, Mom?" and her response to this was just as I'd expected: she came to me with loving, outstretched arms and I instinctively knew, that next, it was time to give Mom a well-deserved cuddle.

Upon my reading this chapter through, I have just had what is, I think, one final, but extremely important thought. As explained, I was only seventeen, still young and naive when all this occurred and just like any teenager, let alone one with my level of physical problems, fleeing the nest for the first time was all a bit of a culture shock and of course, I didn't know what to expect.

I think this experience is also of great testimony to the fact that, just like anyone else, disabled people are still, all very different individuals. We each present our own unique mix of personalities, needs, abilities, strengths and weaknesses. In particular, when accompanied by severe speech problems and the resulting levels of frustration this can produce, it is sometimes virtually impossible to find a suitable solution. The only option here is to simply think of it as just another experience and try once more to resume a calmer and much more peaceful way of life and simply to relieve my stress. At least I tried, however.

16

Coming Of Age In Dudley

My memory of awakening in my own bed on the first morning following leaving residential college will forever remain a very poignant one as I just felt awash with a crisp stillness and a silent sense of calm. I was neither aware of the day nor time, but bright sunlight now slanted through my golden curtains, clearly indicating, it was time to get up.

I started to re-adjust my duvet and I noted that it was almost noon on my alarm clock, so I guessed that Mom had probably crept in and out of my room by now, just waiting until I was ready to start a fresh day.

However, it wasn't long before recollections of my current situation came flooding back to me and, as I lay in the quietness of my room, the question of just what I was going to do with the rest of my life, now seemed to dominate my thoughts.

I also began to ruminate that, living in the close community in which I did, I knew it was imminent that soon my unannounced return would have been noted by all but, looking on the bright side, (well presuming that a bright side existed, discounting that blinding shaft of sunlight which was rapidly beginning to annoy me), at least all those inevitable questions regarding my sorry state of affairs would only have to circulate once, so the sooner the news was out, the better and with this resolute thought in place, I decided that I might as well arise.

I simply felt deflated now, agonizingly conscious that, from hereon in, for the foreseeable future, each conversation was going to turn to why things hadn't worked out for me and all I wanted to do was to forget the whole sorry episode. I felt sick.

My future was hanging in the balance now and it seemed that life was just in limbo. It was pretty apparent that I couldn't just return to school and, right now, this was the last thing that I wanted anyway, inflating my humiliation and sense of failure even more, but what was there left in store for me now? I just felt that my life was just one big fat disaster zone and I wished I could simply go back to sleep like some fairytale character, disappearing into oblivion in a puff of smoke.

Thankfully, the lively outside interest of my sudden return was only short-lived, soon dying down, so after a while things began to return to some resemblance of normality.

As time ticked by, I started to relax, feeling a little more at ease with life. It was becoming clear that sitting around moping all day or fooling around on computer games, was neither going to accomplish much nor did it seem to be doing anything to replenish my rapidly depleting self-esteem. I could now see the need to do something with a little more purpose and so eventually, I concluded that my most logical next step seemed to be to attempt to build up my amateur word processing skills. It was obvious that the days of producing my letters on the typewriter had come to a natural end and that my computer had now taken its place as the most important communication aid of the future. I noticed that there were still a few dusty old typewriting manuals stored on the large dark oak bookcase, so I decided that, maybe, this would be the best place to begin.

From hereon in, I started to spend most of my time industriously copying out letters, memo forms, menus, invoices, neatly arranged tabulated columns and anything else that I felt may teach me more about the complex editing procedures of Wordwise. I probably showed greater patience in this pursuit than most but, after a while, this task was becoming extremely tiresome again and my initial fortitude was soon plummeting into a rapid decline.

During the day, of course, my sisters were both either out at work or school, so I had no-one in my age group to interact with and although my stress levels had now been greatly reduced, I was showing the first tinge of heading toward the next monotonous cycle, this time one of just lamenting desperately for Mom to take me out somewhere, anywhere, simply to immerse myself in some new activity as, at this stage, the days had long since passed when Mom could march me along the garden wall or shut me up with a soggy stick of rhubarb and a saucer of sugar but I still needed something else to do.

On many occasions, we would often end up taking a shopping trip into Dudley and it was during these excursions that I later began to accumulate my colourful assortment of books and magazines, featuring programming techniques written in BBC Basic and so I began to pass many hours industriously keying in reams of strange-looking data, most of which I hadn't the foggiest notion of what it meant.

In fact, for many young geeky types, this now became a very popular interest and, for me, my computer programming endeavours even became a hypnotic replacement for the constant click-clacking of my tired, old Rubik's cube.

Like most of my addictive pastimes, it would often take me virtually a whole day just to key in one game but eventually the moment of redemption would finally dawn, when it was at last time to input the word RUN and I would hold my breath, squeezing my eyes tightly shut, as I knew that the next time I looked, my screen would either be displaying a workable jolly-looking computer game which would keep me entertained for the remainder of the day or just a two-tone soft copy of mindless error messages.

I think my dad began to develop an interest in the computing field too, although he had more of a tendency to use his computer for work purposes than gaming. It seemed that Dad was quite amused by my programming efforts and he would often peer over my shoulder to see what I was up to then saunter back to his armchair, chuckling.

By this time, however, it seemed that Mom was beginning to recognise that I needed something more in my life. I wasn't complaining, or making a bother about my situation but I was still only just turned seventeen and I had no friends in my own age group, so Mom said it was only a matter of time before I became bored again.

Just as I always have been, I was still dead against becoming involved in the local centre, which just catered for mentally handicapped people, so Mom's next move was to telephone the Careers Officer again to see if he could suggest anything else.

However embarrassing this seemed the only logical step left for us to take now if there was still a slim chance of kick-starting my future in some new and positive direction.

Anyway, an appointment was set up to take place at 1:30 p.m. on the following afternoon so I felt that, at least after the initial phone call, the wheels of change had been set in motion again and whatever was in store for me now would probably be better than simply continuing in my current situation. At the time, I don't think this experience would quite have made it onto my most cherished memories list, but it seemed that the first move had been made and, although after our meeting I still felt none too hopeful, my careers advisor went away promising to make a few enquiries.

It turned out, however, that a far more optimistic horizon than I ever could have wished for was about to stretch out before me as he had soon discovered that Dudley College had recently opened a Special Needs division: he informed us that he had spoken to the Head of the department, who had said that I would be very welcome to attend their computer group but what I didn't realise back then was that this one little decision was about to transform my life and I was about to make some lovely friendships, many of which would flourish into several decades and beyond.

Yes indeed, what a terrific breakthrough that was and without further ado, the man in charge of the course arranged to come to meet me. He was a very friendly guy, quietly spoken and smartly dressed but right from the start he seemed filled with encouragement and I probably gave a sly, sideways smile at Mom, as I was thinking, "I'm gonna be alright now phew!"

Little did I know back then, however, that in one capacity or another, I was about to embark upon a mammoth twenty four year relationship with those guys at Dudley, in fact, my student life here seemed to last longer than most marriages.

Well, at first, it seemed like unknown territory although I must admit that I was somewhat chuffed that I was now a student at Dudley College. Many years earlier both Mom and my auntie had trained for their prospective careers at Dudley College, so it seemed a little strange that, for the first time, I would be following in the family's footsteps.

At the time, the college was just running a small class for youngsters with Learning Disabilities and I can recall that on my very first day, the course tutor introduced me to the first two carers, an extremely cheery male and female duo and then he suggested that, maybe, due to my speech problems, the best way to settle me in, acting as a suitable icebreaker, would be for the young man to get to know me a little more by holding a conversation with me via the word processor.

"That sounds good to me", I thought, probably flashing him a nervous smile.

And so, after awkwardly positioning my wheelchair at the desk, we tentatively started to get some dialogue underway, kicking off as usual, with the full repertoire of cheesy comments which as far as I remember, probably went something like this:

Him: "Hi, how are you?"

Me: "Fine thanks, are you ok?"

Him: "Yes, I'm good thank you. So, what are you into, then?"

Me: "Well, err, I like pop music, animals, and watching T.V."

Him: "Let me guess", he chuckled, "I bet you're a typical woman and you're into all the soaps".

Me: "I can't miss Corrie", I replied, "and I occasionally watch EastEnders too, cos I like the dogs."

"Oh my god", I thought, "That sounded really stupid."

Anyway, this tentative exchange probably continued for five minutes or so and then a notion suddenly came crashing down on me. Oh no, I have a feeling that this guy thinks I'm completely mute. He thinks I can't talk at all, but on second thoughts, I contemplated, this could turn out to be my big moment here and really funny, so I decided to show the cheeky side of my character and I bellowed, in my loudest and most articulate voice possible, "OI, I CAN TALK YA KNOW!"

Well, I think that was it, I'd made my mark again. He almost fell off his chair in a heap of laughter and shock but that was, without doubt, the first defining Dudley College moment for me as all my nerves and apprehension just slipped away, only to be replaced by a lovely feeling that I'd not only made the right decision, but I was now in the midst of some really great friends and although I don't think they fully realised it at that point, for many years to come, I was now to become a permanent fixture and life in their Special Needs Section was never going to be quite the same again.

Eventually, we managed to control our giggles and our chitchat via the word processor resumed and by this time some of the other students began to gather round to join in with our conversation too.

"Do you have any pets?" one young girl shyly asked.

"Err, not currently, but I used to have two guinea pigs and a tortoise."

"What kind of music do you like?"

"Well, I like most popular music, but I'm very partial to a bit of reggae", I inputted.

By the end of that first afternoon, I felt really relaxed and comfortable. I didn't quite know what to expect next, or if, in fact, I was going to be expelled for causing too much disruption in class.

Thankfully though, this was not the case at all. This was merely the beginning and as time passed, I was soon addressed by most of the staff as, "a perpetual student" and it was here where I had the very great privilege of working with some of the dearest friends I've ever met it's just a shame their names seem to have slipped my memory (ha-ha!) but let's start from the beginning.

Well for a while, everyone seemed in mutual agreement that, at least to settle in, it would be the best idea for me to continue to build on my word processing skills and so, much like I'd been doing at home, they soon issued me with my first worksheets to practice my document editing skills.

Almost straight away, I began to feel that Dudley seemed to have such a lovely atmosphere in which to work and I found that I began to enjoy learning and making new friends again.

At this point, at least in terms of spending time at college, I settled in well. The experience of joining Dudley College and having the opportunity to meet new friends seemed to have fallen at exactly the right time for me and, placing my faith in the Lord, (which at times, is about the only thing you can do), in view of the desperately sad and vile personal tragedy which was set to unfold just a few months later, then I think the best thing I can do, is to believe that Jesus now provided me with the stabilising effect of Dudley College to get me through (that is presuming you hold the belief that it is always possible to get through). I'm honestly not sure I am.

In March 1985, (despite being totally against my family's wishes), my auntie was persuaded by a group of supposedly trained professionals, who were said to be experts in the care of patients suffering with M.S., to attend a week's respite care and much to our very grave regret, unfortunately, Auntie agreed to comply. Knowing her nature as we did, however, she wouldn't have really chosen to attend but Auntie was renowned for being a very docile, lovely girl and regretfully, much like many other vulnerable disabled people, she always very typically, considered the needs of others in preference to her own, and so she went.

Just one week later, (as up until this point, no-one had either contacted my family or telephoned a qualified doctor to express any need for concern), Auntie's husband went to collect her and upon arrival, he could plainly see that she was very ill and he knew that there was something very wrong.

He decided to bring her home and then he telephoned Nan and the family G.P. Auntie was diagnosed with a very acute and advanced case of pneumonia. She was admitted into hospital, but sadly, despite all arduous efforts, at that late stage, there was nothing that the use of appropriate drugs or the correct medical care could do.

With great sadness, just a few hours later, she lost her brave battle for life and she now rests peacefully in the gentle arms of Jesus.

Much the same as the events which had taken place when I was born, it seemed that now, my auntie, another member of my family, had clearly been denied suitable medical treatment and yet again, Auntie's needs had been seriously misinterpreted as she had become far too ill to deal with this herself.

As I guess it is for anyone who decides to write such a personal story like this and also for those many people out there who, just like us, have gone through such an abhorrent and tragic loss, it now seems virtually impossible for me to pluck out suitable words from my dictionary or thesaurus which could adequately describe how my family and I were feeling when this news began to circulate. It was such a shock - such a sickening and gut-wrenching kick in the teeth but, at least for me, I think about the only thing I can offer here, is just to say that this single event seemed to symbolise the end of my very happy childhood.

However, of course, I'm sure my family would agree, still exercising my strong Christian faith, with which I have always been brought up, then maybe it is true that if a new life on earth is a gift from God, then perhaps the true gift which perhaps I should try a little harder to understand, is just that, despite her many struggles, Auntie was just a great maker of happiness. She was quite simply renowned for being a true ambassador of joy because if there was nothing much going on which struck me as being particularly funny, I'd only have to look across to my auntie, holding her gaze for less than five seconds and, oh boy, was the world a funny place. I didn't even know at times, what we were supposed to be chuckling at but I think those special moments just signify both love and joy in their purest form and I just know that this is something which will stay with me forever.

God bless you and I love you, my dear Auntie.

∞ ∞ ∞ ∞ ∞ ∞

As you may imagine, it seemed even more important now to immerse myself in college life and just a few weeks later, my course tutor said I was making real progress so he suggested that maybe I would like to increase my hours, joining in with the additional class held on Friday afternoons.

Forgive me if I'm wrong here, but I think, these end-of-week sessions took place in a slightly different location as I remember that, back then, the Special Needs students were spread out a little, occupying about two or three classrooms on B Floor.   In fact, while I'm in this location, I think it was in this particular stretch of corridor, where my course tutor later requested me to repeatedly drive my wheelchair up and down, strutting my stuff in front of some T.V. camera guy.   Luckily, I don't think the footage was ever aired although, looking back, whilst at Dudley, from time to time I think I seemed to make quite an impression.

Anyway, it was now that I had access to the college's large, computer network, allowing me to sample a much wider variety of software, most of which was geared towards improving my skills in basic maths and English.

The Special Needs section was a lovely, friendly atmosphere in which to work and, particularly so during the next few weeks, I think having the opportunity to make new friends, having somewhere different to go and just being able to immerse myself in my course seemed to really help, during what was, of course, a time of great personal sadness.

The weeks jogged steadily on again and for quite a while I continued to divide my time equally between practising my word processing and using the programs stored on the network. I was now settled into a good work pattern and at last my new teachers seemed to understand just what I needed.

Soon I reached my next significant milestone and I celebrated my 18th birthday.

Turning eighteen, which is commonly perceived to be the first step into adulthood, did, at the time feel like quite an achievement for me and Mom and my grandparents were all in general agreement that it should be marked in some special way, so I suggested that perhaps, it would be rather nice to hold a party.

At this point in proceedings, I think that maybe it was good to have something positive to aim for, which may, in some kind of haphazard way, assist to boost morale. The show must go on, or at least, for now, attempt to.

On the day of my birthday, however, my older cousin was still away, studying at St. Andrew's University, in Scotland, so I pointed out indignantly, "Yes, I'd love to hold a disco or something. Maybe I could invite some of the staff from college too, but", I concluded, "it's a lovely idea, although any celebration on a major scale will just have to be postponed for a few weeks, as it would be simply unthinkable to go ahead without my big cousin being here and anyway", I added, "this won't matter to me as it will just prolong the fun."

I decided that this should be a party to remember, and I would feel like The Queen, hosting a double celebration, enjoying two birthdays for the price of one. I spent the remainder of the day going around wearing a big smile, as I felt that this revelation sounded pretty cool.

One of the first things I can recall about my eighteenth birthday, just as if it had been yesterday, is sitting by our big, oak dining table, where Mom had arranged my lovely selection of gifts. The collection included a cute purple and white teddy bear from Mom, some musical silver keys and I think someone had bought me a pretty keepsake of an imitation champagne glass too. As I quietly sat by the table surveying all my gifts, I just remember a lovely feeling of just how lucky I was. However this wasn't just because of my presents, despite the knowledge, of course, that they had all been purchased and given with love, I just felt lucky to have been so loved, wanted and encouraged and I knew that the Lord couldn't have blessed me with a kinder and more loving family.

As you can imagine I had an enjoyable day, but as soon as it was over, of course, it was time to call on the help of the family again, this time to make plans for my big, birthday party and with Mom, Nan and Granddad on board, somehow I just knew that whatever happened, this was going to be a night to remember and when at last my big night arrived, I can wholeheartedly impart, that this is exactly what it turned out to be.

One Friday evening, just after my cousin's return for his summer vacation, it was Disco Time and so with everyone piled into three cars, we all headed off to a local hotel. This was the second time that day we'd made this short trip, as Mom and Nan hadn't stopped since early morning as they had been so busy preparing the lovely, evening buffet. If there's anyone still out there who remembers being on my guest list, then I'm sure they will have to agree that the real show stopper though sitting at the head of the buffet and stealing the whole show, was my beautiful birthday cake. It was all white, delicately swirled in pink, fondant icing roses, being crowned by a doll, dressed in a white, feather skirt.

Right till this day I still clearly recall a great sense of pride and the feeling of butterflies in my stomach, at being approached all evening and asked where we had purchased my cake. It seemed the common conclusion that it had been designed at a local patisserie. I was very proud to impart, however, that it was not professionally made. It had been crafted by the most specialized sugar-crafting genius in the business, personally known to me as, Mom.

Just like me, I think my party guests were all, more than a bit impressed. Well done Mom, you did me proud, again.

As usual, of course, Nan and Granddad both enjoyed playing their special roles in all the fun too. During the last few days running up to my disco, my grandparents' house had been another great hive of industry with Nan cooking and compiling her fantastic lists of everything we may need for the buffet: she baked lots of sausage rolls, perfected mounds of butter and cucumber curls, baked and filled vol-au-vent cases;

she produced plates of cling-film covered sandwiches, also cutting a mound of Granddad's home-grown tomatoes into flower shapes. Granddad meanwhile set to work in his shed again, this time covering pieces of plywood in velvet, ready to use as the base for the flower table decorations, superbly arranged by both Mom and Nan.

I don't mean to sound boastful here, but it was just tremendous and really touching to share with so many people, all that my family had achieved and done for me.

Soon it was 6:50 pm; my guests were due to start arriving in ten minutes so I found the perfect activity to keep my little sister busy. I employed her to kneel beside me helping me to receive my presents, safely packing them away into bin bags. Mom and I had agreed on the previous day that this seemed like the best plan, not only minimising the risk of delicate breakages, but it would be easier for me to unwrap everything at leisure, on the following day. After saying my Hello's, I then pointed them in the direction of Granddad, who was stood at the bar, bearing his usual big smile, as he had very kindly offered to buy everyone their first round of drinks.

And so my party was at last set in motion. It was a really lovely atmosphere: I think in the end I amassed something like 150 to 200 guests, Mom had hired a DJ and the function room was trimmed beautifully with clumps of 18th birthday balloons and trailing overhead streamers.

I scanned the room: it seemed as if each of the alcoves and seats placed around the perimeter of the dance floor were all pretty much filled now, everyone appeared to be happy and chatting, so I decided that this was probably as good a time as any to ask Mom to take me to the Ladies' to freshen up a little.

Well, I was just pausing for a minute in front of the bathroom mirror, asking Mom if my hairdo still looked O.K., when my older sister came hurtling through the door.

"Hurry up Sonya, get a move on", she yelled, "the last guest has just arrived."

"What, well who is it?" I asked, now feeling more than a little perplexed. I'd already greeted everyone who'd been invited and I started to mentally run through my guest list: everyone was here as far as I knew.

"My cousins are here, my two, school friends, the neighbours from over the road and everyone's here from college...in fact, my course tutor was the first one to arrive...surely it's not some stupid, drunken gatecrasher". I simply couldn't fathom out who was missing. It was beyond me.

It was all very perplexing, but as time went on, judging by the rising excitement and obvious stifled hilarity on my sister's face, it didn't take too much longer for the penny to drop. Something ridiculous and completely outlandish was about to unfurl.

"O.K. Mom", I said wryly, "what's going on, what...?"

There was no time for Mom to formulate a reply, however, as I continued to be marshalled into the centre of the room. My guests all became upstanding, gathering around and the next thing I knew...I was being attacked...by some mad guy dressed in a gorilla suit.

Yes, it appeared that I'd finally been completely stitched up, but I have to say in all honesty, that my Gorilla Gram just encapsulated and became the true highlight of what had turned out to be a really terrific night.

After my granddad and a few more of my guests had finished off the films in their cameras, the gorilla completed his final circuit, running riot and generally harassing everyone, but what a brilliant surprise that was. I think I'd probably spent most of my first eighteen years of life always wanting to play the prankster, constantly taunting people that, one day I was going to get them, but I think I can safely conclude that on that very special and lovely night, it was Mom and my family who had finally and so expertly, got me.

My only great sadness was that Auntie couldn't have still been around to enjoy my party. However, I know she is still looking down on me and will forever remain at my side in love and spirit and knowing her cheeky sense of humour as I did, she was probably doing her best to egg that gorilla on too.

And so, in terms of joining Dudley College, all the signs were good now. I'd been greeted with a very warm reception and the folks working in the Special Needs Section were all really nice guys.

However, little did I know at this point, there was another terrific trio still concealed just around the next corner and when they came along to join the mix, my time at Dudley College was about to soar from one great success to another.

17

Cooking Up A Storm

Right, where was I? Erm...I was just enjoying a bacon and egg sandwich for lunch, but, while I'm on the subject of food, perhaps I should introduce you to the next addition to Special Needs, who was about to become another of my main teachers.

Well, I think it must have been, roughly around mid 1985 by now and one day, my course tutor suggested that perhaps it would be a good time to introduce me to one or two more subjects and although I cannot be perfectly sure of the exact order in which the following events unfolded, one of the next classes to appeal to my fickle taste, was the Tuesday morning cookery class.

I remember that when I first joined, this class was situated right next to the hairdressing department so each week Mom and I would have to take the lift up a level, arriving on C Floor.

It was here I met a very friendly lady who, in no time at all, seemed to have me completely sussed. Try as I might, however, it became screamingly clear right from the start that I wasn't going to get away with anything with this one, not even my washing up. Ugh, what would she cook up for me next? Mmm...well there was certainly one thing I could be sure of, I still had plenty of hard work before me and with a determination like hers leading the way, I don't think anything could have saved me now.

As I was soon to discover though, the business of splashing soap suds around the cookery room was merely the tip of the iceberg. My new teacher showed a wonderful enthusiasm, being forever ready to embrace a new challenge, (and for her, the more mischief she could dish up, the better).

Well much like her predecessors who had taught me at Victoria School, my cookery teacher was always very keen to egg me on and it wasn't long before she too had hatched her own favourite little catchphrase, especially geared to encourage me to use my hands, "Come on Sonya", she'd say, "get those motor skills working" and although I'd heard the term used before, since then, the mere mention of "motor skills" always reminds me particularly of attending her cookery sessions.

However, probably during my first hour of joining her class, it became plain to see, that our shared passion to overcome my difficulties in the preparation of food, was simply about to become the next great recipe for success.

By a strange coincidence, it just happened that the modern kitchen gadget to be gradually making an appearance into most households was the microwave oven.

Straight away, the microwave proved very convenient for me, providing a far safer cooking method than using a conventional oven. Its easy-to-use control panel and large push-buttons were ideal to operate and it had the added advantage of being able to be sited at an ideal wheelchair height.

Despite all these great benefits though, this is still "ME" I am talking about and as usual, in no time at all, I presented my new teacher with another sticky situation. It appeared that, although the microwave's controls suited me, still only having the capacity to do everything one-handed, I was finding it impossible to transfer my dishes in and out of the oven and all my ardent efforts could easily result in emptying the entire contents of my dish either on the floor or into my lap. Did my teacher really know what she was taking on board when she had agreed to teach me? Somehow, I don't think so.

I was lucky, however, in that this minor setback came to fruition at the start of a new academic year and soon, a young lady who had recently embarked upon a course in Craft, Design and Technology came to visit our department, intending to invent a new aid to make life easier for a disabled person. My teacher swiftly delegated me as the perfect candidate.

Over the next few weeks she came to observe me at my work and through a general process of experimentation and discussion, she concluded that the best thing for it seemed to be to design some kind of new cookery table for me, so together we started to discuss different ideas to devise a feasible plan.

We agreed that the actual problem, in its simplest form, was my inability to raise my dish to the height of the microwave's turntable and so this task ideally needed to be broken down into two, separate actions as opposed to just one:-

a)   To elevate my dish to the desired level

and

b)   To push my dish into the oven

In relation to my time at Victoria, this is a typical example of the well-devised practices I was taught in Peto.

Anyway, after compiling a great wad of notes and rough sketches, the young girl returned to her workshop to set the process in motion, transforming her ideas into the real thing.

Just a few weeks later she returned with the exciting message that, although my new desk still required sanding, plus a few other minor jobs to fix it together properly, the overall design was now completed, so she invited me to view it for the first time.

The sheer level of thought and skill which she had invested into this project still amazes me, but, in the end, she managed to come up with an excellent notion which, with a little more practice and fine-tuning on my part, solved my problem superbly.

She'd built a very basic, large wooden table, probably of a similar style and proportion to a modern computer desk but, most importantly, fulfilling its intended design brief. It also featured a small, rectangular cut-out section, positioned at the front of the desk.

As most people have probably already guessed, this was to be used as the lifting mechanism and could be alternatively raised or lowered with a long piece of dowelling, fixed securely underneath the desktop. In addition to this, of course, when the front section of the desk was raised, it then needed to be locked into the "up" position, so finally there were also two extra planks of timber attached to the underside of the work surface, where I could rest the dowelling pole, hence maintaining the lift.

The end product was superb and it was another great learning process simply to oversee and contribute a few thoughts to its final design. As I have mentioned before, I've always loved anything involving arts and crafts and I find it forever fascinating to seek out new and creative ways to promote my independence.

Time moved on and my teacher delegated me the task of hunting out my own recipes. Unfortunately, however, the Internet still wasn't generally available, (or, not to me anyway) and so I still had to depend upon the somewhat old-fashioned and tedious task of thumbing through Mom's recipe books in search of new and interesting dishes.

My teacher also suggested that it seemed sensible to aim to select ingredients which I could easily blend in the food processor. Looking back, when it came to brandishing sticky wooden spoons around, my teacher seemed to yield little faith in me, although I can't think why.

In addition, the college obtained a mail-order catalogue, marketing a practical range of utensils and kitchen equipment, intended for people with poor hand grip. During my time at college we amassed quite an interesting collection but I recall feeling a pang of excitement when I had taken the big bread knife as I'd take a silent glance around me, secretly thinking, "Right, nobody had better dare upset me now." Its size wasn't dissimilar to a regular knife really, but its only difference was that its handle was set at a right angle to the blade, to facilitate an easy grip.

I had a great time in cookery, (well, more or less), that is, if you can overlook the small, humiliating detail, (acutely to my sheer dismay), that as time went on, one of the young lads who suffered from learning difficulties, seemed to take quite a shine to me. Alas for him, however, although I found his love-struck infatuation somewhat endearing, I don't think his feelings were mutual and as my morning progressed, I think my rising crescendo of rebuffs would steadily progress from my subtle, polite little hint of, "Please could you move back a little more, cos I'm very busy and I'd hate to run my wheelchair over your toes", right up to my intense, nostril-flaring, through-my-teeth screech of "Right, I won't tell you again. If I find you behind my chair just once more, I am seriously going to run you over".

He would then offer his very droll comeback of something like, "What are you making?", or, "You're wearing a very pretty jumper today, Sonya", at which point my hardened heart would just melt again and I would just spend the remainder of my lesson overwhelmed with a lethal mixture of guilt, sympathy and bubbling fury. He did it every time though, the little monkey.

Well, I think I will save a few more tales from my college days for later, as moving a little closer to home, it was in the spring of 1988 that my family and I had the opportunity to move into our first bungalow. Looking back, although my childhood home was located in a very nice area, it had always proved quite difficult to manage my wheelchair on such a steep hill and as time ticked on, I think my mobility needs were becoming more of a strain and particularly as Mom was still transporting me in an estate car, the business of transferring me in and out of the front passenger seat was now becoming particularly hazardous.

For anyone who has ever found themselves in a similar situation, I'm sure you will have learnt, as we soon did, that wheelchair accessible bungalows are extremely difficult to find, so after reaching the decision that our need to relocate seemed to be becoming more urgent, we decided to drive around the whole area, to see if we could find any new building work or anywhere more suitable.

It seems that this period of our lives was another of uncertainty, as particularly within the Dudley borough, quite a substantial number of disabled people in my age group, had, at least, some ability to walk and so they didn't require the perfectly flat wheelchair access. Also, as a result of my many years of experience in travelling around in taxis and buses, picking disabled people up, I had amassed quite a good knowledge of exactly where most of these bungalows were located, but of course, they were highly sought after.

Several months passed by and our search was fruitless and then one day we discovered that in Halesowen, a little town just a few miles from us, a block of low-rise flats were being refurbished: some being modernised, whilst others were demolished but, as luck would have it, we learnt that the plot was going to site just one disabled bungalow.

We only needed one, we could hardly believe our good fortune, almost doing cartwheels with joy. It was just amazing and we felt that once again, the Lord had recognised and met our need. We would still require someone to speak for us though, so as soon as we returned home, it was agreed that our best course of action seemed to be to compose a letter to Scope, requesting them to support our application.

One of their representatives came out to visit us and, upon observing my problems, they kindly offered to help without hesitation and only after a few short weeks, we heard that our application had been accepted and upon completion of the building work, this beautiful, purpose-built bungalow was going to be our new home.

We still had quite a wait though before it was all finalised and ready to move into and I remember the feeling of anticipated excitement, as we would drive over to see it monitoring its ongoing progress, dreaming of how we were going to arrange our things and fill the new garden and back patio. Perhaps it could feature an ornate bench and there would be loads of room for pretty plant pots. Right from the start, Mom decided the fence at the back would be ideal to grow some conifers and maybe Granddad would be able to fix up a trellis to support some sweet peas and trailing ivy. Now with the looming prospect of a lovely new start, I think Mom's creative imagination began to work overtime.

Our bungalow was situated in the perfect spot. Its surrounding pavements were very flat, being ideal for wheelchair users and we would only need to cross two busy roads at the end of our street to reach a lovely, modern indoor shopping precinct.

Finally, after what had seemed like an eternity, Mom received a phone call to say that the agreed work and special adaptations for me had almost reached completion and so the family came around to assist us to pack all our personal belongings into boxes, as we excitedly prepared for our big moving day.

Up until this point, of course, I had always dwelt in a house, so I have a very distinctive memory that, as soon as we moved in, I immediately found a new sense of freedom which I had never experienced before as, for the first time, it was amazing to suddenly have access to every room, even being able to fetch anything I wanted from my bedroom. At first, I just felt like I'd moved into my own private hotel. If there are any disabled people out there reading this memoir, perhaps with similar problems to me, then I'm sure they will wholeheartedly know what I mean when I say it is the ability to perform the smallest and most meagre of everyday tasks independently that really mean such a lot to people like us.

Anyway, it wasn't long after moving in, when one afternoon, we received a telephone call from one of Mom's friends who was living close by. She past on the news that someone she knew had a black cat which had recently given birth to a large litter of kittens. The mother cat and babies were all fine, but the owner couldn't possibly house them all. The prospective cost of vet's bills, cat baskets, litter trays and tins of salmon could potentially leave the poor woman penniless, so Mom's friend had offered to help in the great quest to find the kittens new homes and as you may guess, one of the first people she called, was Mom.

Initially, Mom probably replied with an amused comment which went something like, "Well, don't you think I've got enough to do to look after the children?" She was probably mainly referring to me as, as I think is apparent. I've always been somewhat of a disaster, particularly when it comes to leaving behind a mess.

Eavesdropping into the phone call, as usual, I now felt a hot acidity gradually making its way up from my stomach, bathing my mouth in the bitter taste of imminent failure. Judging by Mom's disposition, I just knew that any prospects of being allowed a mucky-pawed kitten were virtually zero, "Mom will never agree to that one", I thought.

However my little sister soon came in and, as you can guess, it took her all but three seconds minimum before she too tuned in to exactly what was being said, so we now joined forces, each of us now trying to gauge what Mom's decision would be, both of us bearing the saddest of faces and most imploring eyes possible.

"Oh please, Mom", we bleated in unison, "pretty please".

"You've just got to agree, Mom", my sister continued, "cos what if no-one has them and they have to be put down?"

"Good move, Sis'", I thought, still avidly maintaining my authentic, distressed, wobbly-bottom-lip-act, as I knew that our prospective little cat wasn't quite in the bag yet.

Mom was still unsure of what to do, so she sighed to my sister, "well even if we do have one, you'll soon get fed up and I know whose going to be feeding it and cleaning up its mess every day".

"Oh no", I thought, "this isn't looking good", at which point my quivering chin fell another six inches.

"Alright", Mom said finally, "I'll ring and see what Nan thinks."

Well, she did just that and fortunately for us, Nan was looking after my little cousin again and, as you can imagine, upon first hearing the mere mention of the word, "cat", my cousin requested that he should be allowed one too, or it simply wouldn't be fair.

Nan then asked what colour the kittens were.

"I believe they're all black", Mom replied.

"Oh well, that's it then", Nan concluded, "black cats are legendary for bringing good luck, so it seems to point to the fact that we're fated to have them, messy or not. I would probably have thought twice if they hadn't been black, but I think that settles it, cos we clearly won't get any peace until we've both got one. We'll just share the cost."

"YES!!, we'd won, we'd triumphed over every single argument", so it looked like the next job would be to drop into town again, this time to stock up on feline essentials but, in the meantime, Mom contacted her friend again to arrange a suitable time for the cats to be passed over.

I remember when our kitten arrived; almost straight away, it became apparent that ours had the most timid nature of the two and at first she was just cowering right at the back of the cat box, seeming too scared to venture out to meet us. It didn't take too long though until my younger sister managed to coax her into the little doorway and she took the first tentative sniff of her new surroundings. She was so tiny, her little yellow eyes seemed to be skittering nervously all around the kitchen and I remember thinking that her paws looked so delicate on the ends of her little, thin, stick-like legs, that I couldn't understand how she was managing to support herself.

We then began our next lengthy debate; this time to choose what we should call them and it seemed to be a mutual agreement between everyone that, although the kittens would be living in separate houses, they still came from the same litter, so perhaps their names should reflect them as a duo.

As I have already described, their coats were almost entirely black, only with the merest exception of a pretty, white splodge, flickering underneath their chins, appearing almost like a shiny medal. In the end, it was decided to call our tiny ball of black fluff Sooty and my cousin agreed that her miniature match, Nan's cat, should be addressed as Sweep. I wonder where that novel idea originated from?

And so, albeit only for a few short months, we felt that everything appeared to be going well. We all loved our new home and as I have described, living all on one level, in our first bungalow seemed to give me a far greater sense of independence and freedom.

However, our lives can never be that simple, well, it has seemed that way at times. I have often heard the older members of my family say something like, "If we knew what was waiting for us just around life's next corner, then we would never make the turn". As far as my thoughts go, in this respect, I think life must have an incredible capacity to drag us along with it, as once again, my whole family and I were about to be thrown into total turmoil.

It must have been moving towards the close of the 1980s, although I cannot be entirely sure of the exact timescale, when my dad started to complain of chest pain. At first, however, I don't think we thought anything of it, as he hardly ever went to the doctors and as far as his general health was concerned, Dad was regarded by everyone for being a very strong character. Much like most men, I suppose, he would often complain of "man-flu", but after dunking a few biscuits into his cup of coffee, he'd soon rally round again and little more than an hour later, he would reach for his jacket, bustling out on his next journey. That was just how Dad was. He'd always got somewhere to go, or people to see, even if it was only something as simple as going to fill his car with petrol, or to visit family members. He seemed, to me, to just trundle around, anywhere and everywhere. My dad always loved his daily lifestyle of a typical, lorry-driver: driving long distances, spending hours on the road and for most of his life, he had never suffered any major illnesses.

Very unexpectedly though, all this seemed to change and it was shortly after we moved into the bungalow, that Dad suffered a major heart attack, and he was rushed into the coronary care unit of the local hospital by ambulance. He was admitted and prescribed a regime of strict bed rest, also being wired up to a cardiograph monitor.

Just a few days' later, Dad was discharged again, after being diagnosed with angina, now armed with a concoction of pills and under firm orders that he must take things steady.

He forever wished to return to work and I think we expected, as usual, for Dad to reach a full recovery, just as we were all so used to. It appeared that this wasn't meant to be though, as just a little time later, Dad made the very courageous decision to undergo a heart bypass operation, but unfortunately, just a few hours later, it became clear that such an invasive procedure had proved all too much and with great sadness at the close of April 1989, my dad lost his final battle.

Had Dad have still been around today though, I just know that he would have been fascinated by the advances of the Internet and there is also little doubt that he would have been completely kitted out with a great stash of mobile phones, computers and flat-screen TV's, just like me, probably boasting a personal menagerie of digitally-controlled devices in every room and I just know he would have been amazed in how much the age of technology had so totally transformed life for me.

And so, our daily bustling lives just seem to hum on as usual. At least now living in the bungalow had made things a little easier in terms of my mobility needs and, particularly during the summer, it was great to be situated so close to the shops.

Also, as I think this story now fully illustrates, I was still loving my time at Dudley College, often leaving behind a varying mixture of humour and chaos everywhere I went. By now, I think I was building up a reputation of being quite a character but I wonder who was going to make an impression on me next.

18

<u>Computers And Designs</u>

This afternoon I was scheduled for my next computer session, so I'd have to hurry now, as my class was due to start in three-quarters of an hour and I found it so embarrassing if I had to be the last straggler, just scraping in, my late entrance disturbing the whole class.

In general, however, discounting this minor blip, my I.T. sessions seemed to be going well; I'd completed my first module in Introductory Word Processing and if my memory serves me correctly, I think the next large area of curiosity which now seemed to be fuelling my creativity was the business of using computer art or Computer Aided Design packages. Now that I come to think of it though, stripping this wretched tale right down to the blood-curdling truth here, for a while I seemed to develop a weird obsession for creating my own unique range of cheesy greetings cards. In fact, talking of this, before I go any further, I think I'd better offer a sincere apology to any of my ill-fated recipients who may still be experiencing scary flashbacks from actually receiving one of these. It was my initial intention at the time to tailor my themed designs to match the varying character traits of my friends, but that was quite a number of years ago now so I think I can conclude that I was in need of some real help and luckily for me again, it seemed that just the right man for the job was about to come to my rescue.

Back in B17, my computer class, I was sitting at my desk again, ardently trying to fathom out whether I was going to achieve anything at all constructive that day when, unexpectedly, my course tutor arrived and I immediately observed that he was accompanied by another young guy, who I had never seen before but on a fleeting glance, I saw that his most distinguishing feature was his beard.

I remember him standing quietly observing the class where, just like me, my fellow students were all industriously tapping away at their keyboards, each engaged in their own personal projects. Positioned closest to the door, the whole room now seemed completely shrouded in stony silence being almost as unnerving as finding yourself trapped in a deserted graveyard. Well someone would have to be bold enough to speak sooner or later. It seemed like the most obvious candidate to make the first move was me, so extending a shaky hand and giggling a little, I said, "Hello, I'm Sonya."

My new teacher then gave me a huge, friendly smile, shyly stepping forward to greet me.

Well although I didn't realise it right then, most certainly in terms of my continuing computer training, I know that I couldn't have wished for anyone better to join the team and neither could I have met a more true and great friend. He had a lovely, friendly disposition and it was always a tremendous privilege to work with such a kind-hearted and truly dedicated man. He had now been assigned to take over the Special Needs I.T. class, but right from the start, I think his one characteristic which always shone through the most is that he has always really cared about his students and it was soon plain to all that this guy can only be described as a first-class teacher.

Up until now, I seemed to be making steady progress: I think I had just about exhausted most of the brain-teasing puzzles stored on the college network and, probably in desperation more than anything else, I also have some bizarre and fuzzy memory of trying to compile a flow chart based around the storyline and characters of Auf Wiedersehen Pet. I think I wanted to input my data into some kind of program or other but if my imagination had plummeted to such a ridiculous level as this, then I'm sure you will agree that I was certainly in need of help and someone to make me do some real work. Luckily, however, it seemed that our new I.T. expert had arrived to do just that and straight away I could see that this one meant real business and my days of having a sneaky game of Pac Man or Bomber weren't just seriously numbered, they were over. He wasn't strict at all, but finally I was going to receive the type of highly skilled training and expertise which I needed.

This seems to be a very appropriate point to say that in my endeavour to write this story, it has been very necessary to talk about the things I have achieved, outlining my slow, but steady progress. However,

I know that I wouldn't be even sitting at this desk today having the capacity to do any of this, without the help and encouragement of so many highly intelligent and skilled professionals and, as you can probably tell already, this one was certainly going to turn out as no exception.

He always showed great patience and over our almost scary number of years of working together, in addition to gaining so many new skills and qualifications, I feel that through his teaching I seem to have been able to view the resourcefulness of the computer in a completely different way.

Much like anyone else, I guess, I attained the skills and knowledge to be able to manipulate all the major computer applications including Databases, creating Presentation Graphics in PowerPoint, Desktop Publishing, designing and authoring websites and I even survived that one most treacherous and incomparable evil of writing my own spreadsheet. I will never quite understand why I chose to put myself through that one but I remember that I based that particular project on the facts and figures of smoking statistics and looking back, by the time I'd worked out how to do it, I felt like puffing away on a pack myself.

Back then though, during the mid-1980s, the technological explosion which was soon to become the great and global World Wide Web, still wasn't commercially available to us but the field of computing was steadily progressing all the time and in addition to having access to the college network, it was my early introduction to using a database which, in a round-about way, now provided me with my first tiny insight into what was soon to become an exciting and completely new way of life.

The data for this project was stored on a special type of large laser disk which could be accessed by the old BBC Master machines. This was known as The Doomsday Project and, very beneficially for me, its data had been intentionally designed to be retrieved with a trackball.

The information itself was an enormous culmination of more than 147,000 pages of text and over 23,000 photographs which had been submitted to represent the everyday lives and goings-on of the people in Britain.

In the end, I decided, as so very typical of me, to base my final project on creating a database of different species of animals. Implementing the information from the Doomsday disc and therefore being able to produce records in the form of an educational slideshow, seemed to make my final project far more interesting than simply recording my entries in plain text.

This project also allowed me the opportunity to sample a different type of input device which, although I didn't realise it at the time, had also been specially designed for use on the disability market, either known as an "Overlay Keyboard" or a "Concept Keyboard". For people who are unfamiliar with this, it's a device with an early touch screen interface consisting of a sensitive grid which can be used in addition, or as an alternative, to a computer keyboard. I think it can almost be thought of as an electronic storyboard, so it was great to learn how the era of modern technology was moving on, particularly in the disability sector.

It was at this point that I started to consider attaining my first, recognised qualifications in Computer Studies more seriously and very soon my tutor encouraged me to work towards my Cambridge IT Skills Diploma. This course consisted of five modules, each geared to demonstrate competency in a diverse range of computing skills.

I was given a choice of areas of study so I gradually attained qualifications in Word Processing, Spreadsheets, C.A.D., Presentation Graphics and using Electronic Communication. I was particularly enthralled with the last one as it has greatly influenced and shaped my daily online practices covering a whole range of different areas from safe behaviours when using the Internet, to keeping in touch with friends via email and I also studied the very diverse and fascinating topic of how to build a website. At first, I found my web authoring quite a tricky subject, although I am really glad I chose to do this now as, just a little later on, it propelled me towards another fantastic hobby of creating small animations to show online.

I found these projects very helpful in introducing the diverse uses of the computer and, although I continued with my Information Technology studies for many years beyond, this early batch of qualifications seemed to shape how I continue to do things.

In addition to my resulting qualifications though, I didn't look upon my course as being hard work as Dudley College was just tremendous fun and now, the Special Needs Division was beginning to expand, benefitting and attracting many other physically disabled students too. I was particularly pleased that two of my very special friends from Victoria joined me for a while too and I'm sure a few people will know who I am referring to. I will always remember them both with much love as sadly, much like so many of my schoolmates, these nice guys are no longer around.

Well, as I'm sure many of you out there will agree, there are certain points when our daily climate just seems a little dreary: times when life just feels a bit of a drag and it is at these times of despondency that we all probably need another new friend to appear on the horizon, someone to blow away life's murky cobwebs, someone to inspire and encourage, to make us laugh or to just generally relight the fire again and find out where our get-up-and-go has got-up-and-gone-to and as I was about to discover, it was the last of Dudley College's terrific teaching threesome, the resident artist, who soon seemed all fired up to do just that.

It was midway through the 1980s when I started to venture down to the college's art department which was sited just a few miles from the main campus, sharing its ground with a secondary school. By way of introduction, my course tutor approached the guy in charge, enquiring if my friend and I could go along to his Friday morning drop-in session and of course, he didn't hesitate and agreed that we would be very welcome.

This was going to be a new experience for us all, as the resident artist had never taken any disabled students before, but as I soon found out, he was very patient with a terrific sense of humour and upon first hearing his infectious giggle, I was soon thinking, "O.K., I can see I'm gonna have some fun with this one" and if he is somewhere out there reading this story, then I am sure he would agree that we certainly shared a lot of laughs. He turned out to be another great source of encouragement and I think it can be said that his funny stories and kind guidance certainly made an impression on me.

As I soon learnt, my teacher worked in a wide and varied spectrum of art mediums. His drop-in classes attracted students of all ages and abilities and so, for me, this provided a great social environment and an opportunity to meet and chat with other students. It was also a great new experience for me to be involved in a mainstream art facility as the individual projects which were being produced, were so different to which I had been accustomed during my years at Victoria. I remember, in particular, there was a group of three more senior guys also brushing up on their watercolour techniques who were all really nice characters and so, over the weeks, and going into the next decade of attending Dudley's art department, I would find it quite thought-provoking to observe their various aesthetic creations in production.

At this point, Mom was still transporting me to and from college by car and of course, she knew from her many years of experience with me, that if I was going to be allowed anywhere within a ten-mile radius of art materials, then I would ultimately need the largest overall she could find - probably something similar to a surgeon's operating gown or an all-over-body tent would have sufficed, all finished off with two, circular eye holes and a snorkel fitting to facilitate a vital air supply. As I'm sure my art teacher would instantly clarify, I really was that messy.

In fact, staying on the subject of clothing, I think one of the activities I probably found most enjoyable was working on my t-shirt designs. Over time we did two of these. The first of which implemented a stencilling technique I had never employed till then. I remember that my teacher always referred to this design method as silk-screen printing, although following a little online research, it seems that there are a variety of alternative names sometimes used to describe this same technique including screen, serigraph printing, or serigraphy.

Anyway, however referenced, this is a method of transferring a clean printed image onto a blank medium which can either be a piece of paper or, in our case, a plain t-shirt.

I based my first effort on an advertisement I unearthed while skimming through an old magazine boldly promoting spring bulbs. "This would make a good design", I announced to my teacher, pointing at a varied assortment of tulips. "Do you think this would look O.K.?"

244

"Oh that will work brilliantly", he said with great enthusiasm, "that'll be sound, Son'".

Soon I'd selected a bunch of three tulips and, following a little more discussion, we agreed that my graphic would probably be most striking if replicated, completely obscuring the front of my t-shirt, achieving a bright and eye-catching continuity.

The art of silk-screen printing itself, however, all proved a little too tricky for me as to squeeze the coloured ink through its polyester mesh, stencilling the desired shapes, it seemed best to be in a standing position. This aids in forcing constant pressure through the printing squeegee, which in turn deposits an even layer of ink. All in all, it often takes quite a while for the project to reach its completion as this entire process needs be repeated several times depending on the desired number of colours. I found it all very interesting though as it was something different which I had never encountered at school.

Now roughly around the mid-1980s, I was still heavily into Queen music and so on a separate occasion, much to the great amusement of my teacher, I decided to portray this in another of my print assignments, being particularly influenced by one of my favourite pop tracks of all time, "It's A Kind Of Magic".

In this instance though, we decided to create our final graphic in a different fashion, now producing the artwork with fabric crayons.

Even after so many years have passed, I think my t-shirt creations are still tucked away neatly in the back of my chest of drawers somewhere. I don't think I would wear them these days although I can certainly imagine two of my little nephews using them as costumes for their drama classes but, for me, they still serve as a great reminder of enjoying my art sessions.

Over many years, of course, I was able to participate in a vast array of projects and from time to time, I also tried my hand at pottery. Well as you may imagine, despite my keen interest, any notion I ever had of using the potter's wheel soon fell flat but, as an alternative, my teacher suggested that perhaps it may suit me better to try to shape a tureen by compressing clay into one of his varied range of plaster of Paris sculpting moulds. Again, this project took quite a few sessions to complete but it was another different activity for me and, just like my cookery teacher, I think the artist showed great patience in trying to offer new activities, all being particularly geared to further the ability in my hands.

In my opinion, however, the skills in which I seemed to improve most and probably one of my favourite activities was producing my still life sketches. As you can tell, I love my artistic pursuits and as I noticed with these drawings, I always find it completely intriguing how people can each study the same subject matter and yet, when describing what they see with a range of art materials, each artist will interpret it in their own, very unique and personal way.

As I have mentioned, my art teacher had a great personality and was always keen to encourage my writing skills too and so attending his classes not only forms one of my nicest memories, but I think he was one of those people we probably all need to bump into now and then, just to brighten our day and to cheer us along. The other students were great guys too and just like me, they seemed to enjoy the light-hearted atmosphere.

However, thinking back, I don't think I ever did manage to completely get to the bottom of exactly where the unexplained skeleton came from which was hung from a metal hook in a darkened corner of the classroom? As I recall, I did attempt on various separate occasions to tentatively broach this somewhat delicate topic with my teacher. Was it purely just an exhibit used as a creative subject matter or perhaps this was merely the bare bones of something more sinister that only my art teacher knew of?

Despite extensive questioning though, the skeleton's true origin never did come to light although, from my overall impression, anything could arise from the dark catacombs of that art room and with a teacher like mine, it became just another of those humorous tales always sure to hit the funny bone.

And so, as you can see, I just completely loved my time at Dudley College. I think right from the start I knew that I had found some really nice guys. I also particularly enjoyed being partially integrated into the ordinary college environment too and, in my opinion, my main trio of fantastic teachers were all addressing my varied needs, effortlessly.

19

Pushing The Boundaries

I continued to enjoy my happy days in college, with one busy season seeming to speed into the next and it was around the dawn of the 1990s, that my course began to expand again, widening its opportunities and subject range.

Dudley College had now become the only facility in the borough to be offering specialist further education and being their first physically disabled student, I was somewhat amused that my course tutor now often seemed to refer to me as "the pioneer of the course." I wasn't quite sure, however, exactly what I was supposed to be pioneering or whether my efforts were working but, whatever the case, I still felt that my new title sounded quite neat.

Dudley's Special Needs facility was now becoming a popular choice and so, as time passed many more students in the area began to trickle in. Also, as you may have guessed, with its increase in recognition, the staff began to introduce a few other subject areas too and so much like me, my course was now given the new title, "Design For Living".

I remember that many of the students would enjoy participating in our weekly game of bowls. This became a warm-up exercise to get each new week underway, being scheduled for the first lesson of each Monday morning. I tried, of course, although as everyone could soon so embarrassingly see, I was completely unable to engage with the idea of playing sports. I possessed no directional skills whatsoever and my ardent endeavours were just as useless as they always had been throughout school. However, in an attempt to make the game a little more disability-friendly, our sports teacher later came up with the notion of employing an old piece of cut-off drainpipe, which was now transformed into a shoot, down which to roll our bowls, hence achieving the perfect aim.

Despite my literally non-existent sporting skills, my course was still going well and so as a further addition to the college timetable, we were also given two or three more sessions to work in The Literacy Department.

In a similar fashion to my art class, many of the tuition sessions in this division were run on a very casual basis so it seemed that there were many able-bodied students of various ages and multi-cultural backgrounds who would just drop in at a time to best suit their lifestyle, furthering their abilities in everyday maths and English.

It feels only right that I should give a mention to these guys as again, it was just an absolute pleasure to have the opportunity to work with such encouraging and kind-hearted people. As I'm sure you can tell from my story, I've always enjoyed English and for me, the value of this subject has probably been amplified even further by my lifelong problems with communication.

The one ultimate experience though which will forever stay with me, was on that monumental day when my best friend and I joined forces to sit that vision-blurring, finger-numbing and spine-crumbling experience of taking our nine-hour English Language exam. Yes, the exam lasted for the epic duration of almost nine long hours of continual typing. Looking back now, I can still hardly believe how we both managed to keep going, but I think I must swiftly add that at least we were released out of class for food and toilet breaks so, happily, it was a completely amicable arrangement and it was great that we were given such a fair chance.

Our exam itself was overseen by one of my English teachers and we enlisted the support of our I.T. teacher, who also stayed close by to fix any technical glitches with the computers.

I'm sure that my friend and indeed everyone who played a part, would wholeheartedly agree that it was quite an amazing day not only in having the experience, but I must reiterate that it was also very well done by our brilliant English teacher who had worked so hard in persuading the examining board to be so lenient with our resulting time concessions.

Oh, and not forgetting, of course, I should mention my Mom again who had packed me enough fruit pastilles to quench my insatiable desire for a sugary energy boost. In the end, if my memory serves me correctly here, I think my friend and I finished our exam with an approximate half an hour between us but the one thing we did share, of course, is that we were both truly shattered and we spent the whole of the following day tucked up in our weary beds – zzz.

Well time was moving on now and it was midway through February of 1991, when my family once again united in our inconceivable grief, as following his enormously brave battle with cancer, we lost Granddad.

As anyone who has ever met me will know though, for me, my granddad left behind quite an unbelievable legacy, not just in the many happy times we shared, but also in all those brilliantly crafted wooden tools he had so lovingly designed for me in his little garden shed. Courtesy of Granddad's teaching though, if given the opportunity, I can still, albeit pretty badly, tap out the tune of Elvis Presley's "Wooden Heart" on my electric keyboard but in total contrast to the song's lyrics, on a final note, my most enduring memory of Granddad will forever be his "heart of sparkling gold".

I think probably, the next noteworthy occurrence which now seems to be jumping out at me, is that we were soon to re-home another of our much-loved pets but if poor Sooty had been able to talk, I hasten to add, then I'm sure she would have told us that, at least according to the vibes she was sensing in her whiskers, this new addition to the household, was far from purr-fect.

It was my younger sister who first spotted this fussy newcomer: a small tortoise shell kitten who lay curled in a sleepy ball at the back of the local pet shop. Back then, there were numerous children and teenagers living within the immediate vicinity and around teatime and during the early evening, they always seemed to congregate either in the new shopping mall or around the crowded bus station.

Anyway, my sister arrived home one day and rushing down the path looking extremely distressed, she solemnly delivered her tragic lament that she had just seen five kittens for sale in the local pet shop. She said that they were mostly black and white and the four largest ones in the litter were all beautiful little things, commonly featuring wide appealing eyes and so as you would imagine, these were attracting loads of attention and selling very quickly. However, there's always got to be one heartrending exception to the rule and so, cowering nervously at the back of the cage, was a solitary little tortoise shell one seeming to be shunned by all and being treated like the obvious runt.

Well as I'm sure you can imagine, this poignant speech was quite enough for me: Mom could plainly see that there was nothing more that could be said and so within the next half an hour, the new member of the household was teetering gingerly around the kitchen, competitively chasing Sooty to gain the most dominant place around the food bowl.

In colouring, she was a dappled mix of black, brown and light sand, but her most distinctive marking of all was the small ginger splodge right on the crown of her head, which was almost in the perfect shape of a diamond.

"Oh look at her", Mom said, "she's peppered with all colours", and almost simultaneously we all realised that this would be a most appropriate name and so irrespective of the diamond, we officially introduced Sooty, to Pepper.

Pepper was a lovely natured cat but, in contrast to Sooty, it soon became apparent that she was a far more sociable and outgoing cat. She would often curl up on my lap but, by the same token, I think she was pretty quick to ascertain that my electric wheelchair gave her a pretty handy means of transport too, so unlike most other cats, who will get around by leaping from one convenient surface to another, Pepper would simply meow at me for assistance and hitch a ride.

As I'm sure I have made clear many times, I've always loved my many different four-legged companions and I just find it fascinating how, even though they can't voice their thoughts and emotions in the same way as we can, our domestic pets still all possess their very unique and adorable personalities and characteristics. Of course, cats were primarily wild mammals and according to the historical data, they swapped their natural habitat to come and dwell alongside us humans, only a very short time ago. This is probably why many of them still like to be stealthy and solitary creatures... in fact, I have only just realised it, but this point leads me perfectly onto the next very different tale which I think you may find pretty hair-raising, (I know I did) because there is one place I visited where the customary notion of the cat's domestication really wasn't the case at all.

In terms of family life, as I'm sure is self-explanatory, we were still feeling pretty low following the sad and recent loss of my granddad, so it was Nan who made the initial suggestion that it would be of great benefit to us all to enjoy a good holiday and to relax in the warm, rejuvenating rays of the sunshine.

As you can imagine, this idea instantly sparked a reaction from me. My face lit with joy and I said that I would like to fly out to Spain. We had been twice to Jersey many years previously, but I just felt that Spain seemed like an obvious option as it has always been such a popular destination amongst Brits, being strongly associated with its siestas and long, hot summers, so I decided I would finally like to find out what all the commotion was about.

Mom and Nan also agreed that this sounded like a pretty good plan, so without further ado, we went down to the shopping precinct in town, to pay a visit to the local travel agency. They both felt that it was important that we should all go together so that we could stress our special requirements regarding my disability.

From what I remember, we seemed to be in the shop for ages, spending time browsing through the many coloured brochures and trying to decipher from what were quite scanty details, which hotel seemed to be the most suited to our needs.

Anyway, eventually we agreed on a plan and we all went home feeling excited, after having booked a spacious-looking apartment, together with our flight tickets, both ways, between Birmingham and Malaga City, in the heart of the Costa Del Sol.

There were still a few weeks to go after this until the beginning of the summer break, so my college days continued again, uneventfully, but at least now, I knew I had my holiday to look forward to.

Meanwhile, my computer teacher came up with the notion that perhaps I would like to go and spend two hours a week working alongside the guys in an office known as Teaching Aids. This would not only give me something completely different to do, but it was also the first taste I'd had of joining a real working environment. At the time, the Teaching Aids department was managed by a great bunch of guys and, if offered the opportunity, I would have loved to have stayed in there full time, as it had such a friendly atmosphere. This department essentially comprised of one large square room, although in one corner there was also another adjoining area, but this was so small it seemed little more than a walk-in stock cupboard, merely housing a large industrial photo-copier.

Anyway, my I.T. teacher lent me the use of a spare B.B.C. Micro, which was squeezed in next to the window overlooking the college car park and I remember I was given the task of transferring some course notes onto a disk which had been requested by one of the lecturers in Human Biology. Well as I have said, joining the guys in Teaching Aids was just a total buzz for me. I suppose I was a tad nervous at the very onset whilst initially learning about what was expected of me and of course, just like meeting any new people, they had to become familiar with my speech pattern. However, within a few short moments, all my apprehension just slipped away. I could see that, once again, I was amongst great friends and I think it is safe to say that from then on, it was just cheeky comments and laughter all the way. I will always remember them all though for their great encouragement and their lovely senses of humour which not only shone through in their great repertoire of jokes and ceaseless tricks, but was also fully resonated in the décor too as the whole place was filled with comical mugs, posters and ridiculous slogans, so I think I can safely say that, once again, it seemed I'd found just the place for me.

Sadly though, all good things have to come to an end and upon completion of the biology write-up, there were no other jobs available for me but, when I reflect on some of the fun and jollity which we got up to in the small confines of Teaching Aids, this is just another of my great Dudley College memories which never fails to make me smile.

And so, the weeks sped by again: soon it was the end of another year at college and the special treat I'd been longing for was almost upon us. We went to pick up Nan and set out to Birmingham Airport to catch a flight out to sunny Spain - our ultimate idyllic holiday destination.

Looking back, I think my nan was almost as excited as me. In the last few days running up to our trip, she seemed to be wearing a constant big smile and she would often say, "We'll soon be living it up by the sea now Sonya, won't it be exciting?"

"It sure will, Nan", I'd agree in delight. I think my mom was probably looking forward to it too although, knowing her as I do, I imagine she would be feeling a little apprehensive at this stage, although just like me, Mom has always enjoyed air travel.

Anyway soon we pulled into the airport and after checking in at the departure desk, I had to be transferred into one of their wheelchairs, as mine had to be lifted onto the luggage shoot, joining the many holdalls and suitcases varying hugely in colour, size and shape.

We did have to go through customs although upon seeing our obvious problems, I don't think the officer in charge rated us as ardent criminals, so, after a brief frisk, we continued, slowly queuing behind yet another line of bustling passengers.

Next, we entered the long plastic boarding tunnel leading to our awaiting aeroplane and a group of strong, muscular guys came forward, fully equipped with an ambulance chair and effortlessly, they proceeded to lift me onboard the Boeing 747. With a sneaky smile, I wryly decided that this seemed like rather a good start to my holiday.

Well due to my special needs, I was the first passenger to board, so they quickly transferred me into the most convenient seat, although just to add a little more commotion, I requested that a window seat would be preferable so that I could admire the view. I felt this would fully enhance my flight experience so, without too much difficulty, one of the young men kindly shuffled me over.

Soon we'd taxied down the runway and with a whoosh, we were off.

This was my third time on a plane, as when my little sister was very young, we had enjoyed two more family holidays when we had stayed in a really beautiful place called The Hotel de France, in St. Helier, Jersey. Our trips to Jersey had been many years ago by now and, if my memory is serving me correctly, I think I must have been only about ten at the time, so it was a great thrill to be flying again.

Taking a through flight between Birmingham and Malaga usually takes approximately, just under two and a half hours. It's a little farther afield than Jersey, but we all love flying, so in what seemed to be only a very short time, the pilot was soon announcing that we may now experience mild turbulence, as we were about to touchdown in Spain.

The stewardess approached and asked if we could wait until everyone else had exited the aeroplane when someone would be along to help us.

Back on solid ground, we soon noted that there was a large group of holidaymakers being escorted to their various hotels by coaches. We were introduced to our holiday rep and so the first thing we had to do was to climb the steps to get on. I suppose under normal circumstances, I have never felt particularly at ease with making too much of a fuss about my disability but, as you can imagine, for a fully grown adult who can't walk at all, this task was virtually impossible. However, despite my very apparent dilemma and with the help of many kind and willing hands, I just about clambered into the first seat, which a very generous onlooker gave up for me. The seats were two abreast, so from somewhere behind me, I suddenly heard the usual words of wisdom arising from my poor, anxious nan, "We'll hire a taxi on the way back."

Anyway, looking through the coach window, the weather was beautiful and so slowly watching the lightly swishing palm trees, I think we were all, very soon, in mode "Holiday Bliss".

As already outlined, upon our decision to take a trip to Spain, we had spent a long time with the travel agent, trying to formulate the most desirable holiday package to best cater for our needs and as part of this very detailed process, we had clearly stipulated the need for a hotel with ramp access. Well, as we could see on arrival, this is precisely what we were granted, but it soon became apparent that regulations over there aren't quite as disability-friendly as they are in the UK. There was a ramp but, unfortunately, it was horrendously steep and being fashioned from highly polished marble culminated in it being extremely slippery. For most wheelchair users, this would have been totally non-negotiable, although we had to get in somehow and luckily, I suppose, I had taken my manual wheelchair and as long as poor Mom was barefoot, which made things marginally easier, she could just about sprint with me to the top. She needed to run at quite a speed to work up the necessary momentum but, with considerable difficulty, she managed it.

In general, the hotel itself was quite pleasing: our apartment wasn't on ground level, although this meant we had double patio doors opening out onto a lovely private balcony, which overlooked the glistening swimming pool and sun loungers.

After our first siesta, we decided there was little need to go out that day, so we just enjoyed the evening's fare in the hotel restaurant and I remember being particularly amused as we each ordered a different drink, each being unique in colour. I think they were red, blue and green or something, but they were flavoured universally, distinctly spiced with aniseed.

The next morning we arose bright and early. It had been a hot and sticky night but, following a hearty breakfast, we were all keen to go out to explore our surroundings.

We seemed to spend the majority of our day shopping: mostly in small gift shops, many of which were closely packed with souvenirs and wire racks of postcards and so, as is often the case, there was very little room to accommodate my wheelchair. This didn't spoil our mood though: the streets seemed alive with loud Spanish music and as I briefly hinted a little earlier, it was here that I was most surprised to observe quite a sizeable and widely varying group of wild street cats. In general stature, they weren't all that different really to our regular household cats, although they appeared extremely skinny, looking malnourished. However, I don't think this overall impression was aided any by the fact that they practically all belonged to a naturally hairless species.

Time began to tick along now and we would need to return to the hotel so that we could rest a little and freshen up before enjoying our evening meal, but just before leaving town, Mom and Nan agreed to pop into the bank to replenish our supply of Spanish currency.

This we did and then we continued our stroll back, idly savouring the dwindling heat of the sun. We had all had a lovely day and I remember that I just felt happy, probably dreaming of what we could do tomorrow. Our hotel came into view. We only had to descend the final incline in the road and we would be there. Perhaps there would be time to get some nice cool drinks in the hotel again, just before returning to our room.

Everything seemed near perfect in those final few moments. The weather was beautiful, and my wheelchair was laden with small trinkets and gifts to take back for my sisters and niece. We could still smell the warm sand and so being emotionally immersed in that kind of setting, it is very easy to think that nothing can go wrong – nothing could spoil the dream – and then, just within a few short moments, although at the time, it felt like an eternity, we were suddenly dragged right back to horrid, stark reality.

I noticed out of the corner of my eye that a white, Ford Cortina was slowly descending the hill. It seemed quite near to us and for a few moments, I naturally felt there was no cause for concern, but it was soon close enough for me to observe that the two front seats were occupied by two black males and I still clearly remember that the man closest to me had a large, drooping moustache. The car drew ever closer and then, still wearing a very broad, friendly grin, the guy wound down his window and stretching his right arm out as far as possible, he snatched at the bag which was hung on the back of my wheelchair. His nerve was unwavering, and he wasn't going to relinquish his grip – not now.

By this time, Mom and I were both being dragged down the hill by the car at a very high pace, but still the man persisted in clutching on to our bag for grim death.

Meanwhile, from way back in the distance, poor Nan called helplessly from the top of the hill as there was absolutely nothing she could do, except to appeal to everyone for assistance, to watch the whole thing unfurl and to pray for the Lord to intervene and safely deliver us.

Well, eventually the sheer force of the car prised the bag free, also taking with it the rubber handgrip from the handle of my wheelchair. At this point, at last breaking free from the car, I continued to roll to the bottom of the steep incline, where I finally tipped over, still sobbing and dazed with trauma.

Mom meanwhile was just a few moments longer before she too spun free from the accelerating car, also totally awash and trembling with disbelief.

With the car gone, a very kind couple, who I think were Irish and also a nearby garage proprietor, came to our aid, lifting me from the ground and slowly seeing us safely into the door of our hotel, which was merely 100 yards from where this atrocious incident had occurred.

A doctor came and we were treated for severe bruises, grazes, strains and total shock and bewilderment.

After this we were all just too scared to leave the confines of our hotel room again so there we remained for the next three days, still terrified and all experiencing constant graphic flashbacks of the whole, shocking ordeal, before finally being granted a slightly earlier flight back. When it came time to leave, however, we even panicked at the thought of going out to get into the taxi.

We all cried with tears of relief and elation, as at last came our safe landing on British soil, where we could finally rejoin our anxious family.

I think my sisters were both pleased to see us too and I've never enjoyed a cheese on toast supper so much in my life.

20

A Galaxy Of Stars

We are slowly heading towards the close of my story now and up until the early nineties, Mom's branch of the family was predominantly, and almost exclusively female. Of course, there were my cousins, my aunties' two lads, but since the birth of the younger one, in 1974, we hadn't had the need to buy any blue, baby outfits, as my family had seemed to produce a bountiful supply of little girls.

Conversely, though, things were set to change, as we soon learnt that my sisters were both expecting babies together and so within a few weeks, we started looking forward to, not just one, but two new arrivals.

Anyway, I promise to tell you more about how that exciting tale pans out later but first, I think it was more or less around about the same time, for which, even now, I don't feel there was any particular reason, that I suddenly found that maybe I was a little weary with my daily bus trips to and from college and I just felt like, possibly only temporary, trying something completely different.

I had always loved Dudley College, but by this time we were just about approaching the autumn of 1992 and thinking back, although the thought of the harsh weather probably was somewhat of a consideration, I simply felt like a change.

I was still only 25 at this point and upon my first suggesting this new revelation to Mom and Nan, I don't think either of them were too impressed. At the onset though, considering all that I had been through, I guess their initial concerns were perfectly understandable, as much like me, they both feared that if I stopped going into college, then I would just recklessly burn my bridges again, only to bring my college days to an abrupt end, once more severing all ties with both students and staff.

However, it was apparent that for some strange reason I'd obviously got itchy feet and so it seemed like the most logical next move for Mom to make an appointment to meet with the Head of the Special Needs, for us to officially discuss the situation.

Momentarily side-stepping from the plot which right then I thought I'd lost again, I hope people who read this will find it just as amusing as I do in my writing. I can hardly see the letters on my keyboard through my tears of mirth, but at the time the situation felt quite tragic as I just thought I had failed again. Nevertheless, I'd still made up my mind to pull out and just like my family, I felt that the only possible conclusion would be for my relationship with Dudley College to come to an end.

By this time though, my years of being a student were starting to amass and so right from the start I don't think my desire for a break came as too much of a surprise.

"So Sonya", my course tutor began, "what's bought all this to ahead then? Are you really that fed up with us?"

"Ahem, ahem...no Sir...I don't know", I blushed, as I nervously cleared my throat.

And so anyway, without going into too much of the mind-numbing nitty-gritty, I'm sure he would agree that, just like with the majority of my teachers, over the years we had built up a fantastic rapport and so as ever he was extremely patient and understanding. Expressing a similar opinion to Mom though, he suggested there seemed a need to put some kind of contingency plan in place so maybe I could just study in my own time at home which would alleviate the need for my daily bus trip whilst still furthering my qualifications.

We all agreed that this sounded like an excellent idea, so this is just what I did and in what had materialized to be my usual Dudley College trademark, I now became the first student to test out this new way of Distance Learning, known to all as The Outreach Scheme.

My following experiences of Outreach were once again completely excellent and just as it had been in college, the coursework aspect of proceedings was still very much steered by my usual I.T. teacher but, over time, I had the pleasure of working with three more extremely nice teachers who also stepped in to assist me.

The basic working format which we had soon developed is that I would just complete my agreed assignments in my own time and then if I needed help, or when my work was ready to be submitted, my teachers would come along to my house for another tuition session. As time passed the option of joining Outreach became a popular study alternative for other students too.

Attaining further qualifications never proved a problem, apart from the obvious one that is, because no-one particularly enjoys having to sit exams, do they?, but my teachers were great and, just like working in the college environment, they provided fantastic one-to-one support and moderation, assisting me through my various exams in Computer Literacy and Information Technology. Well, quite surprisingly, even for me, I continued studying on Outreach until the summer of 2008, so it often makes me smile when I consider that this makes me the only student to hang around for the whole duration of the course.

Briefly stepping back to early 1992 though, it was now that Mom gave me my next huge surprise as she agreed with perhaps a tad of gentle persuasion, to take in a dog. Up until this point, my grandparents and Auntie had kept dogs although we had always tended to home smaller domestic pets, as Mom often expressed the opinion that a dog would just make far too much mess.

However, thankfully she changed her mind, and we were all excited to re-home a most adorable little Alsatian-Labrador cross, we named Chloe.

We found our Chloe as a puppy, being taken care of at a local animal rescue centre. I didn't go to pick her up, but as soon as she set her paws in our bungalow, for me, it was simply complete devotion on her first, cheery tail wag. Of course, in our traditional British culture, it is nothing out-of-the-ordinary to hear us described as a nation of dog lovers and it is also very apparent that many owners manage to develop quite astonishing emotional attachments with their dogs and it was soon clear that our Chloe would turn out as no exception. She showed a brilliant intelligence and I have no bones in saying she was just total Pet Heaven.

Chloe was only a few weeks old when she arrived and I remember that one of the first things that struck me were her beautiful, floppy ears, textured like velvet. In fact, she was so soft and cuddly that you just wanted to pick her up. I don't think the cats were so impressed though and as for poor Sooty, now with two rivals springing into action, it wasn't difficult to understand why she started to spend most of her days peacefully curled up on top of the freezer.

Contrary to her feline housemates though, now desperately trying to gauge the safest route to their food bowls, our cheeky puppy certainly had no problem in melting our human hearts and as for me, I knew I couldn't have wished for a more loyal and beautiful dog.

When we first bought her home, just like any playful little pup, Chloe couldn't wait to explore her new environment.

By then, Mom had been busily flanking the garden and back patio with two rows of alternatively coloured conifers. This had the dual benefit of adding a little more privacy while also helping to reinforce the fence panels. However, we couldn't believe our eyes one day, as Chloe came bouncing in from the garden proudly wielding a sizable tree in her jaws. Reaching the centre of the kitchen, she continued to shake, widely distributing foliage and clumps of compost all around generously coating every surface. Chasing her around the room, Mom eventually managed to salvage her prized tree, or at least, by this time, the bedraggled remains of it, but tilting her head inquisitively to the side, it was just our puppy's way of bringing us a gift, so I think even Mom had to agree, that it was very difficult to remain annoyed with her for too long.

Well, the months sped by again and it was soon time for my sisters to have their babies. Mom had been convinced all along that one of them would have a girl and so just a few weeks earlier she hadn't been able to resist the temptation of buying a pink and white lacy bonnet.

Anyway, it was just a few days after the New Year celebrations in 1993, when Mom had a phone call from my older sister to say that she thought her baby was on the way, so could we look after my niece.

Happily, just a short time later, we heard that my sister had given birth to a lovely, little boy, so as far as the bonnet was concerned, at least for now, there were no takers.

Approximately six weeks later, however, early on the morning of Saint Valentine's Day, we were blessed again with another very special delivery, as my younger sister also welcomed the arrival of her very precious baby son, but needless to say, Mom's pink hat remained as new in its bag.

I remember that this marked the start of another lovely time for me. Of course, I continued to set aside several hours a week to dedicate to my course assignments, but I now had the enormous joy of being an auntie again.

Back then, digital T.V., as we know it today, was still to be launched and so the old analogue system only facilitated capacity to receive three or four channels through the aerial. Fortunately for the babies, however, home entertainment now entered the age of the video cassette recorder. Our high street retailers now began to promote a vast array of videos aimed to catch the eye of everyone and even the babies were soon babbling along to their favourite Walt Disney Sing-Along tracks.

Well anyway, as the years have slowly rolled on, I am now the very proud auntie to my niece, no less than five fantastic nephews and as we celebrated the new millennium I was delighted to become a Great Auntie for the very first time and I think, at this point, Mom just gave up on the hat as I went speeding into the maternity ward yet again, tightly gripping onto another very special blue balloon. Time moved on again and he now holds the hands of two pretty, little sisters.

And just to round off the subject of children, my youngest cousin and his wife also now have three lovely children – another boy flanked by two more little girls, each one exhibiting loads of beautiful curls.

Although the few paragraphs I have just written spans over quite a few years, I felt I wanted to introduce the children collectively as, in their own unique ways, they are all very special to me. Over the years it has given me such enormous joy to watch them grow and develop their different interests and personalities, but the one thing for which I will always love them all best is that they have consistently shown such an incredible understanding and empathy for my problems.

Of course, I have never been any different. My problems pertaining to Cerebral Palsy have always dictated and shaped my daily life, but I think it has always been the patience, understanding and unconditional love from all these youngsters, which has given me a wonderful opportunity to just draw my emotions back a little from all the constant clamour of difficulties, to simply feel loved and wholly accepted as Auntie.

In other words, "You all smashed it, Kids'. Thanks, and I will always love you all dearly."

Just to conclude on a final note, I suppose the wheels of life have to keep turning and it was amidst the joy of welcoming all these special children, when in May 2001, with terrible sadness, we had to say our final goodbyes to my very precious nan. As I hope I have been able to convey already, I always looked upon Nan as the beating heart of the family, forever overflowing with love and good advice. Nan was a constant friend – always there to help us along in happy times and sad. She was also the perfect companion for Granddad, and I know that just like Mom and the rest of her beautiful family, I would never have been blessed with such a happy and contented childhood without her. Blessings like Nan don't come any greater. Love always, Nan xx.

And so, my story is almost drawing to its conclusion now. Living with a disability has never been particularly easy and like so many other people I guess, if given the choice, it is certainly not a path I would have chosen to travel and I know that my very precious auntie always felt the same. However, I hope that people will find my tale an enjoyable one and if you have reached this point in my tale without either falling asleep or even worse, just using it to doodle your next shopping list on, then that is probably a good sign.

However, my strong faith, which I know I have always needed to cling on to, through good times and bad, has always been guided and lighted by the love of the Lord.

Anyway, thank you so much for your patience in reading this far and now I would just like to leave you with a few final thoughts.

21

<u>New Horizons</u>

Up until the early springtime of 1967, at the time of my birth, my family was no different from any other. Mom and Dad had recently moved into what was, for the time, a very modern, newly built detached house, in a quiet suburb of Dudley. As I continued to describe the events which then unfolded both immediately before and during birth caused a lack of oxygen to my brain, leaving me with permanent brain damage and a lifelong future with Cerebral Palsy.

Glancing back to the opening of my story, it feels natural to wonder what I would have been like if I had been able-bodied and my life had travelled down a different path. Well, who knows? Mom often humorously answers that in terms of relationships I certainly wouldn't have stood for any nonsense, but I don't think there is a great deal of difference there. Ultimately, however, after 50 years of trying to sort myself out and worrying about all this futile gibberish, I think it's hi-time I started to put all my proverbial what if phrases on the backburner and from now on, put my faith in Jesus first and attempt to concentrate a little more on what is essential for my survival today, instead of dwelling on what might have been. I am just me and I feel incredibly blessed that I have always been so loved for it.

The task of producing my story has turned out to be a far more interesting voyage into who I am than I first guessed and mostly, it has been such fun to bring back to mind and revisit so many amusing things from days that have passed. I just hope I haven't overdone it, as there is a strong possibility that when this bizarre tale gets round, I am doubtful if I will ever be viewed in quite the same light again and I don't exactly relish the prospect of having to spend the remainder of my days furtively hiding in the shed. Unlike my granddad, I am not very skilled in the art of woodwork.

As for me though, after reading this memoir, I'm sure you will see that the largest and most important part of my nature, representing the beating heart of my true character, can only be attributed to the constant and unparalleled love and support of my beautiful mother, an extremely determined and hard-working dad and never forgetting, of course, my being massively helped along the way by my very special Auntie, Nan and Granddad, without whom, I just wouldn't have become the person who I am today.

Mom, Auntie, and my grandparents equally loved children and so during my childhood years, my favourite times of all were unquestionably our awesome Saturday afternoons spending time with the family. Yes, my nan was right in what she said, "our problems with disability were, very obvious to the outside world", but so was our happiness, our joy and most of all our unsurpassable ability to cope, our shared faith in our Lord and our very deep loyalty and love for each other.

We weren't just strong as one big, collective family unit either, as they each contributed their own special and unique mixture of love, encouragement and talent that only they could give.

As for Mom, well, she was just born to be a mother, but she's so much more than that too, as she is just the best friend I could ever have wished for. She has always been so incredibly determined that despite my disability and all the many problems it has presented, I should be given as broad a spectrum of opportunity as all the other able-bodied children in the family. This is the reason for which, right from the start, she has always been so doggedly determined to seek out the best treatments and facilities for me that life could offer.

There is little doubt that the characteristics I share most with my dad are his strong work ethic and his unwavering determination. Just like me, Dad always seemed interested in new technological gadgetry and if he had still have been around today, he would have been truly fascinated to witness just how much the field of Information Technology has transformed life for me. As my story probably shows, I also loved my dad's unmistakably unique sense of humour: a particular trait, which right to this moment, never fails to provoke a quiet giggle.

My Nan too was another fascinating and completely adorable character. I don't know if she ever knew, but I just remember feeling so happy and proud when Nan attended the many and varied social events which would inevitably come around at either Victoria School or later in years, at Dudley College. I'm sure all those privileged enough to have met her will agree that she was one captivating, amazing character who, not only could never be forgotten, but she was also renowned for her fantastic capacity to radiate fun and happiness everywhere she went.

As for my dear Granddad, well, where do I begin? All I can say is that he was just a sheer delight to spend time with and quite simply, an extraordinary inspiration. I think he has, probably to differing degrees, passed down his great musical talents to all of us grandchildren, in particular his ability to play the piano and electronic keyboard. For me though, my granddad was simply my best friend and as the years rolled by, his effortless talent in designing and crafting so many ingenious wooden hand tools for me would simply have to be seen to be believed. Granddad was just an amazing, lovely character and I think when you are shown dedication and patience like his, you just know that you were born to try.

There is no doubt that it also helped and encouraged me enormously to be raised in a busy household, forever joining in with the constant fun and, at times, complete pandemonium created by my sisters, cousins, my beautiful niece and all of our lovely children. I don't know if they always realised, but both as individuals and as part of our group, they have all contributed such enormous joy to my life and, just as importantly, it is these few very special people who completely demonstrated to me what it was like to be normal because I just wanted to join in and do things as similarly to them as I possibly could.

I have thoroughly enjoyed the opportunity of re-visiting so many happy times I had during my lovely childhood. I would also like to express my deepest and most sincere thanks to all those extremely kind and dedicated staff with whom it was such a very great pleasure to work with at Victoria School. Of course, there is no doubt in saying that the guys who were there during my schooldays will all have retired by now, but I know that they have left behind them quite an extraordinary and truly priceless legacy, ensuring that every disabled child lucky enough to be granted a place, will receive the very best education and medical expertise possible.

As you have seen, I had a real ball at Dudley College too and I still can't believe that I lasted an incredible 24-year stint of enjoying student life: this certainly was the best choice of further education for me.

When I first started, I really hadn't got a clue what to expect and I recall thinking, "O.K., I'll give it a few weeks to see how it goes", but then everyone was so friendly and such a joy to be around, that my days both in college and afterwards, as I continued furthering my computing skills on The Outreach Scheme, doing all those courses just became a fantastic way of life. I don't think my transition to Dudley was quite the chosen path that my school teachers had originally planned for me, but just as we always sang every year at my art class Christmas party, in the end, "I did it my way", so this is certainly one part of life that I wouldn't have changed for anything.

However come to think of it, now being in a slightly more sober frame of mind, that last statement isn't quite true after all because, in reality, I will always know that I couldn't have achieved any of this without the unfaltering love, encouragement and support of, first and foremost, my very special Mom, Dad, Nan, Granddad and Auntie, the last four of whom still surround me each moment with love, as they watch me from heaven.

Also, when all the younger guys in the family finally get a chance to read this I hope that just like mine, it will fill your hearts with both joy and laughter and maybe go a little way in reminding you that we really do share quite an incredible, delightful and extraordinary family and I just pray that this very special collection of mixed blessings will not disappear with the passing of time, but will live on with love in your hearts forever.

And finally... just to finish, I am now enjoying life living in a beautiful region in Scotland, situated right by the sea.

Well, I'm not too sure whether this was, in fact, a date with destiny but I know that it was always an idea of my nan's, that I should dwell by the sea as, setting out from Dudley, it seemed such a large undertaking to enjoy a picnic on the beach.

It is amazing how the time has flashed by as we have been here for almost a decade now. Like most people in England, I think we were a little unsure at first as to how we would brave the northerly weather conditions but, at least where we are, the climate seems surprisingly similar to that in The Midlands.

I must admit though, the landscape and scenery up here are really beautiful, chiefly as they have maintained many vast expanses of agricultural and farming land. This becomes particularly apparent during summer months when I love to watch the sunset shrink and glisten over the shimmering water.

I am also developing nice relationships with the group of carers who come to lend a hand with my daily personal needs. Many of the ladies have a great sense of humour and after all those years of living in and around Dudley and The West Midlands, it has been especially amusing to learn some of the regional dialects and traditions of Scotland. Thank you all for your kindness and ongoing help, it is really appreciated.

Mom and I now enjoy a busy social life at our local parish church. This is situated in a beautiful little village: another area renowned for its Scottish history and tradition. Moving so far from home, I know Mom will wholeheartedly agree, that it is receiving such a very kind and warm welcome from not only our vicar and his wife, but also many friendly people in the congregation, together with a few more great guys, who have recently taken up a life in Jesus' ministry, which has formed a very essential and key role in helping us to settle in Scotland. We both love participating in their many and varied social events, as together with sharing faith and fellowship, these people really know how to enjoy themselves too.

It was also an enormous pleasure to share my 50th birthday celebrations with family members, carers, and friends at church. Altogether, I think I was treated to three days of partying and the generosity and kindness shown to me by everyone involved was really touching. I just hope everyone who shared this special time with me, all enjoyed themselves as much as I did. Even now, it still amazes me how my mom and all my friends managed to keep this all such a big secret. In fact, right up until the last few moments of my journey, I still held the belief that I was heading to a local restaurant for a quiet meal. For me, by far the best moment was that first magical realisation that my niece and nephew, accompanied by their partners and children had travelled all the way from The Midlands just to share my very special night.

Thank you guys all so much. It was really brilliant.

Well along the way, particularly whilst at Victoria School, I seemed to gather quite an array of strange nicknames, but I never thought that upon my recent northerly travels, I would be appointed with my strangest title yet, now being known by my church Brownie group as, "Barn Owl".

This, again, has provided me with another lovely new interest, presenting me with the great opportunity to make friends in my local community, while viewing my future with a breeze of optimism.

It's just a lovely place and for some strange reason which may, or may not become clear in the future, I feel that this is one special church where only our Lord could gently lead us.

At last, I think I am finally drawing to a suitable close to my story. That just leaves me to say thank you to you all for reading this and being my constant companions, forever uplifting me with love and your kind support.

To my wonderful and truly adorable Mom: Quite simply, I love you and thank you so much from the bottom of my heart, because I know that I couldn't have achieved any of this without you.

Also, maybe we do wonder why things had to turn out the way that they have, but if there was a plan, maybe it was just to enrich our special and very loving relationship in many, many more ways than we could ever have dreamed possible. I wouldn't be at all surprised if any other mother who has given life to a special, disabled child won't agree with this too. Just like me, the Lord just knew you are one lovely and incredible lady.

And, just to round off this hairy tale as only I could, my days simply wouldn't have been the same, without mentioning that we enjoyed the very great privilege of re-homing another simply adorable little cat, named Tobias. I came across this name, via my search engine whilst trawling The Internet, and I felt its definition was particularly nice, as it derives from the Greek version of the old Hebrew name, Toviyah, meaning "God is good" but, most of the time, we shortened this to Toby. Very sadly, though, due to ill health, we had to say our final goodbyes to our Toby far too soon. Of course, all animals are different and beautiful in their own way, but I think we will always remember Toby best for his lovely, sociable purr-sonality, and his incredible capacity to let us know what he wanted. My days just wouldn't have been complete without getting to know such a beautiful and loving little animal, and there is no doubt that Toby has left his paw print on our hearts forever.

Thank you so very much for your time in reading this and to all my family, I love you always and, just on a final note, I hope that everyone who reads this, will in some small way, enjoy my varied and very colourful spectrum of *Mixed Blessings*.

Printed in Great Britain
by Amazon

61939616R00165